HOOVER INSTITUTION PUBLICATIONS

NATO WITHOUT FRANCE

*Research and publication sponsored by the Hoover
Institution and the Stanford Research Institute*

NATO WITHOUT FRANCE

A Strategic Appraisal

By Carl H. Amme, Jr.
with Foreword by
Charles Burton Marshall

The Hoover Institution
on War, Revolution and Peace
Stanford University
Stanford, California 1967

The Hoover Institution on War, Revolution and Peace, founded at Stanford University in 1919 by the late President Herbert Hoover, is a center for advanced study and research on public and international affairs in the twentieth century. The views expressed in its publications are entirely those of the author and do not necessarily reflect the views of the Hoover Institution.

FOREWORD

Whether or not it has been efficacious with respect to its purposes—however those purposes may be interpreted—the North Atlantic alliance has certainly been productive in stimulating wordage. What I have read about it over the years includes a couple of file drawers of clippings and pamphlets and some two dozen full-length books. I skimmed the more recent portion while reading Mr. Carl H. Amme's manuscript on the alliance's strategic problems.

What impresses me about the miscellany is that, on their face, all the propositions sound plausible, and many of them sound equally good with or without a "not" inserted by the verb. In sum, the generalities in which foreign policy is customarily discussed are of small value in relation to deciding issues. The alliance is urged both to be dynamic and to hold the line, to eschew old myths and embrace new realities, and to cleave to old realities while resisting new myths. A proposition for the alliance to branch out into cultural cooperation and joint endeavors in economic development instead of confining itself to sterile strategic pursuits is matched with a homily urging member governments not to forget that the one vital mission of the alliance has been military security. A call for the United States to recognize more fully its primacy and thus to exercise more vigorous and insistent leadership is counterbalanced by a plea for more sharing with and deference to allies, so that even the least among them may become imbued with a sense of equality and responsibility. The unbroken succession of American generals in the top command in Europe is cited to reprove the United States, which is urged to reassure allies by seeing to it that the next commander is a European. Oppositely, the importance of presenting another American for the post is emphasized, lest a disposition to shift to a European be taken as a disturbing sign of waning concern for defense on the Continent. The cleavage of views reflects differences in the perceived vitality of the alliance's *raison d'etre*. At one extreme is a thought that the purpose was dubious to begin with and in any case has lapsed, leaving the structure an obsolete encumbrance requiring only to be abolished. According to a contrasting contention, the necessities which impelled creation of the alliance are unallayed, and the alliance remains indispensable to peace and security for its participants.

Mr. Amme is clearly of the latter persuasion. He does not invoke the idea of a Communist timetable for general conquest, but neither does he discount the importance of Communist beliefs, with their total claim on futurity, in continuing to shape the outlook and purposes reflected in the Soviet Union's policy. The Soviet state remains a fixture of the Communist Party. A Communist Party that completely discarded ideology and turned completely pragmatic would lose its reason for existing and its grip on power. In taking any such turn, the Soviet regime would be undercutting itself—something no regime would ever purposely do. Recession of the danger which various governments in Central and Western Europe felt to be impending two decades ago is to be credited to the measures undertaken to counter the danger rather than to any spontaneous transformation within the Soviet Union. Given renewed opportunity, pressure from the Soviet Union, including military pressure, would be resumed. Without the alliance, having to face this pressure one by one, the states of Central and Western Europe would find themselves in danger again. The consequences would be adverse to our own national interests and security. So runs Mr. Amme's line of thought in arguing for the continuing essentiality of the alliance, and in this regard I agree with him. For all its continuing importance, the North Atlantic alliance has the defect of being conceptually complex—thanks to inherent traits and to a good deal of intellectualizing that has gone on since its origin. "Refined policy," Edmund Burke observed, "has ever been the parent of confusion—and ever will be so, as long as the world endures." Abstruseness palls. Complicated propositions have a hard time competing for public favor. The trouble is that understanding the North Atlantic Treaty system has involved too many interacting stages of comprehension. It takes too much explaining. Expecting the respective publics to rally to the cause is like expecting people to thrill to calculus. For me to attempt to enumerate and to analyze all the relevant complexities would entail writing an essay as long as the text to which these prefatory remarks relate, but certain ones occur to me as appropriate for comment.

One concerns the relationship between strategy and deterrence. Strategy involves designs for using force with the intent to prevail against an adversary in the eventuality of having to fight him. Deterrence involves so impressing him with the efficacy of one's strategy that the necessity of ever bringing it to bear is obviated. Deterrence can work only on the basis of a high estimate of the effectiveness of the strategy in event of failure of its primary aim of deterrence. Thus one can never know whether a strategy will succeed in operation unless and until it has failed of its basic purpose. Three states of mind are relevant to the avail of the alliance as a deterrent—namely the putative opponent's, our allies', and then our own. Confidence on our side is a function of doubt on the Communist side, where, conversely, the estimates of opportunity vary in proportion to Communist assumptions of disbelief among the allies in the effectiveness of the alliance. The entities concerned have to go through a continuous notional warfare involving calculation of interrelationships among the three states of mind. The United States's primary concern centers on the adversary's estimate, because basically the adversary is the one empowered to determine the success or failure of the deterrent design. The adversary's estimate, however, is inseparable from calculation of will and confidence among the alliance members, which in turn can be derived only from estimates of what the adversary's estimates are. The key factors in these interacting estimates are military. The essence of the alliance lies in having a cogent strategy.

A second consideration pertains to the interplay of equality and inequality among the members. The alliance obligations are equally incumbent upon them all, and all are juridically equal in the sense that all have autonomy of decision and power to enter into international contracts. Some are marginal to the functioning of the alliance. Others are central and essential. With some, their strategic concerns may be said to be encompassed by the alliance. With others, the alliance, while essential to their security, represents only a portion of their strategic involvement. In most respects, the United States is indisputably the pre-eminent factor. It disposes the nuclear striking power on which the alliance's strategic cogency must primarily rely. It disposes of that power in its own discretion, separate from the alliance command arrangements. The disposition of nuclear forces and the targeting in event of their having to be employed are matters about which the United States may give out some information and accept some counsel, but they are not matters susceptible of subjection to a dispersed responsibility. Moreover, the United States is pre-eminently the alliance member with the widest scope of concerns beyond coverage by the alliance. United States responsibilities are usually described as global, whereas those of its allies have traditionally been regional, have shrunk to regional, or are in process of so shrinking. In partial contrast stands the Federal Republic of Germany. Germany's central importance as a military factor in Europe is as patent now as it has been for a century. Its essentiality to the alliance is virtually as complete as that of the United States in the sense that if either were to opt out of the alliance, the undertaking would be totally at a discount. On the other hand, Germany's strategic concerns fall completely within the alliance's purview. It has no military existence outside the alliance. Under present conditions, it lacks even the command and staff structure for functioning militarily except within the alliance framework.

A third point relates to interaction between the concept of the alliance as a bulwark against pressure from the east and that of the alliance as a basis for achieving some sort of a settlement of Europe's future with the Soviet Union. This aspect in turn is interconnected with the United States's pre-eminence, the strategic need for the Federal Republic of Germany, and the central importance of both to the alliance's viability. It should be recalled that during World War II and its immediate sequel, the United States premised its policies on a hope of concord with the Soviet Union over the conditions of world politics and security. This approach was epitomized at the Yalta and the Potsdam conferences, which were in the format of a victorious United States and a victorious Soviet Union as the main disposers of Europe's future—and specifically of defeated Germany's. Especially since the induction of the Federal Republic of Germany in 1954 as a factor essential to the alliance's effectiveness, the alliance has reflected the idea of the United States and Germany as collaborators in working out a future in opposition to preferences entertained by the Soviet Union.

The United States, however, has never renounced hope of somehow ultimately working around to an accommodation with the Soviet Union—an aim taken out of limbo and made an active goal half a dozen years ago. This notion underlies a considerable number of United States projects in foreign policy, including the present hope of a pact to arrest nuclear proliferation. Such projects—and I would not wish to be understood as favoring them— raise a vision of the United States and the Soviet Union again collaborating as arbiters of Europe's future. There is a difference between having the United States as a protector against a hostile potential and having it as an arbiter of one's future in conjunction with another outsider. If the Soviet Union has been reoriented to a point bringing acceptable terms on Europe's future within reach, then the states of Europe—and emphatically France— would naturally prefer to bargain on their own. On the other hand, the approach, if premature, renders dubious the role of the United States as alliance kingpin. Trying to hold the alliance intact while questing for an accommodation with the Soviet Union presents a danger of missing on both counts— weakening the alliance while falling short of the sought-after *détente*. It is relevant here to take account also of the interplay between the two principal entities in Europe that were defeated in World War II, namely the German Federal Republic and France.

The German Federal Republic is, of course, successor in part to the Reich, which went down to defeat by the Western Allies and the Soviet Union. It is a truncated state, with a complementary fraction to the east under Communist rule and in clientage to the Soviet Union. The Federal Republic earned its way back to respectability and a measure of renewed statehood in being accepted into the North Atlantic alliance. The terms of that alliance included diplomatic support from its allies on the proposition of eventual reunification with the eastern portion. In turn, the Federal Republic accepted military disabilities in renouncing the making of nuclear, bacteriological, and chemical weapons, and in placing its military resources entirely at the disposal of the alliance coordinating mechanism which, with some want of accuracy, is called an integrated command. The measure of restoration achieved by the Federal Republic has come from its allies. The subordination still obtaining for it is related in part to its alliance obligations and in part to the purchase still held by the Soviet Union over the eastern portion of Germany. It is hard to see how any settlement with the Soviet Union could be achieved without legitimizing the division of Germany and perpetuating military restraints on the western portion. For the Federal Republic, such a development would mean renewal of the Yalta and Potsdam motif. The republic must hope against such an outcome and meantime cleave to the alliance, in which it enjoys a status of indispensability and a significant partnership with the pre-eminent member, namely the United States.

France was defeated in World War II, of course, not by the Western allies and the Soviet Union, but by Germany. During World War II and its aftermath France suffered eclipse by the interim conqueror and by eventual victors. Following the breakup of the victors' coalition, France found an anchor in the North Atlantic alliance. It was reluctant about expanding the alliance to include the German Federal Republic but was in no position to say no. The alliance provided a measure of security but no balm for a sore spirit. France's problem was not how to gain security but how to regain a lost significance. It has brooded over its secondary position first to the United Kingdom and then to the German Federal Republic. Initially it hoped to become a primary client of the United States—an aspiration epitomized in President Charles de Gaulle's proposition, broached and rejected nine years ago, for a three-cornered directorate of the alliance whereby world policies of the United States, the United Kingdom, and France would be under a consortium, and whereby France would gain a veto power over the United States's nuclear capabilities. Denied that aspiration, France has found the alliance frustrating to its hopes of regaining status. The alliance, considered as a bulwark, entails close collaboration between the United States as the strategic anchor and the German Federal Republic as the forward wall, with France in a middling and secondary role. The alliance viewed as instrumental for achieving an understanding with the Soviet Union carries the image of Yalta, where the United States was chief bargainer for the West and France was left out altogether. Neither perspective is appealing to France.

So in latter times France has essayed to become a rival of the United States rather than a competitor in clientage to it. This second quest has brought about France's defection from the alliance. By withdrawing its cooperation, France can hope to force adaptations of alliance strategy to suit France's own purposes. It can hope to impinge on the effectiveness and persuasiveness of the strategy which entails the United States's military presence in Europe. The arrangements involving close collaboration between the United States and Germany may then be sidetracked. In the background, the United States would continue to function as a remote and passive guarantor of European security, giving France opportunity to move to the forefront in dealings over the future of Europe—and hopefully France can edge out the United States in relations with the Federal Republic and also be successor to the United States as arbiter of Europe's and Germany's future in dealing with the Soviet Union. It is not a plausible dream, because it entails disjoining strategy and politics, and it counts on a Germany Federal Republic pliable to French designs, but the implausibility does not necessarily detract from the nuisance value.

Hence Mr. Amme's book. In addressing myself to it, I am aware of having left out of account a number of other factors of complexity, and indeed of having dealt somewhat oversimply with the ones mentioned, but what I have said must do. A happening in Canada and its aftermath, detailed in a sheaf of clippings at hand as I write these prefatory observations, gives point to the timeliness of Mr. Amme's appraisal. Proud of its first century of existence and of the distinguished commemorative exposition, the neighboring federal Dominion invited, among others, France's chief of state as a national guest. He came. He saw. He cankered. Throwing aside the canons of behavior, he publicly voiced encouragement to dissident elements devoted to an aim of partitioning Canada. Initially, the incident was widely accounted for as an instance of over-age ego overstimulated by applause. The French government thereupon negated this explanation. According to its official declaration, the incident was not an instance of mischance or misunderstanding but a deliberate exercise of presumed prerogative.

Some analog of Gresham's Law seems to be operative in great affairs. The process has been gaining in recent decades; perhaps the pace of contemporary communications is a factor. Except by bizarre manners and verbal exorbitance, how is one to compete successfully for printed space and televised time? The purpose here, however, is not to moralize on the decline of civic culture in general or to deplore in particular the decay of decorum in international affairs. What I wish to remark is that the hospitality abused by the French President's conduct, which in an earlier era would have been reprehensible even if directed toward an adversary, was that of an ally. France and Canada are both charter members of the North Atlantic Treaty. By terms of the treaty—which on its face imposes obligations which no party thereto can renounce until a time still two years away—the participants are pledged *inter alia* to uphold each other's territorial integrity and to cultivate peaceful and friendly relations, and so on.

Such flourishes of good intention are customary in treaties, and the North Atlantic Treaty text contains a fair share of elevating thoughts. Its core, however, is in its military aspects. The defection from the treaty's precepts, so vauntingly displayed by the French President's behavior in Canada, is pertinent to the military aspects as well.

As Mr. Amme's text makes clear, France even yet collaborates in certain electronic arrangements related to air defense, whose benefits it could not share without participating. Thus even while professing scorn and standing aloof, France remains a beneficiary in general military protection afforded by the alliance. In truth, France's regime is enabled to essay a bold role at small risk precisely because it is so thoroughly sheltered by the very arrangements which it purports to discredit. "Nothing, absolutely nothing, matters so much as rebuilding, thanks to peace, our substance, our influence, and our power," the French President said recently—without acknowledging the basis underlying that peace. The point suggests a homily about the ethics of playing against a system while making avail of its benefits, but I waive the opportunity, for France and its President are not the first and are little likely to be the last to exploit a situation in that manner, and the invocation of such a moral has scant bearing on strategic problems. The focus should be on the practical consequences of France's decoupling from the military arrangements associated with the alliance—a process begun eight years ago with a withdrawal of certain French naval units from the alliance nexus, and climaxed within recent months by the banishment of the alliance headquarters.

The estrangement of France—here I give Mr. Amme's interpretation—makes a significant material difference. The rub is not so much in the subtraction of ground forces, air components, and naval units from disposition by the alliance's coordinating structure. It is rather in the loss of the geographic position of France itself, with its appurtenant aviation complexes, harbors, wharfage, warehousing, canals, railroads, highways, and the like. All these facilities, which might otherwise be dependably available, cannot under present conditions be counted on in the assumptions which strategic planners must make. In extremity France might return to the fold and make its facilities available again to partners in defense. However plausible, this possibility avails nothing for the problem posed. Such a shift of course would come too late. It would serve only in a contingency of failure for the deterrent purposes of the alliance. Whatever the conceivable value in NATO's being able to make use again of the French position in that exigency, the French disaffection meanwhile flaws a strategy whose plausibility is integral to the effectiveness of the alliance as a deterrent.

Mr. Amme's relevant view—I believe I interpret him correctly in this respect—is that denial of France's facilities to the alliance, besides depriving air defense of important depth, cripples logistic arrangements by forcing a shift of reliance to the far less satisfactory alternative of using points of entry in the Low Countries and Germany, whence lines of communication to putative battle zones would necessarily run parallel to the line of battle and thus be made vulnerable by any appreciable penetration of the front. This prospect undercuts whatever plausibility might otherwise inhere in the idea of using a conventional ground defense in the early stages of a large-scale test of arms in Europe. Such a reliance is a basic element of the strategy of graduated deterrence of which the United States has been the originator and exponent.

As Mr. Amme makes clear, that version of strategy has been a focus of doubts on the part of France and, in some degree, of the Federal Republic as well. To the skeptics' thinking, graduated deterrence disturbingly foreshadows a possible period of conventional warfare waged back and forth over country that has already experienced more than its share of it in this century. Why bother to plan for interim phases of conventional war, then a phase of nuclear warfare for tactical purposes, before resorting finally to a nuclear exchange between the main positions? Any thrust from the east into Central and Western Europe would inevitably eventuate in all-out nuclear war. The best way to deter such an attack is to make that upshot an unequivocal and immediate consequence in the event such an attack should occur.

Mr. Amme's point is that undesirability could now be compounded by implausibility in the thinking of continental allies. The logistical flaw cannot be concealed from alliance participants or from the adversary. Confidence among participants is eroded. The other side is likely to be tempted. The alliance's deterrent value is thus subject to being discounted, according to Mr. Amme's appraisal. The alliance without France—meaning the alliance from here on—must for safety's sake, according to his prescription, resolve its will to resort to tactical nuclear weapons, in event of having to cope with an attack, much earlier and with fewer misgivings than postulated in the strategic plans still entertained. He would add that the decision must be made known to those defended by the alliance and to those whom the alliance would deter. Mr. Amme couples this counsel with recommendations for a system of constraints, with exacting custodial arrangements and a new pattern of interlocking controls—their details I leave to his delineation—to foreclose any possibility of cavalier resort to such weapons. He adds that "no constraint doctrine will be convincing to the enemy as long as NATO has aircraft poised on German air bases in peacetime ready to hurl nuclear destruction deep into enemy territory" or "as long as the United States continues to demand increasing buildups of conventional forces."

These propositions are by no means the only ones in Mr. Amme's informative book, but they are the ones, I suspect, most likely to be a focus of controversy. Mr. Amme can uphold his end of it without need of my advocacy. I myself am inclined to wonder whether a prospect of having their territory exposed to nuclear tactics would be any more reassuring to our continental European allies—I speak especially of the Germans here—than a prospect of being made a theater of conventional warfare. Whether the shift in lines of communication constitutes so weighty a factor of discount for the plausibility of existing strategic concepts is a question which I shall leave to the experts. My closing thought returns to the theme with which I began—the speculative character of evaluations in the field of international affairs, which, like horse racing, owes its zest to differences of opinion. The thought relates to a point collateral to the main theme of Mr. Amme's book. It concerns the episode of five years ago which revolved about the emplacement and withdrawal of the Soviet Union's missiles in Cuba. Evaluating the matter vicariously from the Soviet standpoint, Mr. Amme detects error, humiliation, and miscalculation, and adds, "As soon as the United States raised the stakes, the USSR backed down."

I should say the reverse. The Democratic Party's aspirant in the 1960 U.S. presidential campaign voiced unequivocal opposition to the existence of a position in the United States's environs enjoying the protection of the Soviet Union and serving Communist purposes. And, referring specifically to Cuba, he pledged action for the riddance of any such presence. In early January of 1961 the Soviet Union's Premier gave notice of determination to sustain the position in Cuba as an outpost of Communist-inspired revolution. In his inaugural address a few days later, the new American President reaffirmed the attitude expressed in the campaign. After the United States foul-up at the Bay of Pigs, the Soviet Premier redoubled the strength of his previous assertions. In a somewhat tepid rejoinder, the American President more or less stuck to his guns. Subsequently the Soviet Union deliberately proceeded to raise the stakes in a series of actions culminated by the deployment to Cuba of intermediate-range missiles with nuclear warheads. In the denouement, the United States backed down and gave a hands-off pledge as part of a bargain for obtaining withdrawal of the missiles. The United States, moreover, desisted thereafter on aspects of the bargain likely to result in weakening the Cuban regime's domestic grip.

An appraisal of the outcome of the issue over Cuba in light of its origin seems to me to lead to a conclusion that the Soviet Premier's avowed purposes were vindicated and that the American President backed down. I so wrote during the immediate sequel to the Cuba missile crisis, when the terms on which it had been eased off could only be guessed at by logical construe. I wondered then what all the hurrahing was about and appraised the outcome as deserving, from the United States standpoint, no more than two cheers. The basis of the bargain is now no longer a matter for conjecture. Five years later Cuba persists as a base for Communist undertakings, which the Soviet Union both patronizes and purports to disapprove. From the standpoint of American interests, my original appraisal of the outcome seems to have been a good bit too favorable. If Cuba was a victory for our side, may we be spared many more such!

CHARLES BURTON MARSHALL

Arlington, Virginia
August 15, 1967

PREFACE

This book grew out of a series of studies on NATO military problems that I and others made at Stanford Research Institute during the last five years. We were particularly concerned with possible conflict situations in Central Europe that might require the use of nuclear weapons. The more we examined differences in strategic concepts, elements of the opposing force postures, and practical problems of controlling the use of nuclear weapons, the more I became convinced that a better understanding was needed of the military problems relating to the possible use of nuclear weapons in defending the security of the Atlantic Alliance. The past uncertain role of France in NATO only complicated our studies. The possibility of France's withdrawal was always before us. Now that France's withdrawal is an accomplished fact, a new assessment can be made of NATO's military strategy.

This book deals with the special military aspects of the European confrontation as it now exists. The underlying political problems that plague the alliance, of course, must be dealt with. But the emphasis is definitely on military matters: strategic concepts, force posture,* and the practical matters concerning the use of nuclear weapons for deterrence and defense. This book is an attempt to fill a gap and to contribute to an understanding of these matters in a way that might offer insights to policy makers, military planners, and students of international relations. Because of the uncertainties surrounding the potential use of nuclear weapons in Europe, much of the analysis of the real military and strategic problems facing the alliance must necessarily rest on a conceptual basis. In substance, the book deals with the critical military confrontation in the Central European sector and the emphasis is on the problems surrounding the first use of nuclear weapons in more likely conflicts that might arise out of a crisis or from miscalculation.

Some of the conclusions drawn are controversial; some of the recommendations made are clearly contrary to current policy. The reader may disagree with these, but he will recognize that the problems I deal with are important and that in most cases they are practical problems for which solutions are needed. I do not offer a grand design for solving all the problems of NATO security. I do not present a vision of a unified Europe that could share equally with the United States the responsibility for deterring the Soviet Union—and perhaps later, China. I was tempted to do so. For this would have been a good way to attract wide attention for the book. Someone might even have been persuaded to review it—especially if the vision of the future and the prescription for the ills of NATO were startling and radical. Instead, I have tried to be pragmatic and realistic in my analysis. There is nothing to be said about the military problems of NATO that has not been said by someone before. What is said needs to be said again, and hopefully said in a way that is convincing to makers of strategy.

* The term "posture" is used frequently in this book to connote all the elements of military force including composition, disposition, and tactical doctrine.

Stanford Research Institute provided the funds for me to devote my time to writing this book and I am most appreciative of the members of the Research Policy Council who have supported my efforts in such a concrete manner. I am also grateful to the Hoover Institution on War, Revolution and Peace for the prompt consideration and expeditious preparation of the manuscript for publication.

I wish to acknowledge my debt to my colleagues at the Institute who participated in the earlier European studies from which much of the conceptual analysis was drawn. They are Mr. Richard Foster, Dr. Russell Rhyne, Dr. Richard Loomis, Mr. Richard Laurino, and Mr. Gregory Davis. I also would like to express my deep appreciation to Dr. William Van Cleave and Dr. Morris O. Edwards whose criticisms throughout have been most helpful. Mr. Ray Millican, Mr. Kenneth Field, and Mr. Barry Ryan all gave me valuable help in writing Chapter VIII, "The Use of Tactical Nuclear Weapons in Battle." Miss Ann Greenwood provided considerable assistance in collating the necessary information and in plotting the location of the military forces on the two maps in Chapter VI. Miss Carmen Kitzrow reduced my almost indecipherable scribblings to legible drafts—over and over again.

I want to express my appreciation to those persons in other research organizations and in the armed services and government agencies who took the time to read the draft and offer their criticism. In particular, I would single out Mr. James E. King of the Institute of Defense Analysis, Dr. Malcolm Hoag of the RAND Corporation, Dr. Robert B. Johnson of Johnson Research Associates, Mr. Leon Sloss of the Department of State, Mr. Nathan Rich of the Arms Control and Disarmament Agency and Colonel George E. Tormoen of the Air Force.

CONTENTS

ILLUSTRATIONS

TABLES

NATO WITHOUT FRANCE

INTRODUCTION

President Charles de Gaulle's action in pulling France out of NATO and expelling United States troops from France did not so much mark a profound change in the NATO structure as bring out into the open in a most explicit way the conflicts of purpose within the Alliance that have been glossed over for years. That de Gaulle was against the principle of integrating military forces of the various nations under a NATO commander was known even before he came to power in 1958. That he was going to do something about it became unmistakably clear after the failure of the 1960 Paris Summit Conference. But even prior to that event, in 1959, he had forbidden American nuclear weapons on French soil and had withdrawn France's Mediterranean fleet from NATO. The inclination is strong to single out these disrupting actions, and to accuse de Gaulle of atavism in wishing to return to the loose coalitions that proved so costly in previous wars. To do so, however, would obscure the existence of major conflicting interests on the important issues of security, on German reunification, and on the future course of Europe. In the long run, these are the important issues--not the organizational structure of the military command.

Of these issues, none is more important for the United States and for its allies than the security of the Atlantic Alliance--not as an institution or an organization, but as a practical means for protecting the lives and welfare of a community of 500,000,000 people. The central problem here is a concrete one: how to coordinate Alliance arms and strategies in such a way that defense remains strong and deterrence successful amid all the changes that have taken place and are bound to arise from the conflicts of interests and purposes of the member states. The perception of a diminished Soviet military threat, the growing strength of the European nations, and the vulnerability of the United States to Soviet attacks have all had an influence in evolving strategic differences in the Atlantic Alliance. The improved stability of the military confrontation now permits the nations of Europe to attempt to shape their own individual destinies. Because each nation sees its destiny in different terms, each also conceives of different means or strategy to achieve its objectives.

As the year 1969 approaches, when the Atlantic Alliance comes up for formal extension, there is urgent need to reexamine NATO strategy. From a military standpoint, the serious problems of the Atlantic Alliance can be grouped into three related categories: differences in strategic concepts, potential elements of instability in the military posture, and disagreement on arrangements for the control of nuclear weapons. Many of the fundamental strategic problems revolve around political issues. It does not follow, however, that resolution of the major political problems--some of which are intractable--should be prerequisite to solution of military problems or to improvements in the NATO force posture. This does not say that purely military solutions to Western Europe's security problems are possible. They are not. In fact, political considerations quite properly dictate important decisions concerning military matters and, conversely, military arrangements are occasionally advanced as solutions to political problems.

NATO is, nevertheless, a military alliance and the security problems should be approached from a military point of view as well as a political one. It is largely a matter of emphasis since no evaluation of military force structure, calculations of fire power, estimates of logistic needs, and plans for various contingency threats can be divorced from the political and psychological impact on the nations and the people concerned. This is especially true when dealing with the potential use of nuclear weapons, the ultimate key to NATO security and the stability of the present confrontation in Central Europe. Only twice have nuclear weapons been employed against an enemy and it is hardly likely that useful lessons about their military application can be learned from the strategic situation of August 1945. Human attitudes and political considerations that shape our will to use or not to use these weapons have been subjected to conflicting views that range from unilateral disarmament at one extreme to preventive war at the other. Fortunately, supporters of the most extreme views do not hold responsible positions in the governments of the Alliance.

The first part of this study analyzes the differences in strategic concepts of the major NATO nations. These differences stem in part from conflicting political interests, institutional arrangements, economic considerations, and even personality of leaders. But strategic concepts are also expressions of security interests that have intrinsic rationales of their own. The precarious nature of the nuclear balance, the possibility of a conflict arising out of a political crisis or upheaval, the perception of the military threat, the credibility and effectiveness of deterrence, and the confidence or lack of confidence in American military commitment are all important elements in the development of these conflicting strategic concepts.

Conflicting strategic concepts, moreover, are reflected in the military capabilities and postures of the major NATO nations. Significant shifts in strategy and in military capabilities by the United States have had pronounced effects on the military posture of NATO in Europe. Widespread public disillusionment with the stalemate in Korea and the costliness of raising and maintaining large standing forces impelled the United States to seek an answer in the new technology of nuclear weapons. As President Eisenhower pointed out, the new relationships between men and material . . . "permit economies in the use of men as we build forces suited to our situation in the world today."[1] The failure to achieve the 1953 Lisbon NATO force goal of forty-three divisions for Central Europe was a foregone conclusion and it brought about the Dulles doctrine of "massive retaliation" and the Eisenhower and Radford "New Look" strategy of reliance on tactical nuclear weapons for West Europe's defense. The resulting adjustments in force posture were difficult to make--especially for Germany, which was in the process of building a modern army from scratch. Many anachronisms became apparent. Ground forces that were supposed to fight in a nuclear environment under the "New Look" strategy initially had no tactical nuclear weapons, and little thought had been given to the development of a tactical doctrine for their use. Before these problems were ironed out, there came the shift in emphasis by the Kennedy administration to more conventional forces and a wider range of conventional options in Europe. Air forces in Europe that were geared to the nuclear strategic and interdiction role to supplement the mission of the Strategic Air Command found it extremely difficult to adapt themselves readily to the McNamara concept that stressed conventional options.

The second part of this volume examines the actual force posture in the confrontation as it exists with the withdrawal of France from NATO. Despite France's withdrawal, NATO's military strength is still great. The remaining fourteen nations possess major military forces and resources and are resolved to preserve the integrated military organization of NATO. Readjustments in disposition and organization, however, must be made. Fortunately, there exists something resembling a stable military confrontation in Central Europe. Overall, there is a situation in which both sides are basically resigned to the status quo based upon the over twenty-year-old military demarcation. The two important revisionist tendencies that threaten the stability are related to the issues of German reunification and the status of Berlin. On the first issue, West Germany is revisionist whereas the USSR wants to maintain the present division at the Iron Curtain. On the second issue, the USSR is revisionist whereas the West, including the United States, is unequivocally committed to the maintenance of the right of access to Berlin pending final resolution of German reunification. The significant aspect, however, is that both sides have made clear that they do not plan to use force to effect a change.

In such a setting, then, the apparent urgency to make major changes in the Alliance military posture is admittedly low. The perceived threat of major armed invasion of Western Europe, which was a major preoccupation of the NATO planners during the 1950s, has receded. Few strategists any longer regard a sudden incursion, such as a Hamburg "grab," a serious possibility. Most analysts agree that if there is to be an armed conflict at all the most likely contingency is a conflict arising out of a crisis or one based on a miscalculation of NATO resolve. Nevertheless, instabilities do exist in the NATO military posture that represent elements of danger should conflict occur--no matter what the cause. These instabilities involve not only actual force postures, but also the strategic concepts analyzed in Part I. Both are dealt with in the second part of the book in which means are sought to maintain the stability of the military confrontation and to lessen the chance in event of conflict that escalation would result in holocaust.

The third and final part of the book deals with the problem of arrangements within the Atlantic Alliance for the control and use of nuclear weapons. Nowhere is the dilemma of the United States in its effort to promote cohesion within the Alliance and in its search for a detente with the Soviet Union more apparent. Here all the major political problems of NATO--the desire of the European members to share more fully in the forces that are vital to their own security, the conflicting positions taken by the United States and France on the future form of the Alliance, and the preference of the European NATO nations to rely on deterrence rather than defense--are fundamental issues that bear heavily on the question of control of nuclear weapons. From the adversary point of view, the Soviet Union genuinely fears any arrangement that might give West Germany direct access to nuclear weapons. Proposed arrangements such as the Multilateral Force (MLF) or the Atlantic Nuclear Force (ANF) are regarded as threatening and provocative by the Soviet Union. The introduction of such forces not only might set back East-West relations, but would probably cause further disintegration within the Alliance. Except for Germany and possibly Italy, none of the European NATO nations give approval to these integrated force concepts, and France explicitly rejects them.

Yet this problem of nuclear sharing is not entirely political nor is it completely intractable. Given a sensible resolution or compromise of the conflicting strategic concepts and an adjustment in the NATO military force posture that would make it more responsive to the more likely military contingencies, some mutually acceptable and practical arrangement may be effected in NATO for the control of nuclear weapons. The third part of the book explores the possibilities for such arrangements that would preserve the vitality of the Atlantic Alliance in a military sense, even though some major political problems remain unresolved.

PART ONE—STRATEGIC CONCEPTS

UNITED STATES STRATEGY IN EUROPE

It would be a fairly simple task to document the public utterances of the leaders of the major NATO nations on strategy. Such pronouncements, however, do not tell the full story. It is only natural to expect that statesmen will claim to speak for the nation and will insist that their statements are indeed authentic policy. Obviously such statements on strategy have elements of pretense and it may be expected they will be altered or slanted for political purposes. They may actually be at variance with the actual strategy that would be employed to meet a particular conflict contingency. On the other hand, if the policy pronouncements are confirmed by observing the actions taken by the different governments in relation to the statements of their leaders, then there will be more confidence that the strategic concept advanced is actually the one that would be put into effect. Furthermore, it is clear that the strategic concept of each major NATO nation depends to a great extent on a threat that is perceived differently by different countries. A nation's strategic concepts also interact with those of its allies and particularly with the strategy of the dominant military power of the alliance. Thus, the American strategic concept for the defense of Western Europe provides a point of departure for examining the concepts of the other major NATO nations.

The overall United States strategy with relation to the Soviet Union can be broken down into at least three separate strategic concepts: general war, limited war, and arms control.

General War

The general-war strategic concept is the foundation of the United States deterrence strategy. The concept is based on strategic missile forces and, up until

11

now, on long-range bombers that can attack military targets (missile sites and air bases), cities (population and industry), or both simultaneously or with a delay. The major characteristic of this concept is the achievement of a secure second-strike capability--that is, the capability of surviving an enemy first strike and retaliating in a controlled and selective manner. The size of the strategic force is determined by two requirements:

1. To deter a deliberate nuclear attack upon the United States and its allies by maintaining a clear and convincing capability to inflict unacceptable damage on an attacker, even were that attacker to strike first;

2. In the event such a war should nevertheless occur, to limit damage to our populations and industrial capacities.

The general-war strategic concept is primarily aimed at providing deterrence against a direct nuclear strike on the territory of the United States. A second purpose is to provide extended deterrence to counter the threat of major invasion of Western Europe. Implicit in this American strategic concept is the assumption that all members of the Alliance will seek identical objectives and will have similar national interests during a European war. This does not imply that differences do not exist but it does imply that there would be a closing of ranks and unanimity in making the necessary political decisions when it becomes necessary to defend NATO and to defeat the enemy. In short, in the United States view Article 5 in the original treaty (that an ". . . attack on one or more . . . shall be considered an attack against them all . . . ") calls for an ultimate solution--a highly integrated nuclear force that precludes the possibility of disruption by independent national action.

This view is based on two other assumptions. First, common war objectives and national interests demand a common strategy. Since it provides ninety-five percent of the integrated nuclear force, the United States argues that indivisible control is plainly required and that NATO should logically follow the concept of controlled response as enunciated by the United States. This concept calls for ". . . destruction of the enemy's military forces, not of his civilian population."[2] The option of striking the enemy's cities would remain, however, if that be our choice.

The second assumption is that the American commitment to NATO is firm and uncompromising. Besides the solemn commitment of the North Atlantic Treaty itself, a series of official U. S. pronouncements have reaffirmed this commitment. At the Allied ministerial conference in Athens in 1962, Mr. McNamara gave firm assurances that American strategic nuclear forces would continue to provide defense beyond the capability of the forces directly committed to the Alliance. In his Ann Arbor speech of 16 June 1962, Mr. McNamara said:

> We are convinced that a general nuclear war target system is indivisible ... . . We know that the same forces which are targeted on ourselves are also targeted on our allies. Our own strategic retaliatory forces are prepared to respond against these forces, wherever they are and whatever their targets. This mission is assigned not only in fulfillment of our treaty commitments but also because the character of nuclear war compels it . . . . In short we have undertaken the nuclear defense of NATO on a global basis . . . .

Most of the arguments by the United States for a common strategy, for U. S. leadership, and for total commitment are made in the context of general war. In this context the arguments are compelling--at least from the American point of view. It is virtually impossible to conceive of plausible circumstances wherein Soviet attempts to seize all or part of Western Europe would not trigger American nuclear response. Either the Soviets would strike at the United States first to pave the way for a massive combined arms invasion of Europe, or they would have to face the threat of a NATO and American tactical nuclear defense with all the attendant dangers of triggering an American first strike against the Russian homeland. In general war, there would be a closing of the ranks by necessity. Even President de Gaulle recognizes this--despite the doubts he expresses about American commitment. As long as we are dealing with the canonical threat of all-out war, common sense allows no other conclusion.

But the general-war concept, logical as it may be, is a dead-end strategy for achieving any goal except deterrence to general war itself. For either side deliberately to initiate general war to achieve other goals is literally unthinkable. Nevertheless, since it is possible that conflict might break out either because of aggressive designs or as a result of accident of miscalculation during a chain of events surrounding a crisis, the United States has adopted a second strategic concept for limited war in Europe.

Limited War

The second American strategic concept for limited war in Europe, although intended to augment strategic nuclear deterrence, is aimed primarily at providing a defense for Europe for conflicts below the level of general war.

The major characteristic of this concept is reliance on strong conventional forces backed up by selected use of tactical nuclear weapons. The primary threat is seen as a purposeful invasion in Europe for limited objectives and the possible conflict that might arise inadvertently from a crisis situation. An all-out invasion by an enemy obviously would not mesh with our limited-war strategic concept, but would fall under the general-war strategic concept.

An important emphasis in the limited-war strategy is placed on a larger conventional buildup to provide additional options. This policy is not aimed at sole dependence on conventional weapons and forces for the defense of Western Europe. It is rather to ". . . increase our capability to tailor our responses to a particular military challenge to that level of force which is appropriate to the issue involved and favorable to our side." This policy was succinctly set forth in a statement by Mr. McNamara:

> Although we are still a long way from achieving the non-nuclear capabilities we hope to create in Europe, we are much better off in this regard than we were two years ago. Today the NATO forces can deal with a much greater range of Soviet actions, without resorting to the use of nuclear weapons. Certainly, they can deal with any major incursion or probe. But we must continue to do everything in our power to persuade our allies to meet their NATO force goals so that we will possess alternative capabilities for dealing with even larger Soviet attacks. And until these capabilities are achieved, the defense of Europe against an all-out Soviet attack, even if such an attack were limited to non-nuclear means, would require the use of tactical nuclear weapons on our part [emphasis added].[3]

In the 1965 budget hearings, Mr. McNamara reaffirmed that ". . . a major objective of U. S. military policy since 1961 has been to strengthen the non-nuclear capabilities of the Free World, and in particular, those of NATO."[4] He went on to quote again his own statement made in the spring of 1961 in support of the first Kennedy amendments to the Fiscal Year 1962 Defense budget:

> Even in limited war situations, we should not preclude the
> use of tactical nuclear weapons, for no one can foresee how
> such situations might develop. But the decision to employ
> tactical nuclear weapons in limited conflicts should not be
> forced upon us simply because we have no other means to
> cope with them. There are many possible situations in which
> it would not be advisable or feasible to use such weapons.
> What is being proposed at this time is not a reversal of our
> existing national policy but an increase in our non-nuclear
> capabilities to provide a greater degree of versatility to our
> limited war forces. [5]

This was a clear change of strategy from the "New Look" of Eisenhower and
the officially adopted NATO strategic plans of 1954 based on using nuclear weapons whether the Soviet Union used them or not. At that time, conventional forces
were regarded as a "trip wire" that could not hold back the enemy, but which
could act as an impediment, or a screening force to ascertain enemy intentions,
and could give the alarm that would allow the nuclear forces to strike. The precarious trip-wire concept, however, could lead to mistaking a border incident
for a deliberate invasion. Under General Lauris Norstad, as Supreme Allied
Commander, Europe, the strategic concept envisaged using shield forces--both
conventional and tactical nuclear--to enforce upon the enemy a longer "pause"
so that the aggressor could reflect on the serious consequences of his military
action before the full weight of the West's nuclear forces were launched.

On the surface, the McNamara conventional concept has similarity to the
Norstad pause concept: both sought the achievement of the thirty division goal
on the central front. But the pause concept did not envisage more than a comparatively brief holding action with these conventional forces to enforce a pause,
whereas McNamara would use these forces to defend against a major incursion
or probe and "even larger Soviet attacks." Both concepts recognized the possible
need for using tactical nuclear weapons. But the pause concept would have brought
nuclear weapons deliberately into play immediately after the intentions of the enemy became apparent, whereas the McNamara concept did not propose to employ
nuclear weapons until Soviet conventional forces were overrunning NATO forces.
As he put it, tactical nuclear weapons are needed ". . . to deal with an attack
where the opponent employs such weapons first, or any attack by conventional
forces which put Europe in danger of being overrun. We mean to defend Europe
with every kind of weapon needed."[6]

A second important characteristic in the American concept is the doctrine of controlled response. This is most often discussed in dealing with the general-war strategy. Controlled response, or counterforce is based on the argument that American strategic forces should be so superior, so invulnerable to a first strike, and so well controlled that the United States could possess the controlled capabilities of striking alternative types of targets. City-avoidance, damage-limiting, and selective nuclear strikes could be possible under this doctrine. In short, the controlled response concept seeks to take the spasm out of a strategic nuclear exchange.

But controlled response also has another meaning, one related to the use of tactical nuclear weapons in a selected manner for the defense of Western Europe. Secretary McNamara appears uncertain of the utility of controlled response in tactical nuclear warfare as indicated by his exchanges with Senator Margaret Chase Smith during the defense appropriation hearings in February 1963.

At one point, Mr. McNamara pointed out that "The principal reason for having strong tactical nuclear forces is to cover the intermediate range between conventional war and global war." At another point, he suggested that small nuclear weapons to close a pass or blow up a bridge would ". . . not necessarily" escalate to a higher threshold. "But by using nuclear weapons in this way," he went on, "we must recognize the possibility that our opponent will also perceive an advantage in using them on a similar or larger scale." Later, Mr. McNamara stated that ". . . the uncertainty and dangers of escalation which could arise from the initiation of tactical nuclear weapons must be [as] apparent to the Soviet bloc leadership as to us." Accordingly, he thought that the Soviets would not be likely to perceive an advantage in initiating the use of nuclear weapons, for "they would do so with the full knowledge that the NATO nuclear response would be powerful and immediate. It would in all likelihood mean general nuclear war."[7]

The ambiguity in these statements could be calculated. Mr. McNamara suggests that tactical nuclear weapons are made available to be used under certain contingencies, but to use them would in all likelihood bring on general nuclear war. Again, on 23 February , 1966, Mr. McNamara stated:

> A theater nuclear capability is to deter Soviet use of tactical nuclear weapons in an attack on Western Europe, to permit us to respond in kind if such weapons are used, and to support U. S. and allied forces as may otherwise be required.[8] [Emphasis supplied.]

Except for the ambiguous third clause of this statement, the tenor suggests that tactical nuclear weapons would be used only in retaliation. For, as Mr. McNamara further confesses, "It is not yet clear how theater nuclear war could actually be executed without incurring a very serious risk of escalating to general nuclear war."[9] Coupled with an insistence on providing stronger conventional options, it would seem clear that the United States intends to follow a strategic concept in Western Europe that relies on conventional defense--at least initially--unless, of course, the Soviets use nuclear weapons first.[10]

The initial uncertainty and attendant dangers of escalation to general nuclear war from the initiation of the use of tactical nuclear weapons, which the Secretary of Defense thinks ". . . must be [as] apparent to the Soviet bloc leadership as to us, . . ." are also apparent to our European allies. Our European allies have serious objections to the American concept of conventional defense and a "controlled" tactical nuclear response at the dire moment that NATO forces are in danger of being overrun. The American concept relies on a postponed threat of nuclear retaliation. Nuclear deterrence is thus counted upon to prevent a continuation of an enemy invasion that a NATO conventional defense has failed to stem. Presumably, the threat of using tactical nuclear weapons at the outset is regarded as too implausible for the enemy to believe; however, the enemy would presumably consider the deterrent threat credible at a later time when it appeared the NATO forces faced defeat. We would then expect the aggressor to discontinue the attack!

However, should the hostile force continue the attack, the following hypothetical sequence of events under the doctrine of flexible response would take place: (1) Soviet conventional attack, (2) NATO conventional defense, (3) Soviet breakthrough, (4) NATO counterforce with tactical nuclear weapons (i.e., aimed at spearheads and support), (5) Soviet response with tactical nuclear counterattack in battle area, (6) U.S. controlled or demonstrative strategic strikes against Russia. At any step in the sequence alternatives are offered. This is illustrated by the diagram in Fig. 1.

Most military analysts would agree that NATO could not mount a successful conventional defense against a determined Soviet attack. At the same time, NATO would hardly accept a conventional defeat after the Soviet Union had "overrun our forces" and made a breakthrough. Thus Points X and Y in Fig. 1 can be disregarded

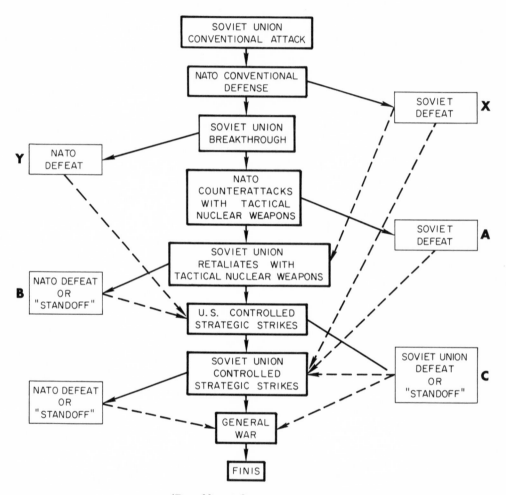

(Dotted lines indicate pre-emptive options.)

Figure 1. Hypothetical Sequential Stages in a
Central European War Under Doctrine of Flexible
Response

for the moment, although it is noted in passing that each side possesses a pre-emptive option of using either tactical nuclear weapons or strategic nuclear strikes, or both. Instead, we will examine three other hypothetical situations (Points A, B, and C) that seem to be implicit in McNamara's flexible-response doctrine. [11]

At Point A, the Soviet Union is assumed to accept defeat and withdraw without retaliating in turn with nuclear weapons. This is admittedly a speculative and most unlikely outcome, for certainly the Soviet leaders would have calculated the possibility of NATO's initiating the use of tactical nuclear weapons before launching the invasion in the first place. It is beyond the bounds of credulity that the enemy would launch an invasion with the firm intention of accepting defeat in the event NATO carried out its well-advertised intent of using nuclear weapons. Nevertheless, if NATO nuclear weapons are withheld until its forces are in danger of being overrun, the people and resources in the path of the invasion would already have suffered a great deal of destruction from conventional weapons. The use of nuclear weapons by NATO to prevent defeat at that time would only add to the local devastation, while the United States and Russia would presumably remain untouched.

The second and only slightly less implausible alternative (Point B in Fig. 1) would be for Russia to retaliate with tactical nuclear weapons rather than to accept defeat and destruction of its forces by NATO's use of tactical nuclear weapons on the battlefield. In this situation the enemy has penetrated into NATO territory and the NATO forces are in danger of being overrun before the first nuclear weapon is used. Both sides now would resort to tactical nuclear weapons in a controlled manner, and tremendous destruction in Western Europe is assured --or at least in the part being fought over. Not only might the military forces of both sides, their bases and command centers be targets for destruction, but civilians and industrial resources would be destroyed in the process. Even the most careful counterforce strikes could not avoid some collateral destruction. Europeans can hardly regard this situation as anything but unmitigated disaster even if some Americans could see it as a limited tactical nuclear war where the nuclear conflict is confined to the battlefield and to the military bases in support of the fighting forces. [12]

The first two postulated situations that would result from carrying out the

American declaratory strategy assume deliberate restraints are employed by both sides to prevent the nuclear conflict from exceeding certain limits. Moreover, it assumes that these deliberate restraints are recognized for what they are, even though there is no real hope of making a sure distinction among nuclear weapons by judging their yield (except in the most general sort of way), by estimating the range and point of origin of the delivery vehicle, or by divining whether the collateral population damage was intentional or not. The falseness of these assumptions only underscores the objections of Europeans to the American strategic concept. [13]

The third alternative situation would call for the initiation of the use of strategic nuclear weapons in a "controlled response" as soon as NATO forces were in danger of being defeated by superior Russian nuclear and conventional forces (Point C in Fig. 1). This alternative could bring on general nuclear war and furthermore would constitute a contradiction in the terms of American declaratory strategy. Whereas Mr. McNamara can contemplate the initiation of the use of tactical nuclear weapons in Europe, he cannot contemplate the initiation of the use of strategic nuclear weapons in the first or preemptive strike. "Because we have a sure second-strike capability," he is quoted as saying, "there is no pressure on us whatsoever to preempt. I assure you that we really never think in those terms." [14]

Europeans strongly object to all of these alternatives implicit in the doctrine of flexible response. In the first place, a major conventional war is considered not only undesirable but unfeasible. The memory of the devastation wrought by conventional weapons in World War II is still fresh, and the Germans somewhat naturally object to having a large portion of their homeland reduced to a battlefield while the homelands of the two super powers remain intact. The distances are short and the densely populated area between the Iron Curtain and the Rhine would make it practically impossible to execute a successful conventional defense without widespread death of civilians and destruction of industry.

In the second place, some Europeans (and Americans) profess to the fear that the explicit dependence on conventional forces to cope with large Soviet attacks might encourage the Soviets to indulge in limited aggressions at lower levels of conflict by a "quick grab" or fait accompli. Implicit to this view is the assumption that the credibility of the U. S. deterrent has been weakened, that some sort of nuclear standoff does exist, and that the Soviet Union could rationally attempt a purposeful, limited aggression in Europe without incurring a risk of reaching the higher level of stimuli that would trigger a NATO nuclear response. Four important factors argue against the validity of this belief. The first is the record of manifest caution exhibited by the Soviet Union in any military confrontation with U.S. forces, no matter how minor. A second factor is the Soviet leaders' apparent unwillingness to subscribe to the distinction between general war and limited war in Europe. The third factor is the added disincentive created by the existence of the independent French and British nuclear forces. The fourth factor, paradoxically, is the very inconsistency in the U.S. declaratory strategy and the disposition and composition of U.S. forces in Europe, organized and equipped as they are for nuclear war. All these factors, which are discussed in more detail later, make it extremely unlikely that the credibility of deterrence in Europe will be degraded in Russian eyes.

It is curious to note that the same implicit assumption that nuclear standoff exists is used by some proponents of a larger NATO capability for conventional defense. Professor Robert E. Osgood advances the idea that the West ". . . should be able to wage effective conventional resistance of a large-scale and protracted nature in order to raise the threshold of violence to a point where limited nuclear resistance would be sufficiently credible to exert its intended political effect."[15] He goes on to argue along lines very similar to the McNamara concept, in favor of limited or graduated nuclear blows (e.g., controlled response) as a concomitant to a conventional resistance strategy, rather than as a substitute for large-scale conventional warfare and ". . . a step on the automatic escalator to massive strategic nuclear exchange."

The use of tactical nuclear weapons might well bring about uncontrolled escalation, but there is no evidence to guarantee that it would. In fact, the initial use of weapons that are so dreaded might have an opposite effect and shock the conflict to a standstill. There is a vast difference between the danger of escalation and the certainty of it. In the abstract, there is a certain logic in the American strategic concept for limited war in Europe that keeps the war from spreading to the United States. A local defense employing a flexible response might succeed or it might escalate to general war. But the threat of such a defense, with the attendant dangers of escalation, is at least a more credible deterrent to local enemy actions than a threat of transoceanic massive retaliation from the United States, if for no other reason than that it is more believable. United States troops and weapons are on the spot and must be dealt with.

Arms Control

The danger that conflict might break out in Europe for whatever reason has impelled the United States to adopt a third strategic concept to reduce the possibility of such an occurrence and to limit destruction if war does occur.

This third American strategic concept has for its purpose some accommodation with the Soviet Union. The threat, more political than military, is epitomized as the "Cold War"; the search for arrangements with the Soviet Union is based on the rationale that both the super powers have similar interests in preventing war with one another. The major characteristic of this third strategic concept is that the military means are cooperative as well as competitive. To identify the peculiar aspect of military cooperation between the United States and the Soviet Union, this third strategy is labeled "arms control. " Arms control and other military strategies are intimately linked to serve U. S. national security policy. Military strategy is designed to deter an enemy from deliberate attack upon us or our allies; arms control bases its measures on minimizing the devastation that will accompany our efforts to prevail over the aggressor. Yet this is not a clean-cut separation. Military strategies themselves are also concerned with minimizing the danger of accidental war or of miscalculation that might lead to war. This fact is frequently overlooked. Also frequently ignored is the fact that national interests may also require arms control action that heightens the risk of war rather than diminishes it. The Cuban blockade of 1962 is a striking example of this.

Yet the Cuban missile crisis is just the sort of nuclear confrontation between the two super powers that might be regarded as the most dangerous threat to international security. It would appear only natural that most arms control concepts and even disarmament proposals should be concerned with the preponderant military power at the disposal of the United States and the Soviet Union. Whether President de Gaulle agrees or not, preponderant power has placed the United States in the role of champion and major spokesman for the West in seeking accommodation with the Soviet Union. The Hot Line agreement[17] can be regarded

as a direct result of the Cuban confrontation. The limited nuclear test ban treaty
was for the most part negotiated by the United States with the USSR, after which
other countries were called upon to adhere. The Eighteen Nation Disarmament
Conference in Geneva is largely a propaganda forum between two sides, with the
neutrals seeking to influence the conditions upon which the United States and the
Soviet Union can agree.

The bilateral nature of the American attempt to seek some sort of arrangement with the Soviet Union on armaments is regarded with distrust by France
and Germany. Determined to develop nuclear weapons of her own, France has
rejected the limited test ban and has refused to participate in the Geneva Disarmament Conference. Germany has strongly opposed arms control concepts for
disengagement and nuclear free zones--such as the Rapacki, Eden, and Gomulka
plans--because they would tend to give recognition to the partition of Germany.
The Federal Republic also regards the negotiation of an anti-proliferation treaty
with extreme suspicion, as it might prevent her participation in nuclear policy
matters that have to do with her vital security interests. In practice, the pursuit
of a strategy based on arms control and disarmament arrangements with the
Soviet Union tends to conflict with what is required to provide political cohesion
in the Alliance. Arms control measures that might promise to enhance détente
with the Soviet Union and to reduce the danger of inadvertent nuclear war must
be balanced against not only the fundamental requirements of deterrence and defense, but also the realities of alliance politics and goals. This places a limit on
how much can be accomplished in pursuit of this strategic concept. Far-reaching
measures of accommodation in such arms control matters depend on a favorable
international political climate which does not now exist. Whereas it is true that
armaments themselves may be tension-inducing as well as tension-reflecting,
it seems evident that until some of the political problems in Europe, such as
German reunification, are resolved, the major thrust of this strategy will be to
achieve some sort of "arms stability" in Europe. This requires a stable military
posture on both sides that can prevent political crises from resulting in drastic
upheavals of violence.

There is an inherent logic in the strategic concept of arms control that de-
rives from the existence of nuclear weapons and the possibility, however remote,
that deterrence might fail. It is no less than vital that the United States continue

to seek means of achieving its aims of lessening the possibility of war. The problem is extremely complex, however. Militarily rational and desirable solutions may not be politically feasible and may impair alliance unity. Solutions that seem to promote unity and enhance the military deterrence might provoke the Soviet Union to actions detrimental to the détente.

The general European view is that the Soviet Union is not militarily aggressive and that domestic communism no longer offers a serious threat to the NATO nations. European leaders see no great threat from the East, except in conjunction with an actual or potential United States-Soviet Union crisis or confrontation. Because such crises do occur (Berlin, Cuba, Viet Nam), they must worry about their security from time to time, especially in the presence of a strong Soviet military force nearby. Basically, the Europeans believe that the Soviet Union is deterred from any use of force by fear of a nuclear war with the United States. So long as such a war is a probable or even possible issue from the Soviet use of military force, the European NATO nations are not seriously concerned about Soviet military power. They would, however, be concerned if the military confrontation in Europe were changed radically in such a way that the Soviet Union might be encouraged to think about possible ways of using military force in Europe--especially if provoked by U. S. actions outside of Europe. Barring a radical change in the European confrontation, the NATO nations are not likely to be as interested in local defense or in seeking arms control arrangements with the Soviet Union as they would be in resolving some of the political problems that give trouble.

STRATEGIES OF MAJOR EUROPEAN MEMBERS OF THE ALLIANCE

Contrary to popular belief the most serious military problem of the Alliance is in West Germany--not in France. The unresolved problems of reunification and of Berlin are major issues of potential crisis. Moreover, West Germany's exposed position, her dense population, and the lack of natural defense positions near the border present serious military technical problems. Despite the fact that both sides have announced that they have no intention to employ military means to achieve their conflicting goals, there is always the possibility that a deep crisis might arise that would precipitate into armed conflict at the critical points of confrontation along the border, along the routes of access to Berlin, or at Berlin. Furthermore, German efforts to achieve security are constrained by the strategies of the other NATO nations. French nuclear diplomacy is to a large extent aimed at weakening German-American ties and substituting French hegemony in Europe. Great Britain's aversion to the Multilateral Force (MLF) is conditioned by her desire to keep Germany from having a finger on the trigger of NATO nuclear weapons.

West Germany

The special circumstances and institutionalized arrangements surrounding the admission of the Federal Republic to the Atlantic Alliance must be understood to appreciate the traumatic effect on West Germany of the major shifts in the U.S. strategic concepts. Germany is a divided country, defeated in World War II, and still painfully burdened by the atrocities of Hitler. Militarily exposed, Germany was and is greatly dependent upon the other members of NATO for her security--

and especially upon the United States. The political instrument for West German rearmament and entry into NATO are contained in the 1954 Paris Protocols Amending the Brussels Treaty (of 1948). Of particular relevance are the provisions that incorporated the declaration of Chancellor Adenauer that ". . . the Federal Republic . . . undertakes further not to manufacture in its territory" atomic, biological and chemical weapons; long-range missiles, guided missiles, and influence mines; warships, with the exception of smaller ships for defense purposes; and bomber aircraft for strategic purposes.[1]

Thus, in an agreement with its Western Allies, West Germany unilaterally renounced the manufacture of nuclear weapons as well as other related armaments on West German soil. It is important to note that it did not renounce either the possession or the use of nuclear weapons. In return for this pledge, Germany's Western allies committed themselves to support eventual reunification of Germany, which was then still militarily occupied by Britain, France, the United States and the Soviet Union. The weak political position of the Federal Republic at the time left her no alternative but to actively seek the closest integration within the framework of the Alliance. Territorial security had to be assured, and the other major goal--German reunification--had to take second place.[2]

The leaders of West Germany were slow to include nuclear weapons in their strategic thinking. From the very start, Adenauer adopted a military policy that emphasized the German contribution of conventional divisions to the "shield" forces of NATO. Constrained by the Paris Agreements, the Adenauer government went about plans for conscripting a conventional army. Neither the acute public reaction to the 1955 simulated nuclear air exercise "Carte Blanche" nor the opposition of the Social Democrats swayed Adenauer. Reports in the press and in the Bundestag on "Carte Blanche" emphasized the "suicidal nature" of nuclear warfare in the highly populated areas of West Germany and provided the opposition with cogent arguments against conscription. Fritz Erler of the Social Democrats stated in the Bundestag that ". . . The strategy of NATO leaves no room for doubting that an armed conflict in Europe--even with 500,000 German soldiers--will not remain a conventional conflict."[3] He went on to argue that SACEUR wanted the German conventional divisions to force the enemy to concentrate in order to provide a suitable target for NATO's nuclear weapons. Thus, it seemed clear to him that even 500,000 soldiers could not protect the German people

". . . against the use of atomic weapons in the event of conflict." Despite this

opposition, Adenauer succeeded in getting the conscription law passed, only to

have his position undermined a few days later by the announcement on 13 July,

1956, from Admiral Radford, the Chairman of the U. S. Joint Chiefs of Staff,

that the United States proposed to cut back its armed services by 800,000 men

and base its strategic concept on the use of tactical nuclear weapons.[4]

After "agonizing reappraisal" and difficult parliamentary battles, the Feder-

al Republic in March 1958 decided to equip its army with the means of delivering

tactical nuclear weapons in accordance with the 1957 NATO five-year plan (MC-70),

which called for thirty combat-ready divisions equipped with both conventional

and nuclear weapons. Having fully committed its forces to the NATO adopted stra-

tegic concept, the Federal Government found itself subject to criticism at home

by the opposition and abroad by some of its allies over its effort to acquire nucle-

ar arms for the German units (as was already the practice for other Allied units

in forward areas in West Germany).

General Heusinger, the Inspector-General of the Bundeswehr, in a talk to

the senior commanders of the three services in 1960 emphasized the necessity

of having tactical nuclear weapons in the "Shield" forces. This talk was condensed

and published under the signature of his deputy, Vice Admiral Friedrich Ruge in

Heusinger's absence.[5]

> The soldiers of the Bundeswehr have a right to weapons which
> are at least equal to those of the opponent . . . . The arma-
> ments of the opponent make graduated deterrence essential.
> This deterrent requires a balance of atomic and conventional
> armament for the shield force as a supplement to the strategic
> air force and navy. . . . Tactical atomic weapons in the sphere
> of the shield forces are therefore an essential step in deter-
> rence . . ."

The text of the statement from which this quote was drawn, according to Ruge,

created ". . . a commotion because it was regarded by some politicians as an

attempt of the generals to meddle into politics and as an attempt by West Germans

to obtain nuclear weapons of their own."[6]

West German Defense Minister Franz-Josef Strauss echoed this plea of

General Heusinger, but he was more careful to indicate that the Federal Republic

was in no way advocating West German production of nuclear weapons. "The government of the Federal Republic," he stated, "has never advocated that the group of nations possessing atomic weapons be expanded. It has always been opposed to such a development. In this instance, it has given particularly strong support to the American point of view that the production of atomic weapons should not be extended beyond the present group of producers."[7]

West German leaders not only requested that German NATO units be equipped with tactical nuclear weapons, but they began to emphasize the necessity of combining the German conception of Forward Defense (which they had insisted upon from the start), with immediate use of these weapons against any Soviet aggression in Central Europe. Such a strategy, pregnant with the danger of rapid escalation to general nuclear war, was considered by the West Germans as the only sure way of ensuring effective deterrence against the Soviets, given the Federal Republic's exposed position and its vulnerability to even a small penetration.

A most detailed declaration of German military policy was given by Minister of Defense Strauss on December 16, 1961. His main point was that Germany recognized that dependence on strategic nuclear deterrence alone was not enough, and that it was equally important to have strong conventional forces and modern equipment including "launchers for tactical nuclear weapons." He emphasized the urgency of having nuclear weapons "within the Alliance" distributed throughout "from the forward to the rear areas," and he endorsed the Mobile Medium Range Ballistic Missile (MMRBM) proposed by General Norstad, the Supreme Allied Commander, Europe.[8]

Seven months later, on July 25, 1962, Defense Minister Strauss formulated the chief aims of German military policy goals. The first and foremost aim of Germany according to Strauss, must be and must remain to achieve the goal of making war in any form impossible, in spite of all changes and revolutionary technical developments that may occur in the future. Should a war break out, however, the next aim must be to end it as quickly as possible and to restore the status quo ante. The deterrence capability of the Alliance, therefore, must be deployed as far forward as possible.[9] In short, Germany wants effective nuclear deterrence above all else--and she wants it effective at the border.

This is all very well, but what if deterrence failed to work? A conventional defense at the border was regarded as impossible and a tactical nuclear defense was looked upon as almost certain destruction of large areas of West Germany.

The destruction experienced in World War I and II and the published results of exercise "Carte Blanche" convinced most Germans on these points. Germany saw her only hope of salvation in making a credible threat of almost immediate use of nuclear weapons, to confront the enemy with the terrible risk of automatic escalation to general war. This Germany cannot do because she does not have nuclear weapons and the Americans who hold the keys to these weapons advocate a strategic concept that is interpreted as being aimed at "war-fighting" capability on German soil.

This poses a dilemma for West Germany. Since the United States was not inclined to give up its strategy of flexible response, the Germans sought to convince the United States to modify its concept to call for earlier use of tactical nuclear weapons at a lower threshold of violence.[10] The German leaders did this by minimizing the danger of escalation and by advocating early use of nuclear barrage weapons (Sperrwaffen) and battlefield nuclear weapons at the very border. But even this nervous compromise was not enough. By minimizing the dangers of automatic escalation to general war, the German leaders in effect suggest that controlled response would permit a limited nuclear war to rage on German soil. They attempt to get around this problem by advocating a few selective nuclear strikes against Russia to insure that the Soviets would recognize the inherent danger of starting a conflict under the belief that the tolerable limits of the nuclear threshold would allow them to achieve limited objectives without bringing on a catastrophic nuclear exchange.

The two most important factors that influence the Federal Republic's attitude to nuclear weapons and nuclear strategy are the problems of reunification and the need for security in the face of a Soviet military threat. In 1954, when West Germany signed the modifications of the Western European Union (WEU) agreements and joined NATO, the consideration of security clearly took precedence over reunification. The Western Allies pledged to support German reunification at some date in the unspecified future, and in the meantime they guaranteed West Germany's security by incorporating it into the Atlantic Alliance system.

Every nation, of course, is preoccupied with its own security above all competing considerations. In the case of West Germany, the problem of security is aggravated by her exposed position vis-à-vis the Soviet Union and its Eastern European satellites. West German hypersensitivity to problems of security is conditioned not only by the dangers of having any part of Germany overrun in the case of a Soviet attack but also by the desire to deter the Soviets from attempting a "quick grab" of Berlin, the symbol of eventual reunification. This view of the Soviet threat is at the basis of the German concept of a forward defense.

The extent of West German preoccupation with the problems of both reunification and security can be gauged by the reservations with which the FRG government greets most arms control and disarmament proposals for Central Europe. West German leaders are quick to reject any proposals of this nature, such as a zone of disengagement along the East-West German border, since they might tend to formalize the political status quo, i.e., the division of Germany, or give the Soviets an obvious military advantage, particularly in the case of a surprise Soviet aggression when superior Soviet conventional forces could play a decisive role.

The two primary objectives--security and reunification--create a quandary for German foreign policy. Germany sees her security interests served best by close association with the United States. The Germans realize that, insofar as events in Germany may provide a casus belli or trigger armed conflict with the Soviet Union, they would much prefer American military backing to the guarantees of France and Great Britain. But the Germans also realize that the goal of reunification can be advanced in the long run only through seeking closer ties with her European allies and rapprochement with the Communist satellite states. Because of this, Germany entered into the Franco-German pact and is reluctant to offend France. For if Germany cannot get along with France, there is even less likelihood that she can reach a rapprochement with Poland, Czechoslovakia, and Hungary.

Furthermore, the means available to achieve these two primary objectives are subject to the influence of a third important goal: dispelling the associations of militarism and feelings of ill-will that accrued to Germany as a result of Nazi crimes and aggressions during World War II.

The Federal Republic's strategic concept and its policy concerning nuclear weapons are affected by these three goals and interact with them. Under the German strategic concept, tactical nuclear weapons deployed by NATO in West Germany would play a key role in ensuring the FRG's security. At the same time the West German option of obtaining a nuclear force--an option which exists, of course,

regardless of the provisions of the 1954 WEU agreements--remains an important
bargaining factor in an eventual settlement concerning German reunification. West
German leaders realize that German renunciation of nuclear weapons along with
renunciation of the territories east of the Oder-Neisse Line most likely would be
important prerequisites in any reunification scheme.[11] For this reason they have
preserved options on both matters. Up to this point, however, West Germany has
not made any obvious attempt to acquire an independent nuclear strategic force
or independent control over tactical nuclear weapons.

West German Defense Minister von Hassel recently wrote that although the
Soviet objective of "Communist world domination" had not changed, "Soviet methods and tactics . . . have been refined and altered." He was quick to add, however,
by way of warning, ". . . that there is no reason to believe that the Soviets would
not revert to ways of force, or threats to use force, if they saw advantage in it."
He also stressed the point that ". . . Europe remains of special importance in
Soviet politico-military objectives."[12] Thus the official West German attitude
appears to be that the present Soviet threat in Europe, while it still exists and
should by no means be ignored, is not one of imminent Soviet military invasion
in Central Europe. On the other hand, Soviet fears of West German "revanchism"--
continually expressed in the press and radio--are one of the factors keeping the
Soviet threat alive for the West Germans, a kind of defensive reflex. Regardless
of whether the nature of the military threat has been altered significantly since
the inception of NATO, hostility and fear continue to exist in both Germany and
Russia.

France

The most significant factor in the development of a French strategic concept
is the accession of de Gaulle to power and the strong personal leadership he has
continued to exercise in restoring the pride and "grandeur" of France. Only by
understanding de Gaulle's purpose and his assessment of what he calls the "realities" of the world situation, can the rationale of French strategy be followed.
This strategy hinges on the development of an independent nuclear force and the
freedom to exploit this force politically to achieve and maintain a dominant position in Western Europe for France. Although the decision to develop nuclear en-
ergy dates back to 1952 and the positive decision to develop nuclear weapons was

taken in 1958 by the cabinet of Felix Gaillard, it was only after the fall of the
Fourth Republic that the major outline of the French strategic concept began to
take shape.

As a result of the "New Look" policy of the United States, both strategic and
tactical nuclear weapons were emphasized over conventional forces. But because
of the vulnerability of the United States to Soviet nuclear attacks, Washington
preferred to find other means than massive retaliation to handle aggression in
Europe. The idea was to store tactical nuclear weapons in Europe, these weapons to be provided to the allies under certain circumstances for their use in defense. The new Soviet medium range ballistic missiles presented a serious threat
to Western Europe. The United States attempted to counter this threat by offering
Thor and Jupiter Intermediate Range Ballistic Missiles (IRBMs) under the "double
key system" to her allies. Great Britain, Italy, and Turkey accepted the offer
but France rejected it. This rejection was based on de Gaulle's clear purpose to
acquire a greater voice in strategic decisions related to French vital interests.
The memory of Suez was fresh in his mind. When France and Britain were
threatened by Russia, both sought immediate assurances that the United States
would retaliate. The only reassurance given was ambiguous: the United States
would ". . . respect its obligations under the North Atlantic Treaty . . ."[13]

In the 1958 secret memorandum[14] to the President of the United States and
to the Prime Minister of Great Britain, de Gaulle proposed a triumvirate to for-
mulate an agreed-upon nuclear strategy, not only for the Atlantic Alliance, but
also for other areas of the world. His argument was that France, Britain, and
the United States were the only Western nations possessing an actual or potential
nuclear weapons capability and the only ones with global interests. De Gaulle considered that the world situation no longer justified leaving Free World defense
decisions in American hands. He also indicated that the achievement of the three-
power arrangement would take precedence over NATO, as far as France was concerned, since NATO did not meet the needs of France's security.[15]

This proposal was turned down by the American and British leaders. If accepted, the proposal would have undermined the American nuclear hegemony
over NATO and placed constraints on American freedom of action in other areas
of the world; it would have threatened the concept of unanimity under which the
NATO Council theoretically operated. It might well have developed an arrangement

that would compete with the special relations enjoyed by the British with the
United States. Whether the directorate of three would have satisfied the French
government's desire to have a greater voice in strategic decisions or not, the
rebuff to de Gaulle's proposal left France with only one alternative to achieve its
aim--a progressively more independent strategic concept with regard to NATO.
In 1959, the French government advised NATO that nuclear weapons could no
longer be stationed in France unless France was associated with their control.
Thereupon, nine U.S. fighter and fighter bomber squadrons were moved out of
France. Also in 1959, France withdrew her Mediterranean fleet from NATO. On
this occasion de Gaulle stated his objection to the NATO concept of integration:

> I believe that the Alliance will be all the more vital and strong
> as great powers unite on the basis of cooperation in which each
> carries his own load, rather than on the basis of an integration
> in which peoples and governments find themselves more or less
> deprived of their roles and responsibilities in the domain of
> their own defense. [16]

Then, following the failure of the Paris Summit Conference in 1960, de Gaulle
emphasized again the need for France to have her own nuclear force and the
government's firm intention of being ". . . the sole mistress of her resources
and her territory."[17] In April, 1961, he was even more explicit: "What I question, therefore, is not the Atlantic Alliance, but the present organization of the
Atlantic Alliance." He made three points: First, "it is intolerable for a great
State to leave its destiny up to the decisions and actions of another State, however friendly it may be." Second, the more exposed European members of the
Alliance ". . . must know exactly with which weapons and under which conditions
their overseas allies would join them in battle." Third, since the threats of war
are no longer limited to Europe but extend over the entire world, the Atlantic
Alliance must revise its organization to cover the areas outside of Europe and
the problems that arise there. [18] In May, 1962, de Gaulle dealt with the issue
of confidence in America's willingness to employ its nuclear force in Europe's
behalf. With America and Soviet Russia ". . . capable of striking each other
directly and, doubtless, of reciprocally destroying each other, . . . no one can
tell when, how or why one or the other of these great atomic powers would employ its nuclear arsenal." Therefore, the French atomic force coming into existence and the gradual return of French military forces from Algeria would

enable France to provide for her own national defense--something de Gaulle regards as ". . . absolutely necessary, morally and politically."[19]

One would be blind not to read into these statements of de Gaulle a consistent
stand against any arrangement that would perpetuate or extend American control
and domination over French policies. Whereas the organization of NATO and the
principle of integration were considered necessary while the United States held
a nuclear monopoly and France was exhausted and weak from defeat in World
War II, the circumstances had changed--as de Gaulle made perfectly clear in
his famous 14 January, 1963, press conference. It is worthwhile quoting certain
portions of the passage relating to the credibility of a U. S. response:[20]

> The Americans, our allies and our friends, have for a long
> time, alone, possessed a nuclear arsenal. So long as they
> alone had such an arsenal and so long as they showed their
> will to use it immediately if Europe were attacked--for at
> that time Europe alone could be attacked--the Americans
> acted in such a way that for France the question of an inva-
> sion hardly arose, since an attack was beyond all probability.
> . . . It can be said that, during that period, the deterrent
> worked and that there existed a practically insuperable ob-
> stacle to an invasion of Europe. It is impossible to overesti-
> mate the extent of the service, most fortunately passive,
> that the Americans at that time, in that way, rendered to
> the freedom of the world.

> Since then the Soviets have also acquired a nuclear arsenal,
> and that arsenal is powerful enough to endanger the very life
> of America. . . . From then on, the Americans found and
> are finding themselves confronted with the possibility of di-
> rect destruction. Thus the immediate defense, and one can
> say privileged defense of Europe, and the military participa-
> tion of the Europeans, which were once basic factors of their
> strategy, moved by the force of circumstances into second
> place. We have just witnessed this during the Cuban affair.

> The Americans, finding themselves exposed to a direct atom-
> ic attack from the Caribbean, acted in such a way as to rid
> themselves of that menace and, if it had been necessary, to
> crush it without its having occurred either to them or to any-
> one else that the game would necessarily be played in Europe
> and without recourse to the direct assistance of the Europeans.
> Moreover, the means which they immediately decided to em-
> ploy in order to counter a direct attack, whether it came from
> Cuba only or was combined with another originating elsewhere,
> these means were automatically set aside for something other
> than the defense of Europe, even if Europe had been attacked
> in its turn.

> . . . In these conditions, no one in the world--particularly
> no one in America--can say if, where, when, how, and to
> what extent the American nuclear weapons would be employed
> to defend Europe.

De Gaulle's argument about the Cuban nuclear confrontation is somewhat spe-
cious. True, this American-Russian test of will did not involve Europe directly;
but the U. S. forces that are located in Europe for NATO's defense, including the
Seventh Army and the Third and Seventeenth Air Forces, were available ". . . if
Europe had been attacked in its turn." Besides, the U. S. Strategic Air Command
was on full alert. It is curious for de Gaulle to suggest that the explicit nuclear
commitment of President Kennedy would be invalid and that the United States
would stand by and allow its European forces to be attacked without retaliation.
De Gaulle offered a more trenchant argument in his February 21, 1966, press
conference that in such a situation as Cuba Europe might have found herself involved against her will. [21]

Throughout, de Gaulle had made his position crystal clear in terms of policy.
Until February 21, 1966, he had been more circumspect in setting forth the specific and practical measures that he would like to see adopted. [22] But on this date
he bluntly announced that he would withdraw the remaining French forces from
NATO, and that all foreign forces in France would ". . . be under the sole control of French authorities." He, however, emphasized that this would not constitute a break with the alliance but a necessary adaptation to restore a normal situation of sovereignty. [23] In an aide-memoire delivered by the French government
to its allies on March 28 and 29, 1966, de Gaulle announced his intention to withdraw French forces from NATO on July 1, 1966, and set the deadline of April 1,
1967, for the removal of allied commands and U. S. and other foreign forces from
French soil. De Gaulle, however, offered to discuss arrangements with the Federal Republic of Germany for keeping French ground and air forces now stationed
in Germany. He also offered to discuss with the United States arrangements in
regard to military facilities on French territory that could be used in a possible
conflict ". . . in which both countries would take part by virtue of the Atlantic
Alliance."[24] Even here, there is some ambiguity as to how far France would go
in negotiation. De Gaulle is above all a realist. If he sees that his policies may
result in isolating France and in decreasing French influence in the affairs of
Europe and of the world, he could well modify his position.

The French strategic concept stems directly from de Gaulle's zeal for sovereignty and independence. It is completely consistent with his rejection of such integrated schemes as the American Multilateral Force (MLF) and the British Atlantic Nuclear Force (ANF). The French official views on a strategy for the defense of Western Europe are quite explicit as articulated by de Gaulle, his ministers, and his military chiefs. French spokesmen advocate an immediate massive reprisal against the Soviet homeland for any attack against "vital interests." In a speech at the NATO Defense College on 26 June 1964, General Ailleret, Chief of Staff of the French Armed Forces (a position comparable to our Chairman of the Joint Chiefs), called for a return to a NATO strategy of immediate nuclear response to aggression:[25]

1. In order to destroy the roots of aggression and its logistic support by means of nuclear strategic bombardment of the power potential of the country which launched the aggression, thus forcing it to renounce the aggression.

2. This action would be completed by a battle having simply for its end the mopping-up and destruction of the remaining forces of the aggressor which already would be susceptible of being broken up and destroyed or thrown back upon their jumping-off points of invasion.

General Ailleret does not make a distinction between "major" aggression and "limited" aggression (as the Americans do) but between "marked aggressions" (penetrations with the use of force seeking to seize all or part of Europe) and "apparent aggressions" (frontier incidents of all sorts).

To give meaning to the strategic concept, France currently depends on her own independent force de frappe of some forty Mirage IV aircraft which, according to Defense Minister Pierre Messmer, "alone is capable of exercising a determining influence on the enemy's will to wage war." France disagrees completely with the U.S. counterforce doctrine as applied to strategic forces and France's Defense Minister Pierre Messmer has said: "The only objectives that have a deterrent value are demographic; to aim for missile sites would be an absurdity."[26] In short, only by threatening immediate retaliation against Russian cities it is possible for France to achieve the maximum deterrent value from its small independent nuclear striking force.

The fact that the official pronouncements are so unequivocal does not in itself

signify that these views are strongly held by all ranking members of the French
government. There are cases where disagreements within the official French
administration on nuclear matters are publicized. For example, the controversy
between General Le Puloch, the Army Chief of Staff, and General Martin, the
Air Force Chief, reveals sharp differences. [27] The army attacks the air force
nuclear concepts in the frame of three basic questions: "Where to strike, whom
to strike, and how to strike." Briefly, the army chief advocates striking the forward units in lieu of the rear (as only engaged divisions offer a concentration of
forces and are therefore vulnerable); attacking targets of opportunity as well as
fixed targets (General Le Puloch maintains that the airplane is not capable of
discovering targets of opportunity and attacking them without delay); using tactical missiles rather than aircraft (speedier, less vulnerable, less costly). The
doctrinal aspects of the debate motivated by service interest should not be over-
estimated; they are reminiscent of American interservice arguments in the Fifties.
By the time that tactical weapons become available, probably six or seven years
hence, both sides will probably have a tactical nuclear role. The real question
narrows down to the strategy by which these weapons may be used. At present,
official pronouncements seem quite firm: the strategic concept advocated by the
Air Force Chief of Staff and General Ailleret appears to prevail.

In contemplating nuclear war, France is interested in establishing the option
of insuring her own survival by an independent deterrent force in the event the
United States is committed elsewhere or fails to live up to its commitment in
regard to France. At the same time this independent capability also provides
France with an option that will permit her to stand aloof from a crisis or test of
will between the two superpowers. This latter option is often overlooked as a
reason why France insists on an independent nuclear force. In the prevalent
American view, the French motivation is derived from a lack of confidence in
American support for France in time of crisis. An independent French nuclear
force would give France the means to "trigger" American response. While this
may be a possibility, there is no denying the fact that an independent nuclear
force also provides France the means to keep out of involvement in a nuclear
confrontation between the United States and the Soviet Union that does not affect
France's vital interests directly. De Gaulle made this point quite explicit in his
21 February 1966 Press Conference: [28] "There are other conflicts in which

America is involved in other parts of the world--as once in Korea, yesterday in Cuba, and today in Vietnam--that could escalate to a general conflagration, in which Europe whose strategy in NATO is the same as America's, would be automatically implicated even if it had not wanted it." (Emphasis supplied.)

De Gaulle, however, is not only motivated by a desire to achieve for France independence from the NATO strategy--which he equates with the strategy of the United States--but also by a desire to sustain France's position as a dominant political power in Western Europe and to establish a French hegemony over the nations of the Common Market independent of the "Anglo-Saxons." To exert leadership over the other European countries, and especially over Germany, France must appear, at least on the surface, to give support to the Forward Defense strategy advanced by Germany and adopted by NATO on 1 September 1963, for defending Western Europe at the Iron Curtain. However, since this concept calls for early use of tactical nuclear weapons to prevent West German territory from being overrun, there are obvious inconsistencies with the Forward Defense concept and the strategy pronounced by General Ailleret.

According to General Ailleret, who rules out conventional defense in Europe except in the case of frontier incidents, even the use of tactical nuclear defense could hardly be judged satisfactory for the French. For even if tactical nuclear warfare ". . . prevented the invasion of Europe, it could not protect the Europeans from destruction." He also stated:[29]

> This situation (limited tactical nuclear war) constitutes a method to be employed only if there is no other way to do it-- that is to say, if the United States, which is the only country today capable of deterrence and the only country which has nuclear stockpiles for conducting nuclear war on a grand scale, decides to apply this method to the exclusion of all others. In view of this hypothesis, it is necessary for the Western forces to be prepared intellectually as well as materially to use tactical nuclear weapons, but they don't recommend their use and they would only be able to resign themselves to it.

The French would use tactical nuclear weapons as a secondary action in the field simply ". . . for mopping up the destruction of the remaining forces of the aggressor . . . "

The inconsistency in these views and those of the Forward Defense Strategy was pinpointed in an editorial in Le Monde:[30]

> Without saying it in so many words, General Ailleret, in
> sanctioning a simple system of alert condemns the "forward
> strategy" which NATO has taken so much pains to put in ef-
> fect. The French government has always declared that it
> would deploy a certain number of units towards the East.
> Only the lack of a coherent group of casernes and territory
> for training has retarded the transfer. It will be difficult to
> maintain henceforth this policy position, first of all dooming
> the manifestation of French good will to the German Federal
> Republic.

The lack of French support for NATO's forward defense strategy obviously
gives the Germans cause for concern. On the other hand, the French concept of
immediate massive retaliation provides the element of early strikes against the
Russian homeland missing in the American strategic concept of flexible and controlled response. The only question is whether France would carry out the threat
against Russia, if only Germany were attacked. De Gaulle recognizes this concern of the Germans, and even in the process of pulling French forces out of
NATO he stated that France is willing to reach an agreement ". . . regarding
the conditions of the cooperation of her forces and theirs (i. e. , the allies) in the
event of a common action, especially in Germany."[31]

There is no question of the sharp differences between American strategic
concepts, with their emphasis on integration of national forces and flexible response, and the French concepts in favor of an independent deterrent force threatening immediate retaliation against population centers. There is little doubt that
the French strategic concept and de Gaulle's withdrawal of French forces from
the integrated military command of NATO stem from motivations of national self-
interests and dissatisfaction with the institutional arrangements of the Alliance
that perpetuate American control and domination over certain French policies.
But this is a far cry from justifying an independent nuclear force as General
Pierre Gallois and others do, on the grounds that nuclear weapons have made
alliances obsolete. [32] Assuredly, de Gaulle does not think so. For, as Raymond
Aron pointed out, ". . . it was the Atlantic Alliance that in the years past enabled
France to commit the bulk of her forces abroad and that, in the years to come,
may make it possible for her to reduce conventional forces in favor of the atomic
program."[33]

Yet there is much to be said for a completely independent deterrent force
for France aside from the reasons advanced by the more nationalist advocates.

French General André Beaufré argues that since nuclear war has become unthinkable because of the inevitable and reciprocal destruction it would entail, nuclear weapons can only act as an effective deterrent to war if there exist a certain amount of instability or uncertainty in the command and control arrangements so as to prevent "nuclear paralysis" from setting in. Several nuclear decision centers are better than one and the plurality of means provide the necessary element of uncertainty that makes deterrence credible.[34] There is little doubt that the French possession of an independent nuclear force adds another uncertain element to the Soviet calculations of NATO response to any aggression the Kremlin may contemplate.

The crucial question therefore is not the existence of a French independent nuclear force--for Great Britain has one also--but whether the nuclear force is to be employed within the Alliance to strengthen deterrence or to be used as a means to further political aims inimical to the mutual interests of the other members.

Great Britain

It is easy to generalize and to attribute the development of the German strategic concept to external pressures and events imposed on a divided country, psychologically inhibited by the shameful remembrance of the horrors of the Third Reich. The constraints and institutional arrangements imposed on a defeated Germany easily account for the lack of freedom of political action and her acquiescence to NATO's strategic direction. It is equally overly simple to blame de Gaulle for the strategy of France. The pronouncements of de Gaulle trace a continuation of France's traditional aspirations for greatness and for becoming the dominant political power in Europe, which adequately accounts for her independent strategic concept.

But when it comes to Britain, no single set of factors or any one personality can be singled out of the confusion of rival political groups, conflicting economic pressures, and opposing traditional policies as dominant in the development of British strategic thought. It is not a case of "muddling through" as the British so often characterize their own actions. For what emerges as a strategic concept is a conscious synthesis of many pressures and counterpressures, an apparent logical adaptation of strategy to the realities of the nuclear age, to Britain's reduced world power position, and to the needs of the Atlantic Alliance.

The changes in British strategy have been profound. Traditionally a maritime power, with the twin strategic problems of protecting her overseas empire and at the same time preventing a dominant continental power from threatening her resources, Britain avoided any binding commitment that would tie down her forces to the continent. Today, all this has changed. Britain has largely liquidated her overseas empire; she has accepted the obligation for maintaining ground and air forces on the continent in peacetime; and she has elected to utilize her limited resources primarily for the nuclear defense of her homeland. Britain's decision to purchase F-111 aircraft from the United States rather than build a new aircraft carrier clearly indicates her choice of priorities. Implicit in all these actions is acceptance by Britain of her role as a secondary power. This does not mean that Britain has abdicated her responsibilites for influencing events in the world. On the contrary, it only means that Britain recognizes the realities of the political and economic constraints that limit her commitments mainly to those that affect her vital national interests.

The first major change in British defense policy was set forth in the Defense White Paper of 1957 that outlined a five-year plan aimed at reducing military expenditures and abolishing conscription by 1962. The significance of this White Paper was in the frank acceptance of the fact that no country can any longer protect itself in isolation. "The defense of Britain is possible only as part of the collective defense of the free world. . . " and the ". . . overriding consideration in all military planning must be to prevent war rather than to prepare for it."[35] Britain obviously took its cue from the Eisenhower "New Look" strategy with its emphasis on nuclear weapons rather than on conventional armed forces.

The events of December 1962 and January 1963--cancellation of Skybolt, the Nassau agreement, and France's veto of Britain's application to join the European Economic Community--forced British defense policy to undergo a second major reappraisal.

The joint Anglo-American Statement of Nuclear Defense Systems[36] agreed to at Nassau underlines a significant shift in Britain's attitude toward NATO and is marked by Britain's acceptance of: (1) assignment of her future Polaris submarine force to NATO; (2) subscription "for the immediate future" of some part of the V-Bomber force to NATO; and (3) the creation of a NATO command and control mechanism for strategic nuclear forces.

British strategic debate, as in France, centers around the independent nuclear force. Under the Conservative British government, the official position
was that Britain's ". . . contribution to the strategic deterrent remains significant. It is by itself enough to make a potential aggressor fear that our retaliation
would inflict destruction beyond any level which he would be prepared to tolerate."[37]
The former Conservative prime minister, Mr. Harold MacMillan, insisted that
Britain would retain her independent nuclear deterrent power: "It is the view of
the Government . . . that it would not be right for Britain to abandon the nuclear
weapon at this stage." He gave four reasons why Britain should maintain an independent deterrent. First, Britain had the nuclear knowledge and capacity to contribute to the alliance. Second, the United States could not expect other nations
possessing nuclear weapons to hand over forever complete control. Third, the
prestige of a nuclear power permits a country to make valuable contributions to
international discussions. Fourth, ". . . there may be conditions, there may be
areas, in which the interests of some countries may seem to them more vital
than they seem to others." This last reason MacMillan considered the most important as it would enable Britain to maintain her position free from threat and
". . . to make her independent decisions on issues vital to her life."[38] This,
incidentally, is precisely the reason de Gaulle gives for France's independent
force de frappe.

On the other hand, Labour Prime Minister Mr. Harold Wilson is acutely conscious of the fact that the effectiveness of the overall Western deterrent does not
stem from the manifestly small British nuclear contribution, but from the marked
preponderance in strategic power that the United States possesses. Wilson would
no doubt agree with the first three reasons advanced by MacMillan, but he would
use these not to justify an independent force but to support Britain's nuclear contribution to the Alliance. He disagrees with MacMillan's fourth reason: that it is
possible for Britain to make independent decisions on issues ". . . more vital
than they seem to others," and therefore calls for merging the British nuclear
force into an Atlantic Nuclear Force under a NATO commander. The British
contribution, Wilson insists, ". . . would be wholly committed for as long as the
Alliance continued."[39] He seeks to preserve above all the American veto on the
use of strategic nuclear forces, and would disapprove of any system of majority
voting for the force. Wilson has insisted, however, that Britain also retain a veto:

"For any combination of NATO allies to override either the United States or Britain would, I am sure both sides of the House will agree, involve proliferation which would be unacceptable."[40] Prime Minister Wilson has outlined three objectives of the British proposals for an Atlantic Nuclear Force: (1) participation of non-nuclear members in nuclear planning, (2) unity of command and integration with other commands in the Alliance structure, and (3) increased and continuous consultation about ". . . deployment of nuclear weapons or situations that might require their use."

The statements of MacMillan and Wilson indicate many similarities in stated policy. Both parties agree to the ultimate veto as to the use of nuclear weapons in the hands of the President of the United States insofar as NATO is concerned. Both favor consultation that would permit Britain to have a voice in nuclear strategy. The Conservatives reserved the right to withdraw and use the British strategic forces assigned to NATO ". . . where her Majesty's Government may decide that supreme national interests are at stake."[41] In 1960, before the election, Labour went on record that "Britain should cease the attempt to remain an independent nuclear power, since this neither strengthens the alliance nor is it a now sensible use of our resources."[42] Since Labour has come to power, however, it has in practice done little to reduce the allocation of resources for the nuclear force. True, as did the White Paper of 1965, the White Paper of 1966 calls for internationalizing British nuclear strategic forces in order to discourage further proliferation and to strengthen the Alliance.[43] Nevertheless, such a NATO command arrangement is not now in force. Latent Labour-Conservative disagreement on the need for an independent nuclear force remains; but for various reasons, including the objections of some of Britain's allies, the Labour Government has not changed the actual situation in practice. There are some good reasons to preserve an independent nuclear force as a hedge against future contingencies. So long as the French nuclear force exists, Britain is not likely to concede to France the role of being the only nuclear power in Europe. A certain prestige is conveyed to the owners of nuclear weapons on strategic matters, which is not conferred upon the lesser powers. There may be possible commerical advantages in future nuclear technology. With the present course adopted by France, Britain would do well to stand by as an alternative European nuclear catalyst should political changes loosen the ties of Europe with the United States.

When the British contemplate a possible nuclear war, the small size and dense population of the British Isles are foremost in their thoughts; they see no hope of defense against a thermonuclear attack. Accordingly, most of their strategic thinking deals with the problem of deterrence rather than defense. The British also perceive rather clearly that the ultimate success of deterrence rests with the United States; they are threfore motivated to maintain close bonds to ensure that they can influence American action in matters of Britain's survival. Alternatively, some commentators see in Britain's vulnerability to nuclear attack an incentive to seek neutralism or non-involvement in a U.S.-Soviet confrontation or conflict. This thesis is bolstered by the stand of the Campaign for Nuclear Disarmament (CND) and by some left-wing members of the Labour Party. However, other major values or objectives supplement the desire for close collaboration with the United States: namely, the long history of traditional exercise of world power by Great Britain, her continued interest in wielding influence in the world today as evidenced by her commitment to members of the Commonwealth and her experience of friendly and mutually beneficial relations with the United States during and after World War II. These values are conditioned by British preoccupation with alleviating a serious balance-of-payments problem and with defending the pound sterling that make the economy incapable of supporting important increases in military expenditures.

Britain's assessment of the threat also supports the position she takes for continual involvement in world affairs and cultivation of the "special relationship" with the United States. Only a perceptible increase in the Soviet threat coupled with a clear indication that the United States is withdrawing from involvement in European affairs--both of which are exceedingly unlikely--would cause the British to reassess their relationship with the United States. A major armed attack by the Soviet Union on Europe is considered extremely improbable; but there is always the risk of war arising out of misunderstanding or miscalculation, such as when the origin of the conflict is uncertain or where the intentions of the enemy are obscure. For such conflicts in Europe, the British consider that ". . . the number of ground formations already available is probably sufficient."[44] The British oppose automatic resort to nuclear weapons. On the other hand, they reject the concept that nuclear wapons can be used in a controlled and selected manner-- even if confined to the battlefield: "Once nuclear weapons were employed in

Europe on however limited a scale, it is almost certain that, unless the aggressor quickly decided to stop fighting, the conflict would escalate rapidly to general
nuclear exchange, in which the whole of America's nuclear forces would be engaged."[44] This view is also shared by the Conservatives.

British actions during the Berlin crisis of 1961 reveal some interesting aspects of British official thinking on strategic concepts for defense.[45] While
supporting U.S. definition of vital interests in Berlin, the British government
balked at the new element of a conventional tactical probe up the autobahn, which
President Kennedy wished to insert in the strategy for dealing with the crisis.
Britain favored maintaining the threshold of nuclear weapons as the transition
point to armed conflict. In other words, Britain preferred to stand pat on nuclear
deterrence to force the Soviets to back down on their planned course of action in
Berlin. Thus the NATO concept of the pre-nuclear conventional "pause" advanced
by General Norstad and supported by British official public pronouncements appears to have been rejected in favor of a "trip-wire" concept in this particular
instance.

On the whole, the military posture of the British in Western Europe appears
to support their pronouncements. Despite heavy balance-of-payments problems,
Britain has maintained a commitment in continental Europe in the form of a
British Army of the Rhine (BAOR) of eighteen battalions or three divisions and
a Royal Air Force contingent of Canberra strike squadrons for both the conventional and nuclear role. It is interesting to note that the BAOR is larger than the
strategic army reserve maintained in the United Kingdom proper. It is clear that
Britain's commitment to NATO is strong. However, it is perhaps indicative of
Britain's distaste for strategic concepts for limited tactical nuclear war that she
has opposed the mobile medium-range ballistic missile (MMRBM) concept and
has declined to incorporate shorter-range tactical nuclear missiles into the BAOR.
Mr. Denis Healey has rejected ". . . the American concept of a prolonged defense
of Western Europe by conventional forces supported by tactical nuclear weapons."
Instead, he suggests that greater nuclear power be given to the NATO commander
to indicate that ". . . any attack could lead to a nuclear war and the destruction
of the Soviet Union."[46] (Emphasis added.) These statements and actions would
seem to confirm the British view that such weapons could not and ought not be
distinguished from other strategic weapons (UK Bomber Command) and that their
use would almost certainly escalate to general war.

SOVIET STRATEGY IN EUROPE

One of the remarkable aspects of the current strategic debate within the Atlantic Alliance is the lack of discussion and almost total lack of concern for the Soviet strategic concept in Europe. An essential element of that conflict is the strategic concept of the Soviet Union's use of its armed forces in a possible war in Europe. Specifically, what can NATO expect the Soviet Union to do militarily in the event of conflict? Here we face the difficulty of viewing the conflict in the same terms as the Soviets. So much of the theoretical debate on strategy within the Soviet Union is concealed in the dialectics of Communist ideology that it is difficult to discover just what the firm aspects of its strategic concept are and what are merely declaratory statements.

There is no question that many of the actions of the USSR are dictated by national self-interest, as are the actions of any other powerful state. In such cases, Communism is used as an ideology by which the Kremlin rulers seek to justify or explain their actions. We should not, however, dismiss the idea that "scientific" socialism, as a totally new concept, has necessarily influenced the development of Soviet military strategy. The Communist claim on the world's future through a proletarian revolution may be just a visionary notion, but its validity depends on its operational significance. Often when Soviets say and do things that seem to indicate that they are advancing the cause of world communism, we react with hostility and assign to Communist ideology a large part of the offensive character we perceive in Soviet global strategy. Whether the Soviet Union's actions to expand its power and influence is motivated by revolutionary zeal or national aspirations is moot. The evidence would seem to support the

view that the Soviet Union is strongly defensive in a military sense although its
overall strategy may be characterized as offensive in a political sense. Whenever the Soviet Union has seen an opportunity to advance either national interests
or revolutionary aspirations at low risks, it has done so by a variety of means--
even military. The subjugation and absorption of the Baltic States, the seizure of
territory from Poland and Romania, and the imposition of Communist regimes
on East Germany, Poland, Hungary, Romania, Bulgaria, North Korea, and finally, Czechoslovakia, all come in the aftermath of the Nazi and Japanese defeat.
A power vacuum existed that was adroitly filled by the Russians. The presence
of the Red Army quite naturally played a part--at low risk. [1]

The mixture of the political offensive and the military defensive in Soviet
strategy can be attributed to certain characteristics of the Russian people as
well as to certain characteristics of the Soviet hierarchy and precepts of its
ideology. For example, Soviet revolutionary pretensions and aggressive political purposes are colored by the same fear and distrust of foreigners as were
felt by the leaders of Tsarist Russia. This, and a strong desire to conserve and
hold on to the material gains, has tended to make the operations of Soviet strategy conservative: adventurism is eschewed though opportunities are seized when
the risks are low, as the Soviet Union seeks to assist the advance of the historical design. Cuba was a mistake. What appeared as an opportunity to make striking gains at low risks turned out to be a humiliating "adventure." The Soviet
leadership completely miscalculated American reaction. As soon as the United
States raised the stakes, the USSR backed down.

The Russians have historically displayed an understandably defensive concern for their homeland, and especially for Moscow, traditionally regarded as
the "Third Rome." The need for defending the physical security of the homeland,
whether against the medieval Tartars, the seventeenth-century Poles, the eight-
eenth-century Swedes, the nineteenth-century Turks, or the twentieth-century
Teutons has been a basic factor in Russian strategic considerations. The ghosts
of past invaders have had a definite influence on Soviet Russia's attempt to establish security by a cordon sanitaire in reverse, a chain of buffer states bordering
Russia, dominated by the military, political, and economic policies of the Kremlin. This aim was finally achieved on the western flank at the end of World War II.

In short, conservative and defensive tendencies have clearly influenced the

Soviet doctrinal approach to strategy. As Sokolovsky put it, "Military doctrine. . . is formed on the basis of the entire life-experience of a state and is the result of an extremely complex and protracted historical process . . . [as] determined by the general policy of the social class ruling the state and by the economic and moral resources at its disposal."[2] Whatever means the Soviet select for carrying out the "protracted historical process," however, they will be such that the supremacy of Soviet power and the survival of the Soviet Union will not be put in jeopardy.

Since the first days of the United States' atomic monopoly, the Soviets have had a primary aim to break out from "capitalist encirclement." The fact that this encirclement was a reaction of the West to the Soviet consolidation of her war gains by setting up a puppet state in the Soviet-occupied zone of Germany, by engineering the coup d'état in Czechoslovakia, and by establishing Communist regimes in other buffer satellite states, is of course not at issue. By 1960 the Soviets believed that their successful development of nuclear weapons and means of delivery had neutralized American strategic superiority. As Khrushchev once pointed out, it was no longer clear who was encircling whom. The Soviets' assumed strength in missiles and in space had a terrific impact on the entire world. Most of all it had an impact on the Soviets themselves. Very likely they began to believe their own propaganda and saw themselves in a position of growing invincibility. The conversation reported between Premier Khrushchev and President Kennedy at Vienna in June 1961 indicated that the Soviets had decided to put to the test the United States resolve--already, in Soviet eyes, weakened by the Bay of Pigs fiasco--and to pursue the expansionist foreign policy plainly called for by their ideology.[3] The Berlin crisis of 1961 and the Cuban missile confrontation of 1962 no doubt had their origins in a mistaken Soviet assessment of United States' resolve.

It is important to recall these crises and the subsequent dénouements to understand the Soviet strategic concept. For although the Soviets clearly want to alter the balance of world power in their favor, they do not want to jeopardize in any way the security of Russia in doing so. The battle is waged increasingly on the diplomatic, economic, scientific, and ideological fronts, with the objective of establishing "peaceful coexistence" on Communist terms. "Peaceful coexistence must be correctly understood," said Khrushchev. "Coexistence is the continuation of the struggle between two social systems, but a struggle by peaceful means, without war . . . ."[4] The Soviet leaders have by no means given up the use of threats to further their goals. It is only that they have found it advantageous in the present circumstances to get the confrontation with the United States on grounds less dangerous to Russia's survival.

Two significant developments during the last fifteen years provide a key to understanding the Soviet strategic concept. The first was related to the death of Stalin's "permanently operating factors." War was a struggle between one social system and another, and the outcome would be determined by permanent factors, which denied the relevance of many of the principles of warfare. Nuclear weapons were assimilated within the conceptual framework of these factors, but the element of surprise was not. The permanently operating factors were the stability of the rear (i.e., as we understand it, the zone of the interior), the morale of the Army, the quantity and quality of divisions, the armament of the Army, and the organizational ability of the Army Commanders. Nuclear weapons were important considerations, but not decisive.

Soon after Stalin's death, Major General Talenskii wrote an article that started a train of new thought which ultimately rejected the Stalinist formula. Emphasis was placed on armed might and combat. The importance of nuclear weapons was more clearly assessed. Communist theory could not accept the view that the initial nuclear attack would achieve victory and end the war because of the possibility that the West would strike first. However, it did recognize that early nuclear success could very well bring on ultimate victory. The element of surprise was given unprecedented recognition and this, in turn, through the logic of dialectics, demanded that the Soviet Union be prepared to launch a "preemptive or forestalling strike" against an enemy poised to attack.[5] However, Soviet declaratory policy on preemption has remained ambiguous and perhaps deliberately so. In the first place, U.S. air generals, with massive first-strike forces under their command, had talked about preemptive strikes for years. Second, the evidence would seem to indicate that the Soviet Union has not undertaken to build a strategic force capable of rational first-strike use. There are obvious disadvantages to advertising an ability and intention to preempt as a key element in a deterrent strategy. For one thing a convincing Soviet case for preemption might prompt the United States, Britain, or France to entertain a similar concept in turn rather than to place complete reliance on a secure second-strike posture. Second, it would mar the image of the Soviet Union as a peace-loving nation interested only in defending itself against the armed attack of the imperialist nations.[6] On the other hand, there are practical advantages in a military posture capable of launching a preemptive nuclear attack both in strengthening the deterrence and in reducing the magnitude of destruction in the event of war. Since it has become clear that the United States' invulnerable strategic posture of hardened Minuteman sites and concealed Polaris submarines would prevent the Soviets from achieving a decisive advantage, there are signs that the Soviets are also putting effort in a second strike posture. As McNamara pointed out in 1963, there is increasing evidence that the Soviet Union has begun to adopt measures for hardening its strategic missile sites to acquire a reliable second-strike posture.[7] Furthermore, the missiles shown in the May Day parade in Red Square in the last few years are indication that the Soviets are also placing emphasis on mobility to reduce vulnerability.

At the same time the development of a strong nuclear force posture--clearly dictated by national security interests--was taking place, a second development occurred that was related to the deposing of Malenkov and to the ideological arguments on strategy that attended his downfall. In March 1954, Pravda reported Malenkov as having pointed out the possible "destruction of world civilization" with the present means of warfare. He also was quoted as having said that he knew of ". . . no objective impediments to the improvement in the relations between the Soviet Union and the United States." These two statements were anathema to Communist theoreticians. To suggest the possibility of destruction of the Soviet Union, as the first statement implied, was "defeatism." To suggest that a state of mutual deterrence could exist and that accommodation with the United States could be made was "heresy." It only took a short time to bring Malenkov to heel. On April 26, he made a complete reversal and predicted that a third world war "would inevitably lead to the collapse of the capitalist system."[8] Whatever were the true reasons for the dismissal of Malenkov from the office of Premier, it would appear that the ideological aspects of strategy contributed at least partially to the grounds or to the justification for his ouster.

Two important doctrinal considerations have emerged from these events that illustrate how Communist ideology and Russian national security interests were reconciled in the development of the Soviet strategic concept. First, the basic Communist tenet that the USSR will emerge victorious was upheld. This doctrine requires a strategic concept based on military superiority. The imbalance in the strategic postures in favor of the United States does not prevent the Soviets from advancing the claim of military superiority.[9] To emerge victorious, the USSR must obviously possess superiority in the most advanced nuclear weapons and be prepared to use these weapons not only against military targets, but also against communication networks, industry, and population. The idea of placing restraints on the use of nuclear weapons to limit damage could suggest that one side or the other might concede defeat before resorting to the use of the most destructive weapons. The Soviets categorically reject the idea that a war can be kept limited and claim that ". . . armed conflict will inevitably develop into an all-out nuclear war if the nuclear powers are drawn into it."[10] According to Sokolovsky:

> The annihilation of the enemy's armed forces, the destruction of objectives in the rear, and disorganization of the rear will be a single continuous process of the war. Two main factors serve as the basis for this answer: the need to defeat the aggressor decisively in the shortest possible time, for which purpose it will be necessary to deprive him simultaneously of the military, political, and economic means of waging war; secondly, the real possibility of [our] achieving these goals simultaneously with existing weapons.

Whether one believes the Russian statements is not so important as the objective evidence of their capabilities. Stephan T. Possony points out time and again in his analysis of Communism that the statements made for public dissemination and the interpretations of Marxist-Leninism cannot be accepted at face value.[12] The large numbers of rockets and medium- and intermediate-range nuclear missiles in the Soviet arsenal, however, indicate that the Soviet Union does possess a capability of carrying out the above strategy--at least against Europe.

This leads one to the second doctrinal consideration, which is based on a more realistic appreciation of the dangers of nuclear war to the survival of the USSR. The Soviet Union could well adhere to the doctrine of military superiority and the tenet of emerging victorious as long as there was no war. But there was a certain incompatibility with this doctrine and Lenin's prediction of "inevitable" catastrophic war between the capitalist states and of a ". . . series of frightful collisions between the Soviet Republic and the bourgeois states."[13] Khrushchev resolved this doctrinal dilemma at the twentieth Party Congress in 1956 by

revising the party line to claim that war was no longer ". . . a fatalistic inevita-
bility. "[14] But the proviso is implicit that the danger of war remains as long as
imperialism survives. He made it clear then and later that, whereas general war
is no longer considered inevitable, the same statement did not apply to local wars
and wars of national liberation that are favorable to Communist purposes. The
Kremlin leaders undoubtedly recognize the dangers of escalation to general war
by any use of nuclear weapons. This does not inhibit them, however, from em-
phasizing the dangers of escalation for political purposes as long as they believe
the risk of a nuclear war occurring can be rationally controlled. As Marshall
Malinovskii stated in November 1962, "No matter where a 'tactical' atomic weapon might be used against us, it would trigger a crushing counterblow."[15]

The sometimes incredible inconsistencies between Soviet military capabilities
and Soviet announced doctrine, according to Robert D. Crane, may be explained
by three hypotheses. First, the Soviets, with a lack of sophistication by American
standards, might not have realized that many aspects of their force posture (e. g.,
unhardened missile sites) were inconsistent with the Soviet strategic concept for
protracted war. Second, the Soviets might consciously be trying to manipulate
the strategic thinking of the opponent over an extended period of time. Under this
view, Soviet military doctrine is not designed as a guide for actually waging war,
". . . but rather as an instrument of psychological warfare. . . " In other words,
the Soviet doctrine of superiority that would assure Soviet victory in an all-out
war might convince the West that the Soviets would be willing to wage such a
general war if provoked by American action. Third, the Soviets do not regard
doctrine by itself as an adequate and true reflection of Soviet military thinking,
and therefore are not necessarily bound by it in a practical sense. [16] All of these
hypotheses may be correct to some degree. As far as the Soviets' declaratory
strategic concept is concerned, however, the Soviets reject the American idea
that a distinction can be made in general war between counterforce strikes and
strikes against population centers. Furthermore, the Soviets assert unequivocally
that local war would escalate to general nuclear war, if (1) the nuclear powers
are participants, and (2) nuclear weapons, even tactical nuclear weapons, are
employed. The American strategic doctrine of flexible response is opposed as
". . . an adventuristic reckoning by the American imperialists to wage war on
foreign territory."[17]

Whether or not the Soviets would adhere to this strategic doctrine in the
event of conflict in Central Europe is questionable. Putting aside ideological considerations, it would appear that the same rationale that applies to the U.S. concept of flexible response would also apply to the Soviet Union. A limited conflict
in Western Europe may well jeopardize the vital interests of the Soviet allies in
the Warsaw Pact, but it would not inevitably jeopardize the core of the alliance
that is the Soviet Union. The question is similar to the one asked by our NATO
allies. Whether the United States would sacrifice American cities to defend Paris
or Copenhagen could also be asked by Czechoslovakia and Poland of the Soviet
Union. Whether Russia would be willing to sacrifice Moscow to defend Warsaw
or Prague is a moot question. In fact, it would seem that the Soviets' conventional superiority and geographical position in Europe would make a strategic doctrine
of conventional defense even more attractive to Russia than to the United States,
especially if the Soviets sincerely believed in their vaunted military superiority
for a protracted war and the hazards of nuclear escalation.

Thomas W. Wolfe has pointed out that there are some signs of change in the
Soviet doctrinal position with regard to limited and local war.[18] But even the signs
of change he points out are ambiguous. The Soviets recognize the possibility that
". . . the imperialists . . . might launch against us one form or another of war
without supplying nuclear weapons." Therefore, the Soviets must be prepared to
deal ". . . an appropriate rebuff also with conventional means."[19] However,
". . . once matters reach the use of nuclear weapons, the sides will be forced
to put into operation their entire nuclear strength. Local war will turn into world
nuclear war."[20]

Robert D. Crane also makes a persuasive case for Soviet acceptance of the
concept of limited war and controlled response through an analysis of Soviet military writings. He cites various quotations, such as ". . . The imperialists may
engage us in one or another form of war without the use of nuclear weapons. The
practical conclusion from this is that our armed forces should be ready to respond
in an appropriate manner with conventional weapons . . ." "'The methods of con-
ducting war against an enemy,' wrote Lenin, 'must be changeable when circumstances change.' . . ." "If things develop in one way then military actions will
be characterized by the massive use of nuclear weapons, if in another way then
by their partial use, and if in still a third way then by complete abstention from

their use. It all depends on the conditions, the place, and the time . . ."[21] Whereas, on appropriate occasions, the Soviets may continue to insist that the conduct of a war in Europe with nuclear weapons cannot be limited, these selected statements would at least indicate that some military writers are having second thoughts.

An indication that a Soviet strategic doctrine for limited war in Europe has been developed is found in the Warsaw Pact maneuvers that took place the last week in October 1965. The war game began with a surprise attack by the West deep into Thuringia, a part of East Germany, employing conventional tank forces, artillery, and air support. By the third day, the Warsaw Pact forces had repelled the attack and launched a counteroffensive--all with conventional weapons. At this point the Western "enemy" began to use nuclear weapons, that were responded to by "mighty atomic counterattacks."[22] The scenario used for these maneuvers would indicate that, on the military side, the Soviet military plans envision employing a conventional defense, at least initially. Perhaps the Soviets are swinging around to an operational strategic concept of a flexible response to defend what they already hold. This would seem logical, particularly if it is coupled with the threat of nuclear retaliation or nuclear escalation to dissuade the West from employing military force to oppose Soviet advances by other means.

In a later chapter it will be shown rather concretely that the Soviet forces in East Europe are oriented for defense. The ten armored and ten infantry divisions are disposed in East German casernes in such a uniform manner that they could be used either to defend against a NATO attack or to suppress an uprising in East Germany, Poland, or Czechoslovakia. The Soviet Air Force disposition is even more significant. The primary emphasis on defense is made evident by the considerable size of the Soviet interceptor force dispersed widely at many airfields throughout East Germany. In connection with this, the Soviets place great reliance of their surface-to-air missiles (SA-2s) to protect Communist territory from high-altitude attacks. As time goes on, the Soviets are expected to deploy large numbers of the SA-3 missiles, which are similar to the U.S. Hawk surface-to-air missile, to destroy aircraft at lower altitudes.

The record also confirms this defensive orientation. Since the fall of Czechoslovakia and the commitment of the United States to the Atlantic Alliance, the Soviet Union has exercised extreme caution in making advances and has not hesitated to back down (Cuba, Iran) or limit its commitment (Greece, West Berlin,

Korea, Vietnam) when faced with a direct confrontation of American force. On the other hand, once a gain has been made (Hungary, East Germany, the Berlin Wall) the Soviet Union has not hesitated to use its superior conventional force to protect the advantage.

Viewed from the record and available evidence, the Soviet strategic doctrine in Europe begins to become somewhat clearer. Her large conventional forces permit the Soviet Union to maintain and protect the gains that she has achieved, whereas her strong emphasis on nuclear rockets and the threat of an "inevitable" escalation is designed to inhibit NATO from opposing Soviet minor or political and strategic advances. By the same token, the American strategic concept of flexible response--despite the objections of the NATO allies--is exactly tailored to oppose these advances. The Cuban missile crisis is a classic illustration. The Soviet attempt for a fait accompli was based upon the mistaken belief that Soviet nuclear capabilities would deter the United States from interfering. The attempt failed, not because President Kennedy warned the Kremlin that an attack against any nation in the Western hemisphere would be regarded as a Soviet attack against the United States ". . . requiring a full retaliatory response," but because the United States ignored the implied Soviet missile threat and opposed the Soviet move with a conventional military force: the naval "quarantine" or blockade. American strategic nuclear strength, of course, weighed heavily in Soviet calculations, but the naval blockade placed the burden of escalation upon the Kremlin and exposed the Soviet nuclear threat as a bluff.

For the Soviets, as well as for the West, the major issue of contention is still Germany. Premier Kosygin has reiterated what has been said time and time again by Communist leaders:

> The main requisites for ensuring European security are the
> inviolability of existing frontiers, including the Oder-Neisse
> line and the border between the two German states, as well
> as the prevention of West Germany's access to nuclear weap-
> ons in any form. [23]

The Warsaw Pact meeting in July 1966 noted that "the question of frontiers in Europe has been finally and irreversibly settled."[24] (Emphasis supplied.) The Russians are genuinely afraid of German designs. But they also would prefer to deal with a Germany that is not backed by the United States. It is thus a necessary part of Soviet policy to seek the disengagement or noninvolvement of the United States in Europe.

The Soviet Union will therefore continue to seek to divide the NATO alliance. It is quite clear that the Russians have no intention of permitting Germany to re-unify; nor would the Soviet leaders jeopardize Russian hegemony over the satellite states or Russian core interests by major military adventure. However, the Soviet Union might possibly employ military forces in a sort of "salami tactic" to achieve minor gains, relying on the threat of nuclear escalation to keep NATO from opposing her move. In the unlikely event that the Soviet Union should resort to force or threats of force in such cases, the NATO strategy should be to oppose the action with resolution and dispatch at the lowest level of conflict.

NATO STRATEGY AND FLEXIBLE RESPONSE

Essential Differences

The security of European NATO nations is no longer completely dependent upon the United States as it was immediately following World War II and the fall of Czechoslovakia to the Communists. The perception of a diminished Soviet military threat, the growing strength of the European nations, and the vulnerability of the United States to Soviet nuclear attacks have all had an influence in the evolving strategic differences in the Atlantic Alliance. The improved stability of the military confrontation now permits the nations of Europe to attempt to shape their own individual destinies.

Because each nation sees its destiny in different terms, each also conceives of different means or strategy to achieve its objectives. Although there are limited alternatives, the basic strategy of each sovereign nation is largely determined by considerations of national self-interest, the nation's primary values and objectives, and the means or capabilities it possesses. Thus attempts to arrive at an enduring agreement on an Alliance strategic concept in peacetime can result, at best, only in compromises.

In each dimension of warfare there are differences among the four major nations in the Atlantic Alliance. Table I highlights in simplified form the salient features of the different strategic concepts for the defense of Western Europe. Despite these differences, the views of Britain, France, and Germany on nuclear policy have a common theme: every country is more concerned with deterrence than with defense.

The West European nations are mistrustful of American attempts to build up

Table I

SALIENT FEATURES OF STRATEGIC CONCEPTS
FOR DEFENSE OF WESTERN EUROPE

Country	Conventional Warfare	Tactical Nuclear Warfare
United States	Prolongation of conventional defense as long as possible	Employment of tactical weapons in a selective manner
Great Britain	Short conventional defense to ascertain Soviet intentions	Employment of tactical weapons in demonstration of resolve and then in conjunction with strategic force
France	No conventional defense except for border incidents	Immediate nuclear retaliation on Russia
Germany	Short conventional defense at border to ascertain Soviet intentions, but with a very low nuclear threshold	Almost immediate use of battlefield nuclear weapons in zone of conflict, with possible demonstration strikes on Soviet territory

military forces in Europe sufficient to defend the borders against major attack with conventional means. They see this action as degrading the credibility of deterrence, and they fear the consequence of a large-scale conventional war in Europe, an implication of the U. S. concept of flexible response. As Professor Henry Kissinger points out, a Soviet penetration of even a hundred miles in the fluctuations of conventional combat is a vital matter in which the national existence of a state is at stake.[1] Europeans, viewing the success of the NATO deterrent posture in the last seventeen years, are reluctant to change from a strategy that threatens an aggressor with massive destruction to one that reduces losses for a defender. They want the continuance of a nuclear deterrent that is reliable and credible. To some, the presence of American forces assures reliability and credibility, and the buildup of conventional strength is either unnecessary of harmful in its effects. To others, such as France, credibility rests on the direct control of nuclear forces by the country whose vital interests are at stake.

Deterrence, in the final analysis, is a psychological and political posture. The means may be fixed but the deterrent effect is relative. As Bernard Brodie stated, it must be measured ". . . not only by the amount of power that it holds in check, but also by the incentives to aggression residing behind that power."[2] In the French view, the fact that the United States has sufficient strategic nuclear arms to destroy the Soviet Union several times over does not of itself invalidate the deterrent effect of the fifty or so nuclear-equipped Mirage IV aircraft and the planned interim missile sites, even if they are vulnerable to a Soviet preemptive strike. Certainly, the existence of these forces will weigh on Soviet calculations, and the Kremlin must also consider the possibility of U. S. retaliation in the event the French force de frappe were struck first. This French force, as well as the NATO-committed British nuclear force, which is ultimately under the orders of its own government, would simply erect new disincentives to counteract whatever incentives the Soviets may have to attack.

Since deterrence is the key problem in European eyes, strategic concepts revolve around this issue and the strategic nuclear forces that provide the means to deter. In regard to tactical nuclear weapons in Europe, no country other than France questions the arrangements whereby these weapons are under sole American control to be released to our allies in the event they are needed in time of war. As has been pointed out, Great Britain and Germany regard tactical nuclear weapons mainly as a direct but intermediate step in deterrence. But when it comes to the final arbiter--". . . the credibility of a nation's will to confront an adversary with a war that no one can win"--each of the major allies wants to have its own voice in the control of strategic nuclear weapons. In such considerations Professor Robert E. Osgood points out ". . . national views on military logic are bound to be heavily infused with the logic of politics and psychology."[3]

France has chosen the way of an independent nuclear force. Great Britain, under the Conservatives, has regarded its V-Bomber forces as an ". . . independent contribution to the long-range strategic forces of the Western Alliance." Under Labour, Great Britain seeks to exercise more influence on U. S. control and all that it implies. Mr. Harold Wilson, the Prime Minister, has called for ". . . much closer cooperation in NATO for deciding not only questions of targeting, guidelines, and the rest, but deciding . . . the consensus, the circumstances in which the bomb should be dropped."[4] The position of Germany on strategic forces is clearly in the formative stages. There are conflicting political forces operating upon the government. On one side, there are the pressures from President de Gaulle and some politicians of the right wing of the Christian Democrats to choose a continental coalition. On the other side, there are pressures from the United States, Great

Britain, and some of the smaller European nations to choose a wider basis of collaboration within the Atlantic Alliance. There is very little articulated demand from the German people for Germany to become an independent nuclear power. But the government leaders are keenly aware of the dangers of an incipient trend that might develop in this direction.

On the whole, Germany recognizes that the United States is the only country with the strength and will to protect German vital interests. Consequently, the German position is to seek closer collaboration with the United States on strategic nuclear forces and thereby exercise more influence on U.S. strategy. At the same time, the Germans will try to avoid alienating France in order not to jeopardize the possibility of reunification of Germany and closer political integration in Europe.

There is a clear incompatibility between the American concept for the defense of Western Europe and the strategic concepts of the European nations that put more emphasis on deterrence. Europeans would prefer to alter our strategic concept for Europe, which stresses deterrence through defense (denial), to one similar to our strategic concept for the United States, which stresses deterrence through punishment.[5] Although we proclaim that our strategy is indivisible and that we have ". . . undertaken the nuclear defense of NATO on a global basis," some of our pronouncements and actions to create a strong conventional defense in Europe, or even to increase the number of tactical nuclear weapons (as was advertised by Secretary of Defense McNamara[6]), are viewed by Europeans as an effort to confine the fighting to Europe and to leave the United States untouched. The American argument for adopting a common strategy of flexible response based initially on conventional defense is seen by many Europeans as a desire to raise the nuclear threshold on issues that may be vital to the Europeans but not vital to the United States. Even when faced with a bona fide threat in the 1961 Berlin Crisis, the proposed American strategy which incorporated a conventional probe along the autobahn was not wholly subscribed to by the other NATO nations involved. West Germany, in particular, wanted to preserve Berlin as the future capital of a reunited Germany and stressed the importance of preserving the quadripartite status of East Gerlin. Boon wanted no dimunition of resolve on that score. In the end, this quadripartite status was lost by allowing the Berlin Wall to be built. As long as European national interests and objectives vary from this, the attainment of a common strategy is hardly likely. One only has to recall the Suez crisis to bring home this point. There should, however, be opportunities for clarifying and coordinating arms and strategies for the crises that arise.

Deterrence and Defense in Central Europe

The American strategy for limited war is a war-fighting strategy in the traditional sense. It has the objective of defense and a successful defense implies victory, or at least stalemate, on the battlefield. How well the American concept of flexible response can stand up to enemy attack in practice and achieve victory-- a standoff, a restoration of the status quo ante, or even positive political goals-- depends to a large extent on the military force postures of both sides. The presence of sufficient well-deployed military forces is essential to provide a successful defense; what constitutes sufficiency, however, depends on the kinds of action the enemy might undertake. A range of contingencies and alternative courses of actions must be examined. Timothy W. Stanley has pointed out that some of the ". . . most disastrous military mistakes in history have resulted from trying to make a choice of terrain, tactics, timing, and weapons for the enemy. One has to assume not one or two possibilities, but a full range of actions of which the enemy is capable."[7] On the other hand, one does not have to emulate Lewis Carroll's "White Knight," by trying to anticipate every conceivable contingency.[8] There is a limit to the range of actions that are remotely plausible in the European context. In the first place, any outbreak of conflict in Europe would take place under the umbrella of strategic deterrence. Before various conflict contingencies can be examined, it is necessary to ask why any conflict--aside from a border incident-- should take place at all.

In the overall context, stable nuclear confrontation is generally assumed to exist--at least insofar as a nuclear exchange between the two superpowers. This stability is based on the firm conviction, verging on certainty, that nuclear retaliation would result in such unprecedented death and destruction to the attacker that no nation would initiate the first strike. Such stability depends on (1) a redundant supply of strategic missiles which are highly invulnerable to enemy attack and which possess the assured capability of overcoming enemy defenses, and (2) the continuing assessment that there will be no technological advance which will radically change the vulnerability of either side to the nuclear attack of the other.

But nuclear deterrence may be used for other things such as deterring a non-nuclear attack. Here the element of uncertainty creeps in. Such a deterrent strategy can still be successful so long as the threat is made to appear to the opponent as commensurate with the vital interests of the nation making the threat, and so long as the strategy raises doubts in the mind of the opponent as to whether the objectives he seeks are worth the risk. If the stakes seem at the time to be relatively minor or peripheral, it will be difficult to make the threat of nuclear retaliation credible. The enemy may then take the chance of achieving certain modest goals (e. g., the Berlin blockade of 1948 and building the Berlin Wall in 1961) particularly if the means available to the other side appear insufficient to deny him success.

Uncertainty in the effectiveness of nuclear deterrence to cover every kind of threat has impelled the United States to seek a range of options between what is clearly vital to U. S. national interests in the true meaning of the word and what is not. For what threatens our vital interests, nuclear deterrence is based on certainty of retaliation; for what threatens national interests that are not considered vital, nuclear deterrence has an element of uncertainty about it. In an attempt to remove the uncertainty from the latter category, the United States has attempted to structure a careful series of graduated threats and commitments that would be more credible than the threat of nuclear retaliation alone. The measures structured consist of a mixture of (1) attempts to convince the enemy that the U. S. national interests are vital, (2) not-so-credible threats of nuclear retaliation, (3) more credible threats of conventional defense backed by the postponed threat of using tactical nuclear weapons, (4) the actual commitment of conventional force to battle in the event that the first three fail to deter, and (5) the ever-present articulated or tacit threat of escalation that accompanies any armed conflict.

These measures may not, however, remove the uncertainty. The argument can be made that the United States would not intervene with nuclear weapons in Europe because of the risk that the continental United States might be attacked. The implied threat, that France might use her _force_ _de_ _frappe_ to trigger an American nuclear response can similarly be discounted. These are legitimate arguments. At the same time, the credibility of the threat of a Soviet invasion of Western Europe must be taken into account. The two sides of the credibility equation must be considered together. In other words, how plausible or credible would be a major Soviet invasion of Western Europe coupled with American and French abstention in the use of nuclear weapons? The record over the last twenty years and the force deployments in Western Europe would suggest that the combination of these two credibility factors balances out. Stated differently, the probability that the Soviet Union would refrain from an attack in the face of American and French threats to use nuclear weapons is exceedingly high. The probability that the Soviet Union has no intention to attack is also high. This indicates that deterrence is credible or that the Soviet Union has had no intention of attacking Western Europe, or both.

The prevalent view that a Soviet military threat in Central Europe has receded (if it has not disappeared entirely) appears to be based on evidence and logic. The historical evidence is a record of manifest caution by the Soviet Union in any military confrontation with the United States--particularly in the face of the strong United States commitment of the Seventh U.S. Army, Third and Seventeenth U.S. Air Forces, thousands of tactical nuclear weapons, the implied threat of the U.S. strategic nuclear forces, and the support of the not inconsiderable European NATO forces in West Germany. The logic of this U.S. commitment would indicate to both sides that the decision in fact has actually been made to defend West Europe with all means necessary. This decision immediately places the onus on the Soviet Union to decide whether acquiring all or part of Europe is worth the cost. This is different from the arguments on relative military capabilities that deal only with the comparative cost of defense versus offense. The value of the objective to be gained must be judged, and this is almost always more valuable to the side in possession.

Surely it must be clear that the leaders of the Soviet Union must calculate beforehand the cost of military action in terms of nuclear destruction and lives to be lost. It is generally conceded that the NATO military forces cannot defend against a major conventional invasion without resort to nuclear weapons. Should it be otherwise, the Soviets would be unable to achieve the military objective desired without resort to nuclear armaments.

Assuming the Soviets place a high value on a particular objective, high enough to command acceptance of the cost of aggressive military action against Western Europe, the question must be asked--what objective and at what cost? For instance, should the high-value Soviet objective be seizure of Western Germany in order to prevent the Federal Republic from acquiring an independent nuclear force, the almost-certain cost would be a nuclear war. This war might be initiated by the Soviet Union (in accordance with its preconceived military strategies), or--as the Western forces are overrun--by either the NATO Alliance or the United States.

Now, if the above reasoning holds true, why should the Soviets not use nuclear weapons immediately and benefit from the tremendous advantage of surprise? Further, can it be imagined that the Soviet Union would plan a deliberate invasion to seize Western Germany--without significantly reinforcing its forces or without having the satellite states mobilized? Would the Roumanian, Polish, Czech, and Hungarian Communist political and military leaders help plan, or even agree after-the-fact, to a deliberate unprovoked military aggression? And can anyone doubt that the reinforcement would be immediately noticed by NATO, which would in turn alert and mobilize its military elements?

It has been suggested that the Soviet Union might seek a more limited objective, such as a probe, e.g., the seizure of a border town such as Lübeck or even Hamburg. The idea would be to achieve a _fait accompli_ quickly and place the burden of escalation upon the West. It is conceivable that such a surprise military operation could be successful in the initial action, provided it were mounted as a Blitzkrieg with a substantial force of at least three or four assault divisions. But it is difficult to conceive that the Soviet Union would undertake major aggression for such limited objectives. First, such purposeful, large-scale conventional attacks are not consistent with Soviet war doctrine which stresses combined nuclear and conventional attacks in an attempt to seize the strategic initiative. Neither are they consistent with Communist doctrine of peaceful coexistence and the avoidance of "adventurism." Second, such adventuristic moves clearly place Soviet core interests in jeopardy. The Kremlin leaders could hardly be certain that the thermonuclear standoff would prevent the United States from launching a strategic strike against the USSR, or from even using tactical nuclear weapons on the battlefield to prevent the seizure. In any event the Soviets still would realize that the West could not accept such a sacrifice without taking immediate military steps to restore the _status quo ante_ or at least to exact a comparable loss from the Soviet Union. Third, once committed to the defense of so vital an area with the NATO military forces at hand, the war would rapidly expand to a full-scale European war and the pressures for nuclear escalation would be almost irresistable. This

would hardly be an acceptable price for the Soviets to pay for a limited objective.
A limited Soviet military aggression of the size of a probe seems on the face of
it even more implausible than an all-out invasion. Yet since it has been suggested
as possible by responsible spokesmen on both sides of the Atlantic it should be
examined as a contingency.

The third and final contingency is the conflict that might arise out of a crisis
or a miscalculation of NATO resolve. Such a conflict is considered by most military analysts as the most likely contingency. The crisis might be an uprising in
East Germany, the attempted seizure of power in West Germany by a resurgent
nationalist group, the hemming-in of an important military convoy on the East
German autobahn in connection with a crisis at Berlin, or even a serious riot and
storming of the Berlin Wall. A crisis might be managed or exploited by the Soviets to achieve what they consider minor or peripheral gains--gains that might
be achieved by deterring NATO's military opposition with the threat of escalation.
(The burden would then be on NATO.) This type of limited engagement would be
in keeping with the Soviet strategic concept and with the Communist doctrine of
eschewing adventurism. If effectively opposed by NATO, and an armed conflict
results, the Soviet Union would have the option of backing down, of holding to the
gains so far established, or of pushing further. The last option represents the
greatest chance of miscalculation and the greatest danger that the conflict would
spread.

Coordinating Arms and Strategies

Crucial to the task of coordinating arms and strategies in an alliance for
dealing with these contingencies is a definition of common political goals in the
event of conflict. In the Atlantic Alliance these have not been defined beyond the
commitment of collective defense against an unidentified aggression laid down in
the Treaty itself. It is fashionable to say that, in Europe at least, nuclear weapons have made war obsolete as a means of achieving political objectives. The
truth of this assertion depends on the objective sought and the military means
employed for achieving the objective. Certainly, armed conflict cannot be ruled
out entirely in Europe. Long before writers began to quote Clausewitz, it had
been recognized as axiomatic that the political aim of war should be within the
military means. It never is as far as the defeated nation is concerned. The

political objectives of Japan in World War II proved in the end to be beyond her military means. The political objectives of the United States, however, were well within her military means, and peace was restored with Japan on reasonably satisfactory terms. On the victorious side, there is always the strong temptation to expand the limited political aims to conform with the full extent of the military capacity. This is dangerous; for example, when the United Nations changed their political objective of merely repelling the North Korean invasion to the complete military defeat of that country, it brought on a quite unexpected war with Communist China. On the other hand, the vague political objectives that accompanied the policy of "unconditional surrender" in World War II caused the Western allies to lose opportunities to achieve political goals well within their military capabilities. In Europe, nuclear weapons afford both sides the means to expand the military action up to general war--a result that neither side would deliberately seek. Therefore, the ability to exercise restraints on the use of force in Europe is just as important as to expand the use of force to achieve the objective sought.

If conflict breaks out in Europe, for whatever reason, the Alliance should at least have an agreed purpose in mind and certain clear political objectives. Yet each local conflict situation will vary according to the circumstances surrounding the initial crisis, the value of the objectives, and the conscious decisions of the two sides to commit armed forces in battle to achieve a local victory. For when military forces do battle there is only one purpose: victory. It is extremely difficult to conceive of circumstances where one side or the other would deliberately decide to resort to force to attain an objective, and to then refrain from throwing the necessary resources into battle to achieve the objective and to avoid defeat. It is not impossible, however, to imagine that limitations and constraints would be imposed by both sides on the objectives to be sought and on the use of nuclear weapons in battle to prevent the conflict from escalating to general war. Too much is at stake. From 122 to 149 million fatalities could result from a Soviet strike against United States cities and military targets.[9] There is no doubt that the Soviet leaders understand well that Russia could expect carnage of similar monstrous proportions; but still, exercising constraints on force implies a limited political objective. The only sensible objective for the types of conflicts examined would be the minimum objective of restoring the territorial status quo ante bellum on the least disadvantageous or unsatisfactory terms.

There are some practical problems that must be dealt with. The question is not the abstract one of whether we can restore the status quo with the military means at our disposal. The question rather is whether we can defeat the enemy's armed forces in a specific locale over a particular issue. Once armed conflict takes place, the tendency on both sides is to take additional measures necessary to achieve a favorable outcome--but not measures that would worsen the outcome. To suggest, however, that both sides would be mutually deterred from using nuclear weapons out of fear of a worsened outcome suggests also that a conventional defeat is a more acceptable outcome. This may well be true, provided the conventional defeat is not one of vital proportions--or perceived as vital. But then the question should be asked if there are any conceivable conventional victory-defeat outcomes of armed conflict in Europe that would not be considered vital by one side or the other.

The record would indicate that whereas the Soviets have made threats, they have committed no acts of aggression against the Alliance. True, the Berlin blockade on the autobahn and railroads in 1948, the construction of the Berlin Wall in 1961, and a number of lesser infringements on what the United States regarded as rights of access were accepted by United States without recourse to force. None of these issues were vital, however. Whereas they could all be regarded as infringements of rights, they could hardly be classed as acts of aggression. The United States, on the other hand, has taken special pains to create in Berlin a symbol of vital interests, if not an American vital interest per se. The United States and the other occupying allied powers have made the freedom of West Berlin an unambiguous symbol of the West's determination to resist further Soviet encroachment. To acquiesce to the loss of Berlin's independence (no longer a marginal matter) would cause such a serious blow to the West, that it is hardly conceivable that the Atlantic Alliance could survive. It is even less conceivable that the city's absorption by the Communists could be carried out without a fight. Finally, considering the absolute commitments made by the United States and its allies to Berlin and the impossibility of mounting an adequate conventional defense, there can be little question that the United States would respond elsewhere at places of its own choice, as well as at Berlin itself, and that we would use nuclear weapons if needed. In fact, this was made clear during the Berlin Crisis of 1961. The Soviet threat of signing a peace treaty with East Germany and of creating a "free

city" of West Berlin was resisted firmly by the United States. It could hardly be
asserted that United States vital interests were involved at this stage. But President Kennedy saw larger political effects in the move and stated:

> If we do not meet our commitments in Berlin, it will mean
> the destruction of NATO and a dangerous situation for the
> whole world. All Europe is at stake in West Berlin.[10]

He reinforced the Seventh U. S. Army, called up certain units of the reserves
and National Guard and resolved that the United States would go to war, even to
nuclear war, if the Soviet Union took action aimed at destroying the freedom of
West Berlin.[11]

Three factors would indicate that nuclear weapons would be used under important circumstances. First, McNamara's idea that the European nations would
come up with the additional forces to make a forward conventional defense-
deterrence successful ". . . for dealing with even larger Soviet attacks" has been
dashed. The Alliance can no longer even reckon on the French divisions and aircraft. The war in Vietnam is placing a strain on U. S. resources and already
15, 000 special American troop ratings have been withdrawn from Europe. Britain is also suffering from a chronic financial drain and there are pressures to
reduce the British Army of the Rhine even further. Secondly, the very existence
of nuclear arsenals and elaborate plans for their use on both sides would indicate
that any large conflict, which cannot be terminated early enough would in all probability escalate to nuclear conflict. A third factor is the continuing nature of deterrence. Deterrence--whether it relies on conventional forces, nuclear forces,
or a composite mixture--does not fail once and for all. The effectiveness of deterrence depends on the opponent's belief that the necessary military action would
be taken to match the value of the objective sought. Each deliberate step in escalation would signify a higher value placed on the objective. For example, if it
were possible for one side to use nuclear weapons in a distinct, obvious, and
discriminate way on the battlefield to prevent the loss of a vital objective, that
side would do so rather than surrender. The burden of expanding the nuclear war
beyond the battlefield would then be placed on the other side. Since each step in
the escalation ladder brings the contestants nearer to general war--an outcome
that neither side would want--it would appear that at some point along the line
graduated deterrence would work, and restraint would be exercised by each side

from the very start to keep the issue from becoming vital to either. Therefore, in pursuing the minimum objective of restoring the status quo, NATO must have a force posture that permits it to react quickly to oppose any enemy move and to prevent the move from developing into a vital issue.

It is strongly suggested that the most likely issue would be small at the start and would arise from a crisis or a miscalculation of resolve. Since the most likely locale would be along the border partitioning Germany or at Berlin, strategic concepts should be examined in these contexts. Certainly, a response to low-level conflicts in line with the French strategic concept that hurls nuclear destruction upon the Soviet Union can hardly be considered a rational response, since it fails to consider that deterrence is a continuing phenomenon. If conflict starts by miscalculation, the proper response would be to take the necessary steps to prevent the conflict from continuing or from enlarging. Whether one accepts the American concept of a conventional response with a high threshold or the German concept of battlefield nuclear and atomic demolition mine (ADM) responses at a much lower threshold, one can certainly rule out the French concept of massive retaliation as a sensible way to defend Western Europe or to keep the lid on the fighting.

If France is serious about her strategic concept of "massive retaliation" for everything but border incidents, one can only wonder why she desires to keep her two divisions in Germany. Their location in Germany is much too far from the Iron Curtain to be useful in a border incident, and anything larger than a border incident is theoretically ruled out under her concept. But France may perhaps plan on using these forces to block on German territory a larger "probe" or incursion before it threatens France.[12] France's true reason for wanting to keep her forces in Germany is more than likely political: to influence Germany's action by retaining rights stemming from the Occupation that relate to the stationing of armed forces in Germany until a peace treaty is signed for all of Germany. This would give France increased weight vis-à-vis the Soviet Union: Russia stations troops in East Germany and France stations troops in West Germany.

De Gaulle's calculated move to get American forces out of France will have a serious effect on the operation of the American strategic concept of flexible response in the case of any sizeable penetration. The idea of depending on a conventional defense until the ground forces are in danger of being overrun before employing tactical nuclear weapons is unrealistic, at least in terms of the logistic difficulties and the lack of strategic depth. Preoccupied as we have been with the central sector and the Thuringian gap, we nevertheless have recognized the possibility of being outflanked through the north German plain where the much weaker British Army of the Rhine is on guard. Theoretically, we could always have fallen back to a defense line along the Rhine and Weser--perhaps comforted by the thought that we still had some strategic depth in France and our logistic lines behind us. If the scenario just described ever had any relevance to reality, it has all been changed with de Gaulle's unilateral action. The one thing de Gaulle has done is to force us to re-examine our strategic concept for limited war--especially as it relates to the defense of West Germany.

However, too much importance should not be attached to erecting the straw man of a sizeable Soviet penetration for the purpose of downgrading the American limited war concept. Clearly a conventional defense in such a case would be the worst possible application. Yet for the more likely contingencies mentioned--a border or a Berlin crisis--an initial conventional response could very well be the only sensible one to employ. The chances are, both sides would act to snuff out the conflict as quickly as possible with the minimum of violence. But if the conflict gets out of hand and conventional defense/deterrence proves inadequate, then the problem would be when and how to initiate the use of nuclear weapons-- keeping in mind the assumed minimum objective of restoring the status quo ante bellum--with the least possible devastation and the maximum possible control to prevent escalation to a Europe-wide or a general nuclear war.

A Conceptual Variation of Flexible Response

This brings us face to face with the problem of escalation and the idea of a firebreak or distinguishable threshold of violence. The two are intimately related. The clear distinction between the nonuse and the use of nuclear weapons is considered by many as a threshold of violence or firebreak that, once crossed would quickly cause the conflict to escalate to general war. Leading defense spokesmen of the major NATO nations have expressed this belief. The difference is that the American concept calls for maintaining this firebreak at a high level of violence and provocation whereas the European members would establish it at a low level to enhance deterrence.

That the so-called nuclear threshold, or firebreak, is clearly distinguishable
is widely accepted. Hardly anyone subscribes to the view that a tactical nuclear
weapon is just another weapon, as was advocated by some enthusiasts in the early
1950s. Furthermore, the nuclear firebreak is the kind of unambiguous distinction
which facilitates tacit agreement on constraints that prevail in war. History has
shown that constraints defined in such clear-cut categories are more reliable
than those defined in quantitative degrees within categories. Thus, "no gas" in
World War II was an easier limit to accept than "a little gas" or just one type of
gas. Tacit acceptance in Korea of "no atomic bombs" was easier to understand
than "small atomic bombs" on certain kinds of targets.[13]

Admitting that a distinguishable firebreak exists, however, does not support
the belief that crossing the firebreak would inevitably result in uncontrolled escalation to general nuclear war. The danger of escalation exists, of course, but
establishing a firm ceiling on the conflict by adopting a policy of postponing the
use of nuclear weapons until allied territory and ground forces are in danger of
being overrun is not the answer. For then the issue becomes vital and demands
for tactical nuclear weapons to stem the invasion would be quite large and the
unprecedented combat losses on both sides would exert pressures on the political
leaders to expand the aims to something greater than the restoration of the status
quo.

There exist two possible alternatives to this dilemma. First the United States
could adopt a strategic concept more in line with German desires. Such a concept
would call for lowering the violence threshold or firebreak and giving an unambiguous commitment to West Germany that tactical nuclear weapons would be used
much earlier than is now contemplated. There are dangers to this approach. A
miscalculation of enemy intentions might be made, and nuclear weapons might be
used when none are needed--thus precipitating a nuclear battle that no one wants.
There are also practical difficulties in establishing an arrangement for giving an
unambiguous nuclear commitment to West Germany, difficulties that go beyond
the obvious political problems involved. It is basically a matter of credibility.
All the assurances in the world won't convince the Germans or the Soviets that
the United States would use nuclear weapons unless it were clearly perceived
that U.S. vital interests are threatened. As Secretary of Defense McNamara put
it, ". . . a credible deterrent cannot be based on an incredible act."[14]

Deterrence is, in effect, a psychological posture. We attempt to create in the mind of a potential enemy a fear or a belief in our willingness to act. Certainly no rational enemy would deny that we would have the will to employ nuclear weapons if the stakes are vital. On the other hand, he would hardly conceive that we would be irrational enough to use these weapons if the stakes are minute. In the final analysis, the problem is a matter of making the perception of the United States commitment to West Germany "vital" enough to risk a thermonuclear exchange.

The second alternative rests on the same psychological premise. It seeks to improve the credibility of deterrence not by enhancing the "vitalness" of our commitment but by making the consequences of using nuclear weapons less horrendous and by establishing other firebreaks or thresholds of violence at an intermediate level between the first use of nuclear weapons and general nuclear war. The problem here is making the threshold distinguishable. As pointed out earlier, making a distinction between nuclear weapons during war by judging their yield (except in the most general sort of way), by estimating the range and point of origin of the delivery vehicle, or by divining whether the collateral population damage was intentional or not, is for all practical purposes impossible in the confusion of battle. About the only hope of establishing a difference between nuclear weapons in time of war is to base the distinction on the use to which the weapons are put. For example, nuclear weapons with impact only in a certain area and in no other may be distinguishable provided the accompanying dialogue is made explicit and unambiguous in both words and actions. Also, atomic demolition weapons (ADMs) can be very distinguishable as battle field weapons because of their emplacement on defended territory and their immobility. However, there are three objections to their use. They must be prepositioned before hostilities to be of much use in fast moving actions, and this prepositioning seems to be presently politically unacceptable. Present defensive concepts call for attempts to stop incursions conventionally before using nuclear weapons. If ADMs are placed near the violated borders, they are likely to be overrun before decisions to use them can be made. Finally, there is the dangerous and unmanageable problem of radioactive fall-out.

Nevertheless, it may be possible to distinguish "battlefield" nuclear weapons from other tactical nuclear weapons used for purposes of interdiction and penetration attacks on military bases deep in enemy territory--not only by their smaller yield and lesser range but mainly by the fact that their bursts are confined to the immediate battle area. If the other side did not perceive the limitation, it would be because it did not want to perceive it. The precedence already has been established in Korea and Vietnam that certain targets could be treated as sanctuaries-- as long as it appeared advantageous to do so. If one side struck at airfields and other military bases outside of the battle zone, the action would be deliberate. Such an act could hardly be considered an unintentional violation of a limitation that the leaders had failed to perceive. Whether such a distinction can be made in practice or not, efforts to do so by peacetime and wartime actions and pronouncements would at least create a presumption in the mind of the enemy, and among our allies, that the United States would be less reluctant to cross the first-use nuclear firebreak in certain circumstances. This could only have the effect of reinforcing graduated deterrence. This conclusion is supported by the expressions of concern by Soviet leaders over the U. S. concept for limited war and for the use of tactical nuclear weapons to keep a European war limited.

The logic of the American strategic concept of flexible response is judged by United States national security and the geographical position of the United States. But the same considerations of national security apply to other nations within the Alliance whose territories are not geographically separated from the scene of potential battle. The obligation of a state to protect its citizens and its territory is conditioned by the understanding that threat to any part is subordinate to the preservation of the state as a whole. The state may be forced to sacrifice part to preserve the whole, but the obligation is compelling for a state to protect its security and to devote whatever resources are needed to preserve the harmony of the whole without destroying the vitality of the parts.

The same obligations in theory apply to an alliance; in practice, however, the obligation is not as strong. History is full of broken treaties, abandonment of allies and reversals of alliances. The Europeans are conscious of this and they are determined not to subordinate their own national security to preserve the alliance. They have no intention of permitting their homelands to be regarded as a part that might be sacrificed in time of war to preserve the vitality of a so-called indivisible alliance, the core of which is the United States. The Atlantic Alliance is to them, as it is to the United States, an instrument to preserve their own security. Alliances are made for national purposes, not the reverse. Thus European fears

center around the flexible American strategic concept for a limited war in Europe
that might be limited or terminated at the expense of the allies. That the American
concept has wide acceptance among Americans is quite natural. The point of this
discussion is that it does not enjoy wide acceptance among Europeans.

European leaders recognize that the United States depends on a general war
strategy for its own survival. They also understand that the limited war concept
of flexible response--as it serves to protect the allies--is based on the logic of
U. S. national self-interests. They see nothing wrong in having a choice of conventional as well as nuclear options to deal with various contingencies. What they
do object to is not having the same choice of options for their nations. They mark
well the United States priorities that emphasize nuclear options as the most vital
for survival. From Secretary McNamara's Ann Arbor speech, they are aware
that the United States reserves to itself the choice of at least two strategic options--
striking enemy cities or striking missile sites and airfields; perhaps they suspect
there are more. Many of the European nations do not have nuclear options--nor
the early commitment of the United States to use nuclear weapons when their vital
interests are at stake. It is hardly any wonder that these European nations are
reluctant to expend their resources on additional conventional forces before a nuclear option, vital to their ultimate survival, is provided.

This is an important point. Some of our European allies accept without question our commitment to come to their defense. For the smaller nations, it is
practically the only alternative available to them. They have neither the incentive
nor the resources to become nuclear powers. The problem is mainly with Ger-
many--for France and Great Britain have at least one nuclear option. Since the
interlocking legal, political and institutional restraints prevent Germany from
becoming a nuclear power, how does one provide an unambiguous commitment
to use nuclear weapons? And how do we create other nuclear firebreaks which
will prevent uncontrollable escalation to general nuclear war? Official pronouncements and assurances will not do it alone. Practical and credible military arrangements may.

In a real world, however, things do not happen exactly as they are conceived
in the abstract. The debate over conflicting strategic concepts by its very nature
is largely a dialectic for political discussion. In a real crisis, a series of actions
would very likely take place that would reveal how vital the issues are and the

governments would act accordingly. The logic of the situation--even to the French-- would indicate that certain intermediate steps would be taken before inviting holocaust. The problem then is to provide a force posture that will allow these intermediate steps to be taken and if nuclear weapons are needed, to permit their use in such a controlled and discriminate manner that holocaust does not result. This critical problem is examined in the second part of this book.

PART TWO—THE MILITARY CONFRONTATION

IMBALANCES, ASYMMETRIES AND INSTABILITIES IN FORCE POSTURE

Barring accidents, the stability of the military confrontation in Central Europe rests on the perceptions and actions of the leaders--especially of the major nations--in the two alliances. Decisions that might result in disrupting this stability and bringing on conflict are subordinated to the perception of two technical factors. First, there are the large numbers of tremendously destructive nuclear weapons in the arsenals of the United States and the Soviet Union. By the very number of weapons and characteristics of relative invulnerability of some of the strategic weapons systems, both sides have the greatest incentives not to engage in combat with each other. Second, a truly revolutionary technological breakthrough would be required to invalidate the more or less secure capability for causing intolerable destruction of either side. The chances of such a breakthrough are assessed--at least for the present--at a very low probability. Moreover, such a wide variety of lethal weapon systems exists that it is even more doubtful whether a single new development or even several breakthroughs could provide either side with a decisive advantage to overcome the entire range of weaponry before the other side could reestablish the stability of the confrontation by technological countermeasures.

These two technical factors, which tend to create military stability on one hand, make the nature of warfare monstrous should it occur. In the imbalances and asymmetries of the two opposing force postures are potential instabilities that are of major concern. Hazards exist in the nature of the force postures, the offensive and provocative nature of some of the weapon systems, the widespread diffusion of nuclear weapons, and the ability to command and control their use.

These are the elements that relate theory to fact, and that make miscalculations possible and the threat of escalation to general nuclear war real.

In analyzing the military force postures of both sides in Central Europe it is important to make judgments about those military options which go beyond the suppression of a low-level conflict, even though such a conflict is judged the most plausible. To do so requires not only an understanding of the imbalances and asymmetries that exist, but also an appreciation of the potential instabilities in the existing confrontation which create major uncertainties or enhance the danger of escalation to higher levels of violence. Judgments need to be made of the effects of these potential instabilities not only on deterrence but also on the possible consequences of using tactical nuclear weapons under certain conditions. This is a large order. The lack of empirical data as to consequences, both military and psychological, of using tactical nuclear weapons only complicates the analysis. The most that can be hoped is to derive insights that indicate the directions we might take to improving the stability of the military confrontation.

The Overall Balance

In the overall strategic picture, the United States and its allies are stronger than the Soviet Union and its Satellites. At the level of strategic deterrence the United States alone has about 1000 land-based ICBMs, 512 Polaris missiles in submarines, and 680 long-range bombers.[1] The Soviet Union has about 300 intercontinental ballistic missiles and about 200 long-range bombers. Americans seem to take comfort by McNamara's periodic reminders of this better than four-to-one superiority. Europeans are more interested, however, in the some 750 Medium and Intermediate Range Ballistic Missiles (MRBM and IRBMs), the 120 fleet ballistic missiles, and the 900 Badger and Blinder supersonic bombers that can be targeted on Western Europe. In European eyes, the eighty V-bombers of the Royal Air Force and thirty-six Mirage-IV light bombers of the French force de frappe are regarded as an extremely inadequate counter to this Soviet threat.[2] Of course, the United States' spokesmen frequently point out that the American overall superiority, including the tactical fighter bombers of the Third and Seventeenth Air Forces and the Sixth Fleet in the Mediterranean, would more than make up this deficit. Nevertheless, the asymmetry that exists fosters a feeling of being "hostage" to the Soviet Union and makes the Europeans realize more than ever that Western Europe is in the final analysis dependent upon the United States' commitment.

The fact that the NATO nations have more men under arms--about 5. 8 million compared to 4. 4 million in the Warsaw Pact[3]--is relevant in the sense that the greater number of men in the armed forces contributes a "reputation" of superior power. The same is true of the vastly superior NATO naval forces. However, as far as actual defense capabilities in Europe at the confrontation along the Iron Curtain, the forces immediately available are more significant. There is an equivalent of about twenty-seven NATO divisions to cover the Central Sector. The Warsaw Pact has about fifty-six divisions, if one counts the twenty-two Soviet divisions in East Germany and in Poland, the six East German divisions, the fourteen Polish divisions, and the fourteen Czechoslovakian divisions. However, all the NATO and Warsaw Pact divisions could hardly be employed in the early stages of a conflict--especially for the type of low-intensity conflict which might arise out of a crisis along the dividing line between the Federal Republic and East Germany. It would seem more realistic to consider that only part of twenty NATO divisions (five plus U. S. , two British, twelve German divisions, and one Canadian brigade) would be available during the initial stages of a conflict and that only part of twenty-six divisions (twenty Soviet and six East German divisions) would be available on the Communist side. Table II shows the approximate numbers of mobilized ground forces in the territories of West and East Germany that could be considered available in the early stages of a conflict along the German partition. Since the NATO divisions are generally larger than the Soviet and East German divisions, the ground forces of NATO and the Warsaw Pact could be said to be fairly well balanced along the East-West German partition, at least in numbers.

Balance, however, is never achieved in practice by equating similar categories of military power. Actually, categories of strength on one side are likely to be offset by a different kind of military strength on the other. One side may have more tanks, whereas the other side may have more aircraft. One side may have more and better nuclear delivery vehicles, whereas the other side may have more conventional firepower at the scene of a possible encounter. Furthermore, so many variables (state of training, weather, competence of the leaders, logistic bottlenecks, intelligence, the "scare factor," etc.) exist and have effects upon a

Table II

GROUND FORCES IN EAST AND WEST GERMANY

West Germany			East Germany		
U. S.	5+ Divs.	225,000 men	USSR	20 Divs.	407,000 men
U. K.	2 Divs.	51,500 men	GDR	6 Divs.	85,000 men
Canada	1 Brigade	6,500 men			
FGR	12 Divs.	279,000 men			
Total	20 Divs.	562,000 men	Total	26 Divs.	492,000 men

(The 2 French divisions at Trier and Freiburg in West Germany are excluded because of doubts as to France's participation in the early stages of conflict unless her vital interests are directly threatened.)

crisis or conflict that is extremely doubtful whether any a priori measurements or judgments as to military balance will have much relevancy to the actual situation. For example, in a given military setting it may be shown that the modern anti-tank weapons, such as guided missiles and recoilless rifles, can handily defeat a tank. But interjecting the "scare factor" raises some pertinent questions: "Will the crew manning the anti-tank weapon fire it accurately? Will it fire at all?" A survey taken by S. L. A. Marshall during the Korean war showed that a large percentage of the troops in combat never fired their rifles.[5] Furthermore, there are other factors that bear on the military balance. Quincy Wright has selected four somewhat disparate elements as the constituents of military power: (1) armaments in being, (2) economic potential, (3) morale, and (4) reputation.[6] The relative importance of these elements depends on the duration of the war. A nation may have a stronger military posture at the start of a war, yet lose in the final outcome because the other side could marshall stronger forces during the course of the war, either because the economic potential and civilian morale were superior or because the potential capabilities and general reputation of the nation permitted it to gain additional allies. On the other hand, in a Blitzkrieg or nuclear war, armaments in being are by far the most important factor in assessing the relative military power or balance in a given confrontation.

Yet there is something to be said for attempting to at least assess the consequences of military imbalances in a real geographical locale for dealing with the more "likely" conflict contingencies.[7] At the same time, it is important to recognize that in any conflict <u>all</u> military forces are relevant--even though only a few may be employed. Both the United States and the Soviet Union have at their disposal nuclear power which could submerge any battlefield action in Europe. The mere existence of such power will weigh heavily upon the kinds of military actions the two sides might employ. In the cases of a conflict along the German partition or at Berlin, the Soviets might well have a local superiority in one or more dimensions of military power. The consequences of local imbalances in such cases, however, while important, can hardly be regarded as important as the major elements of instability in the overall "balance of imbalances"[8] which cause the confrontation to be so fraught with the peril of nuclear escalation. The essential military requirement for NATO is to have a defense posture adequate for suppressing and containing a conflict without allowing it to get out of control. This is not to suggest that large conventional forces are needed to stem an invasion, or that only a fire brigade is needed to quell an uprising. Even though the sizes of the forces that can be engaged profitably in the early stages of a conflict may be relatively small, there is still the need for fairly sizeable forces and for nuclear weapons in case the conflict gets out of hand. It is only prudent to possess a range of military options between a low-level conflict and nuclear war.

Ground Forces

As pointed out earlier the number of ground troops immediately available on both sides to handle a crisis or low-intensity conflict is roughly equal. However, some asymmetry does exist since the USSR has an additional forty to fifty divisions that could be brought up as reinforcements, whereas the NATO nations would have to mobilize. Furthermore, the ground forces of the other Warsaw Pact nations have improved. For a long time the Satellite nations lagged behind the Soviet forces in modern equipment and armament. Over the past few years, however, the East German, Polish, and Czech forces have been provided with up-to-date weapons. New artillery with increased cross-country mobility, new tanks such as the T-10 and T-54, and short-range nuclear capable rockets mounted on tank chassis have been introduced to these forces.

The peacetime locations of the ground force divisions and headquarters are shown on the chart (Fig. 2).[9] As can be seen, the divisions' casernes are fairly evenly dispersed in both West and East Germany. Their locations, however, carry little significance. In most cases the locations of the casernes were undoubtedly determined by the availability of barracks at the end of World War II. Neither an offensive nor defensive orientation can be inferred from the chart. Actually, in a conflict the troops on both sides would be deployed to their defensive (or possibly offensive) positions, or at least to the point of confrontation in the event of a serious crisis.

Nevertheless, some imbalances do exist in the peacetime disposition. The United States maintains five full-strength combat-ready divisions and three armored cavalry regiments in southern Germany. Only part of these forces, however, cover the most threatening route of invasion into West Germany. This is through the Thuringian Gap where a number of open avenues give access to Frankfurt, the "hinge" of the Rhine at Mainz, to the Leine valley leading to the British and West German flank towards the north, and past Kassel, and to the Weser defenses through Paderborn to the Ruhr. Further to the north, the historic invasion routes over the German plains to the North Sea and to Cologne and the Ruhr are guarded by much weaker British, Dutch, Belgian, and German forces. The areas of both of these invasion routes are critical because border incidents or crises that might result in conflict are more likely there for two reasons. First, there is the chronic problem of allied access to Berlin through the Helmstedt crossing where the principal rail, highway, canal, and air routes into East Germany commence. Second, as Robert B. Johnson pointed out, "Nowhere along the frontier of the 'Two Germanys' does the partition cut through an area so densely inhabited and originally so closely tied together."[10]

Finally, there is the acute imbalance at Berlin, the symbolic importance of which is transcendant, and the function of which as a potential "trip wire" for Allied military reaction is most credible. The freedom of West Berlin can only be assured by deterrence. There is unanimous military opinion that it could not be defended successfully if the Communists attempted to seize the city by military force.

There are also some differences in composition of the ground forces. The average Soviet division has about 12,000 troops, whereas the NATO divisions

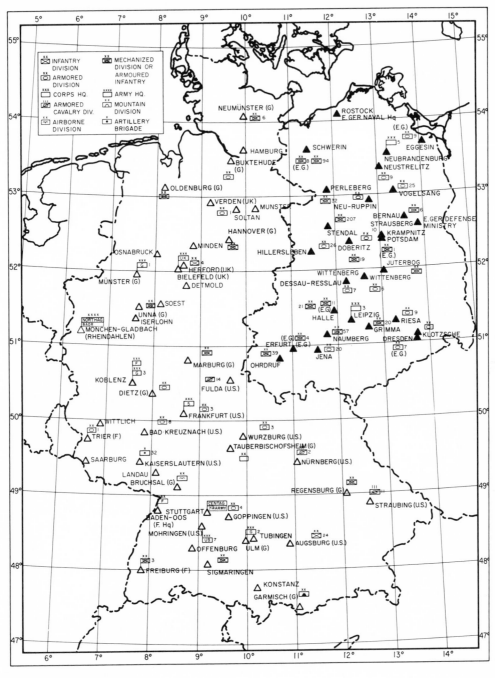

Figure 2. NATO and Warsaw Pact Divisions and
Army Headquarters in Germany

in West Germany average better than 15,000 men. Furthermore, there is a larger number of support elements for the West. For example, an American division slice[11] is about 43,000 troops whereas the Soviet division slice is about 20,000 men. The average number of tanks per division is about equal although the Americans have a few more artillery pieces organic to the division than the Soviets.

The quality and combat readiness of the ground forces on both sides are also important. The combat readiness of the American and Soviet ground forces are generally considered high. The Bundeswehr of the Federal Republic of Germany, which was adjudged in 1962 to be only "conditionally fit for defense,"[12] has improved greatly, but the combat support and logistic arrangements are still weak. Further, the Bundeswehr lacks about thirty percent of junior officers and non-commissioned officers. With a full employment economy, the West Germans are finding it difficult to flesh out the ranks. The Soviet military leaders have rated the combat readiness and effectiveness of the Nationale Volksarmee (NVA) of East Germany sufficiently high that in 1965 five of its six divisions were assigned to the "first strategic echelon" of the Warsaw Pact. The NVA is firmly under the control of the Soviet Supreme Commander, Marshall Andrei Grechko--even in time of peace. Practically all of the military equipment of the East German army comes from the Soviets who are beginning to provide more modern offensive weapons. This reflects less Soviet distrust in the reliability of the NVA than formerly. The NVA has even received the atomic carrier weapons: the 50-kilometer Frog and the 165-kilometer Scud--however, without their nuclear warheads.[13]

The East German NVA, however, cannot hope to stand up against the Bundeswehr in a fratricidal war. It is less than half the size. But then it is hard to imagine circumstances where the FRG and the East German armies would be fighting each other or, if they did, that either the NATO or the Soviet command would allow German soldiers to shoot at their blood brothers across the border without intervening with United States, British and Soviet troops. The key reckoning in the military force postures is the presence of foreign troops on both sides. This is especially true of the Berlin enclave, the most likely spot for a crisis to arise and the spot where the most pronounced imbalance exists.

Logistical support, however, is a major asymmetry and the arrangements in NATO are much more vulnerable to attack. Prior to the withdrawal of France from the NATO military organization, the major lines of supply were from the rear--through France for U.S. forces and through the Low Countries for British forces. The chart (Fig. 3) gives some idea of the former logistical arrangements for supporting the Seventh U.S. Army in time of war. Lacking even the small strategic depth that France formerly provided, logistics must now come through the north German ports or through Belgium and the Netherlands. All of these routes approximately parallel the Iron Curtain. In some cases the lines of communication are closer to the border than the casernes of the troops being supplied.

To give some idea of the size of the task of keeping the troops supplied, it is estimated that for the Seventh U.S. Army alone some 120,000 vehicles would be needed during initial deployment, requiring more than 750,000 gallons of fuel per day. Even in peacetime, more than 500 tons of food, 225 tons of equipment, spare parts and other consumable material, 800 tons of fuel and 125 tons of ammunition are required each day.

In contrast, the Soviet ground forces have shorter lines of communications directly from their rear. Although they have minor bottlenecks such as river crossings and, at one point, marshalling yards where the width of the railway tracks changes from the wider Russian gauge to the narrower East Prussian and Polish gauge, they have no long overseas supply lines nor the vulnerable bottlenecks of ports where supplies must be unloaded from ships and reloaded on land transports. The problem of logistics is one of the most important reasons for maintaining a substantial United States armed force in Europe. It is somewhat easier for the Soviet Union to bring up reinforcements than for the United States to do so.

During peacetime, the NATO patrols perform surveillance and security operations along the border between West and East Germany and along the Czechoslovakian border. In the American sector, which ranges from Kassel in the North to the Bavarian Alps, armored cavalry units conduct these patrols in cooperation with German border police agencies that man more than 200 stations in the villages and small towns along the border.

The Soviet and East German border patrol measures are strikingly different. Along the border on the Communist side there are continuous barbed wire fences--some of which are charged with electricity. The Communists have watchtowers, armed patrols with dogs, and a plowed strip of land ten meters wide that is raked frequently to reveal footprints of persons crossing the border. In most places,

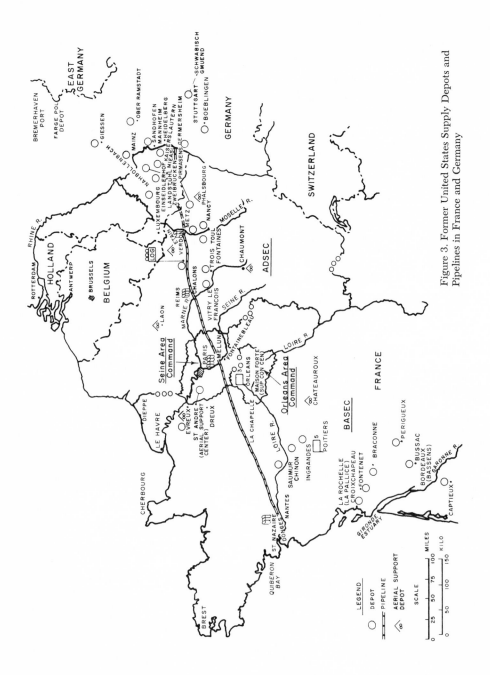

Figure 3. Former United States Supply Depots and Pipelines in France and Germany

the Communists have even placed anti-personnel mines to keep defectors from escaping to the West.

Should a conflict develop, NATO could not hope to provide a forward conventional defense along the entire border that would hold against a determined Soviet attack. The division frontage of about forty to fifty kilometers would spread the troops too thin. The great length and lack of maneuvering depth, the dense population, the excellent East-West roads, and the lack of a natural defense barrier East of the Rhine would make it extremely difficult to stem a rapid penetration of the Soviet ground forces along a broad front. As General Beaufre points out, ". . . the Red Army which was able to cross the big rivers of Russia and Poland would not be stopped by obstacles as the Weser and the Meuse."[14] As discussed previously, however, this is not really the critical problem. The problem is to move sufficient ground forces to the crisis locale to snuff out a border conflict, to decisively defeat a limited attack, or to stem a larger assault. Whether the NATO forces, operating under the doctrine of flexible response, can do this will be explored in a subsequent chapter.

Air Forces

Because of range and speed, aircraft could be brought to bear in a conflict much more quickly and from greater distances. In a 1963 compilation, the Institute for Strategic Studies listed 4,672 interceptors and fighter bombers for European NATO and 11,050 for the Warsaw Pact.[15] Here, too, the significance of this two to one Communist superiority is difficult to gauge. Actually, the aircraft that would probably be used initially in a local conflict--if aircraft are used at all--are located in the Federal Republic and in East Germany. Here the numbers are approximately equal--about 1,000 for each side, but there are asymmetries in the air situation that makes judgment as to the balance difficult.

First, there is a difference in doctrine and in the emphasis placed on various roles which tactical air forces may be called upon to perform. For example, although the Soviets possess bombers, they have never emphasized manned aircraft as an independent means of warfare as have the American military strategists. Aviation has traditionally been intimately geared to the operations of the ground forces. Indicative of this is that Soviet aviation is organized in air armies and air regiments rather than wings and squadrons. Whereas the trend in the United

States is to emphasize the use of fighter bombers for precision delivery of conventional and nuclear weapons of small yield in interdiction strikes, the Soviets appear to be relying on bombers as a supplement to the strategic rocket forces and for delivering nuclear rocket attacks against enemy ground forces without entering the air defense zone. [16] Such strikes could hardly be regarded as precision attacks. Although the Soviet Air Force would like to build up their bomber force, the indications are that the Soviet manned-bomber will be gradually phased out. The Soviet Union has announced on a couple of occasions that it was cutting off production of bombers.

The major emphasis in Soviet Air Forces as well as Satellite military aviation, however, is on air defense. The interceptors are dispersed over a large number of airfields throughout East Germany (see Fig. 4). [17] In connection with this, the Soviets place great reliance on their surface-to-air missiles (SA-2s) to protect Communist territory from high altitude attacks. The Soviet ground forces also have large numbers of 85-mm anti-aircraft artillery that can reach planes up to 35,000 feet and 57-mm and 37-mm weapons that can reach up to 18,000 and 10,000 feet respectively. As time goes on, the Soviets can be expected to deploy in large numbers th SA-3 missiles, which are similar to the U.S. Hawk surface-to-air missile, to destroy aircraft at lower altitudes. Tactical fighters also are considered in support of ground action, but usually the role is envisaged as a followup to surface-to-surface missile and rocket attacks. In this role they would be closely coordinated with the ground armies in combat operations employing either conventional or nuclear weapons.

The situation in West Germany is quite different. The NATO air forces do not place the same emphasis on air defense as the Soviets do. Instead, greater emphasis is placed on interdiction with fighter-bombers. NATO aircraft generally have both a longer range and a larger capability for carrying payloads of conventional munitions. [18] U.S. fighter bombers ". . . on the average can carry twice the payload twice as far as the Soviet counterparts."[19] But the major difference is the current requirement for NATO to maintain many of its fighter bombers on an alert status to deliver nuclear weapons against enemy targets under any weather conditions. Because of the large number of tactical and strategic missiles available to the Soviet Union--presumably targeted on the major NATO military bases and complexes, these nuclear strike aircraft would have to be launched

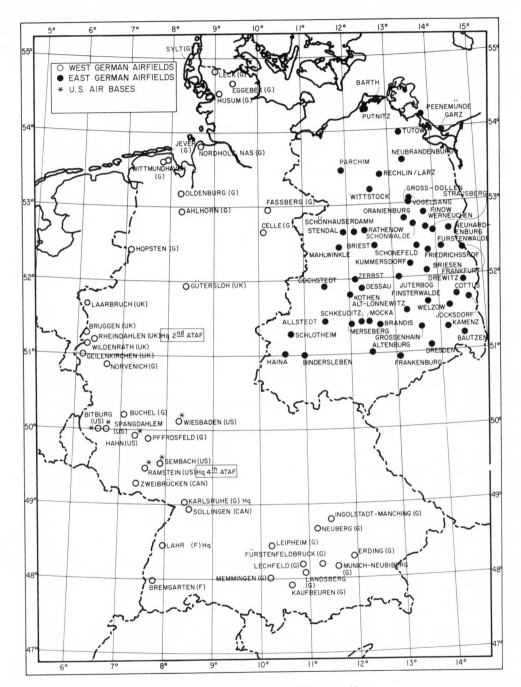

Figure 4. Military and Other Major Airfields
in Germany

almost immediately to prevent their being destroyed by preemptive Soviet missile attacks.

Related to the asymmetries in the air force postures in Europe ". . . is the lack of adequate forward area air defense for our (i.e., U.S.) forces."[20] As far back as 1958, NATO has been trying to find agreement on an integrated and automated air defense system for early warning and control which would be able to cope with high speed interceptors. Whereas many of the components of such a system have been installed under national auspices, the plan for NADGE (NATO Air Defense Ground Environment) has gone through several studies and committee work, with the cost estimates climbing from $150 million in 1960 to $900 million in 1962. In 1964, agreement was reached on a scaled-down NADGE plan and this was agreed to at a cost of about $330 million.[21] Only recently, after France decided to withdraw her forces from NATO, has the contract been finally awarded.[22] True, we have a belt of Hawk and Nike-Hercules surface-to-air missiles. But the missiles may not be necessarily emplaced at the scene of the actual conflict. Furthermore, more mobile systems are required to fill the gap in the combat zone. Because of the disappointing progress with the Mauler surface-to-air missile, the United States has been forced to seek an interim solution to this air defense deficiency. If a low-level conflict develops at a point along the border and aircraft are employed in a conventional close support role, the initial advantage in air defense would appear to be with the Communists. The Soviets' greater resources in interceptors, surface-to-air missiles, and antiaircraft artillery might cause serious attrition to NATO air forces.

The situation would be improved somewhat with the conversion to the F-4 fighter bomber, which has a significantly better air-to-air capability than the F-105, both in detection and kill. The F-4 carries the heat-seeking Sidewinder and the radar-guided Sparrow III air-to-air missile. The F-4 and the later F-111 aircraft could perform quite admirably as interceptors. But this is not their primary assigned role.

Coupled with the American strategic concept of flexible response and an initial defense using conventional weapons, the NATO air force posture provides an element of great vulnerability in the military confrontation. This is especially true of the Seventeenth U.S. Air Force in Germany which is largely concentrated on five major airfields deep in West Germany near the French border. These five airfields are located in a circle of about 35-miles radius. It is hard to conceive how the United States could operate its aircraft from these air bases in conventional support against an enemy attack--no matter how small, and still maintain a nuclear alert posture in the event the enemy carries out its own proclaimed strategic concept of employing nuclear rockets in the decisive initial period of war against the "imperialist" states. For security against a nuclear attack, the U. S. aircraft would have to be dispersed.

Some critical questions here need answers. Should the aircraft earmarked for nuclear strike be sent aloft at the commencement of hostilities to prevent the enemy from "preempting" them on base? Should the nuclear-armed aircraft be dispersed to other airfields during a low-intensity conflict or a crisis that threatens to erupt into violence? Would the Soviets interpret the intent behind such dispersal as defensive or offensive? If indeed we are to fight a conventional war at the border, these aircraft and airbases would have to depend on the sufferance of the enemy for their survival from nuclear attack.

By merely glancing at the map shown in Fig. 3, which shows the military and other major airfields in West and East Germany, some very interesting implications can be derived. The more uniform distribution of airfields in East Germany and the closer proximity of many of them to the Iron Curtain are in keeping with the Soviet's emphasis on air defense. On the West side, the concentration of airfields deep into Germany is compatible with NATO's mission capabilities and emphasis on fighter bombers in a tactical nuclear and conventional support role. The greater distance from the border makes these fighter bombers less vulnerable to the threat of Soviet air attack than if they were based closer to the Iron Curtain. Yet because of their longer range, NATO aircraft can still reach targets in East Germany.

An impartial observer would no doubt detect a major inconsistency between NATO's avowed defensive intent and the tactical doctrine, composition, and disposition of its air forces, organized as they are mainly for nuclear interdiction deep into Communist territory. A major inconsistency is also apparent between the oft-perceived threat of military aggression on the part of the Communists in Central Europe and the emphasis on air defense clearly implied by their air force doctrine, equipment, and disposition.

If we postulate a conflict where nuclear weapons are not used, these NATO high-performance aircraft could probably survive on base with the protection of surface-to-air missile defenses. These aircraft could also perform a worthwhile role in close support. The concentration of fire that may be delivered by aircraft could be very useful against infantry, but it would probably have lower kill probabilities against tanks.[23] In the interdiction role, however, aircraft losses to enemy surface-to-air defenses would probably make the cost of conventional deep interdiction prohibitive for the benefit obtained. This last assessment might be disputed because of the advent of electronic countermeasures (ECM) that have been developed to counter the surface-to-air missiles. Yet if we examine the attrition rate in the somewhat more primitive environment of Vietnam which is on the order of about one percent and compare this with the kill rate of fifty percent credited to the later version SA-3 in certain studies,[24] one can reasonably expect at least an attrition rate of five to ten percent which would effectively discourage a protracted suppression campaign.

It is conceivable that a low-level conflict might develop along the Berlin air corridor or over Berlin itself without in any way engaging the ground forces. Under these circumstances, the all-weather capabilities of our new fighter bombers, especially the F-4, would be advantageous against enemy interceptors, but it would probably suffer high attrition if Soviet SAM defenses were brought into action.

The main problem is the maintenance of a NATO tactical nuclear alert posture, if large numbers of NATO aircraft are employed in the conventional role. Most of these aircraft have been assigned the nuclear strike role against military targets in the satellite countries separately and in conjunction with the strategic nuclear strikes of the Strategic Air Command and the Polaris submarines. If the nuclear alert posture is maintained, the conventional air capabilities are degraded proportionally.

There is consensus among military analysts that NATO air forces could not gain air superiority over the local battlefield without knocking out the Soviet airfields in East Germany. Although we have no experience relevant to the Central European situation, the experience in Korea and Vietnam would suggest that air defenses would make the task of destroying enemy aircraft on the ground with conventional weapons a very unprofitable undertaking. In Central Europe the attrition undoubtedly would be high and the pressures would be great to adopt the alternative of using small precision-delivered nuclear weapons in a saturation attack to suppress enemy air power. This might do the job. For example, the F-105 is a remarkably effective precision-delivery system. Frequent evaluations prove that we can expect a high degree of success of delivering nuclear weapons under the most adverse weather conditions, using auto pilot, Doppler navigation, ground map radar, and toss-bomb computer. Whether or not the airfields are attacked with conventional or nuclear weapons, the conflict would have extended beyond the battlefield with all the attendant pressures to escalate further. During the early stages of a conflict, the Allied Command would have to weigh carefully the advantages of aircraft in air suppression attacks against certain expansion of violence and possible escalation to even higher levels.

Nuclear Weapons

Before turning to the analysis of the possible consequences of using tactical nuclear weapons in battle, the imbalances and asymmetries in the force postures related to tactical nuclear weapons in Europe should be discussed.

Large quantities and varieties of tactical nuclear weapons are located in West Europe. In 1961, Mr. McNamara announced that there were "thousands" of nuclear warheads in Europe; in 1965, he predicted that the numbers of nuclear weapons in 1966 would be "100 per cent higher than in 1961."[25] From this, an elementary deduction can be made. "Thousands" with an "s" must obviously be at least 2000, and "100 percent higher" doubles this amount. Hence, there are at least 4000 tactical nuclear weapons in Europe. Mr. McNamara resolved such speculation by announcing that there were about 7000 nuclear warheads in inventory for NATO forces in Europe.[26] These weapons are under strict American control, to be released to U. S. forces and to our NATO allies on the decision of the President of the United States. Whether tactical nuclear weapons are stored in the Warsaw Pact satellite nations is not known. If they are, it can confidently be assumed, on the basis of Soviet concern over nuclear warfare, nuclear proliferation, and reliability of East Europeans, that nuclear weapons are kept under Soviet centralized control. As reported earlier, however, tactical nuclear delivery systems in the form of rockets and missiles are present in the satellite states and reportedly in the hands of the East German army.[27]

From open discussions on the Test Ban Treaty, it would appear that the United States possesses a great variety of small yield weapons, but what constitutes small yield is a matter of sharp differences. Colonel Reinhardt pointed out that the Institute for Strategic Studies in 1963 claimed for Davy Crockett a yield of 1/4 kiloton. Newsweek Magazine in 1964 claimed for the same weapon an explosive charge between twenty and forty tons of TNT. Former U. S. Deputy Secretary of Defense Roswell L. Gilpatric claimed that the typical tactical weapon has several times the yield of the Hiroshima weapon.[28] The most recent estimate from the Institute for Strategic Studies states the ". . . average explosive yield of the bombs stockpiled in Europe for the use of NATO tactical aircraft is about 100 kilotons and of the missile warheads about twenty kilotons."[29] The strategic bomb for France's Mirage IV is reported to be a sixty kiloton weapon-- somewhat less than the average for NATO tactical aircraft.[30] Future yields are, however, expected to be as high as 300 kilotons. If it is indeed true that Soviet tactical nuclear weapons are of even higher yields, as is generally believed,[31] there is great danger that a Soviet tactical nuclear response to even a discriminate NATO use would cause such widespread destruction that it would be extremely difficult to confine the violence to the battlefield.

Tactical nucelar weapons provide an important element of stability to the confrontation. As discussed earlier, these weapons are regarded by NATO nations as an essential link in strategic deterrence. But paradoxically, their very existence in relatively vulnerable West German storage sites, some necessarily not too far from the border, creates an element of instability, in the event deterrence fails and the conflict develops into a fairly large size engagement. The very physical presence of nuclear stockpiles in Europe creates a need for sizeable conventional forces just to protect them. This especially applies to atomic demolition weapons (ADMs) that to be effective should be prepositioned near the border on defended territory and, in a lesser degree, to the Honest John 12-mile missiles and artillery pieces. The 85-mile Sergeant missile and the 350-mile Pershing can be sited well to the rear of the NATO lines. Unless they are attacked by other enemy nuclear missiles or aircraft, there would be time to assess the operational needs and select targets before they are overrun. A second element of instability is the fact that nuclear weapons delivered by aircraft in support of a ground battle are not as accurate as nuclear weapons launched by short-range missiles and from ground troops. By far the most serious element of instability, however, is a lack of a workable doctrine for using tactical nuclear weapons by either ground or air

forces in the event a low-level conflict gets out of hand Nuclear weapons would
then be required to prevent the conventional forces from being overrun (under
the American concept), or to prevent a definite border penetration (under the
German strategic concept). This important problem is discussed later.

Command, Control, and Communications

Essential to the operations of ground and air forces in conflict, and especially in conflict where nuclear weapons may be employed, are the command and
control arrangements and the communications systems. There is a natural tendency in times of crisis to overload communications networks. Particularly since
the advent of nuclear weapons, the trend has been toward increasing centralization of both information and control in the highest political authorities. This tendency towards centralization is further complicated by the fact that there has been
only maneuver and exercise experience in atomic battle on which to base estimates
of information requirements, or to assess the success of command in controlling
the use of nuclear weapons.

The complicated procedure of disseminating alerts, requesting and obtaining
authorization to use nuclear weapons, assigning targets, and passing on damage
assessments are just a few of the essential functions that must be accomplished
in order to keep the conflict under control and moving towards a recognized objective.

Suffice it to say, the decision to use atomic weapons of any yield will be a
momentous one, and the time it takes to arrive at such a decision will be shorter
or longer depending on the nature of the crisis, the information available, and
the personalities of the President and other leaders. Although there is apparently
little that can be done to shorten the presidential decision-making process by
further technological improvements in communications, it should be quite obvious
that a communications slowdown or failure could be extremely hazardous in time
of conflict or crisis. Further, there is no such thing as a fool-proof communications system. Breakdowns can occur from saturation of message traffic, poor
atmospheric conditions, enemy actions, and power failure. A communications
failure at the critical juncture when the first nuclear weapon is being released
could be disastrous. At this point, the pressing need to contact allied governments,
to monitor results, to redeploy forces, to regird for restrikes, and above all to

communicate unambiguous intentions to the enemy, create almost overwhelming demands on the communication network. Without some carefully thought-out doctrine for discriminate nuclear release and control, it would be extremely difficult to keep the conflict from escalating to general war.

Search for Stability

Most military analysts would agree that President de Gaulle's action in pulling France out of NATO and expelling United States troops from France has altered the capabilities of NATO--mainly by denying to the allies use of lines of logistics and dispersal airfields on French territory. Yet, as a practical matter, it does not appear that the NATO force posture in the rest of Europe is likely to be altered in a significant way as a result of France's defection, at least in the near future. The peacetime disposition of ground and air forces and the infrastructure investment in casernes, supply depots, pipelines, and air bases represent considerable capital investment. Both the United States and Great Britain are suffering from balance of payment problems. None of the NATO countries seems disposed to increase its military expenditures to improve the NATO force posture. The only major change in the offing appears to be the necessary readjustment occasioned by France's action. This adjustment could hardly be counted as an improvement. From all indications, the actions being taken to relocate American forces formerly stationed in France are dictated more by financial and political considerations then by strategy.

There remain now, as before, asymmetries, imbalances, and identifiable hazards and vulnerabilities in both force postures which create potential instabilities in the event of conflict. These unstable elements derive their significance mainly from the existence of nuclear arsenals on both sides and the possibility, however remote, that these powerful weapons might some day be used in anger.

Over the period of years, various plans and schemes have been advanced on both sides to eliminate hazards. Some were aimed at attacking the various asymmetries and imbalances directly. For example, the mobile medium-range ballistic missile (MMRBM) was advanced as a counter to the large Soviet MRBM and IRBM force. The possible contribution of such a force, however, has seemed to many to be offset by the disadvantages and dangers inherent in the introduction of MRBMs in Western Europe. These missiles, having the capability of reaching the

Soviet Union, would certainly be regarded as a direct threat by the Russians, who would then have considerable incentive to preempt in a serious crisis. Realizing this, the West would have similar incentive for early use of the weapons to prevent them from being destroyed before they could be used to strike the enemy.[32] The resultant situation in time of crisis or limited conflict would be quite unstable. This element of instability is accentuated by the fact that MRBMs or MMRBMs could not be made invulnerable, and both sides would realize this.

Even if the enemy attempted discriminate counterforce blows against these missiles, collateral damage would be substantial. If the MRBMs were fixed and hardened, they could be pretargeted and the hardening might merely prompt the enemy to direct higher yield warheads against them. Mobile missiles could not be pretargeted and on that account might be somewhat less vulnerable than hardened missiles, but this attribute could bring the enemy to use area saturation strikes to ensure their destruction. In either case, collateral damage would be so intensified as to render a counterforce strike practically indistinguishable from a countervalue war.

The possible value of a European MRBM force is further reduced due to reluctance of Europeans to accept such a force, either as an American system or as an allied or dual-control force. European attitudes have been more favorable toward the sea-based Polaris missile than the land-based MRBM. Especially in the case of the MMRBM, there would seem to be political and psychological drawbacks. Serious anxieties would probably be produced by constantly moving missiles, and adverse psychological effects could be expected to be reflected in political pressures. Propaganda offensives, demonstrations, and possible riots against MMRBMs could diminish the effectiveness of the force and perhaps make it a political liability. Such happenings would also disrupt the mobility of the system, adding to the already great problems posed by congested traffic and command and control. Even a mobility-on-demand system, rather than a continuous-mobility one, would face similar difficulties.

These considerations detract from the military potential of a NATO MRBM system. But the major reason for rejecting the NATO land-based MRBM system was political. France has rejected American nuclear weapons on French soil and Denmark and Norway refuse to have nuclear weapons on their territory during peacetime. This leaves only West Germany and possibly Belgium and the Netherlands. The last two are extremely reluctant to have strategic weapons sited on their territory. The Soviets have made emphatic their opposition to giving the West Germans a share in strategic nuclear weapons. Germany's allies are only slightly less apprehensive. To establish a NATO strategic nuclear force in the heart of West Europe in which only the Americans and Germans were participants would seriously divide the alliance and disrupt the detente with the USSR.

Various disarmament and arms reduction schemes have also been considered to correct the imbalances and asymmetries. Some of the proposals were geared to grandiose Utopian schemes of general and complete disarmament. Others sought various reductions of forces in confrontation and reduction or elimination of certain weapon systems including the most destructive armaments--nuclear weapons. This is not the place to examine the various disarmement plans considered or proposed. The fact remains that all such proposals have been perceived by one side or the other as giving the other side a relative military advantage or, more importantly, as undermining the basis of stability in the present confrontation believed to be conferred by the very fact that each side has the nuclear means to deter the other.

Plans for rectifying asymmetries and imbalances themselves do not necessarily improve stability. Even if NATO were to succeed in building up its ground forces to the thirty division force goals for the Central Sector--thus correcting what is commonly regarded as an imbalance in conventional firepower--some of the major hazards and vulnerabilities in the military confrontation would continue to exist. Proposals for dealing with the potential instabilities themselves--all aimed at reducing the chances of conflict and to alleviate the damage of warfare-- are discussed in the next chapter.

ARMS CONTROL IN CENTRAL EUROPE

The various arms control proposals aimed at improving the military stability or at alleviating the possible damage of warfare in Europe can be divided into two categories. First are those measures or arrangements in which explicit agreement is sought between the Soviet Union and the West in the military confrontation. Second are those measures that could be undertaken unilaterally by one side or the other to enhance stability.

In the first group were the Eisenhower "Open Skies" concept and the Eden "joint inspection" proposal of the July 1955 Summit Conference, which sought to strengthen confidence in the peaceful intent of the opposing sides and provide insurance against the danger implicit in the military confrontation by a system of advance warning of surprise attack. The Rapacki plan (named for the Polish Foreign Minister) and other nuclear free zone proposals sought to reduce the dangerous elements in the confrontation by eliminating nuclear weapons in the Central European area entirely. Various schemes of disengagement--of withdrawing troops on both sides--would extend the ban to conventional forces hoping thereby to keep the conflict from starting in the first place. Others have suggested a "no-first-use" doctrine declaration and doctrine for both sides, the establishment of sanctuaries and the use of nuclear weapons for defense only to reduce the dangers of nuclear war and to limit damage if war should occur.

Some of the above proposals also fit into the second category of unilateral measures that may be taken by one side. For example, the "no-first-use" doctrine could be undertaken unilaterally as well as the nuclear weapons for defense only. Some unilateral proposals envisaged a separation between tactical nuclear

forces from conventional forces by setting up separate operational commands
for the two forces in the hope of resolving the contradictions between nuclear
and conventional deployment and operations. Other plans were aimed at establishing clearly defined constraints and limitations on the use of nuclear weapons
to keep the conflict from escalating to general war.

Inspection Against Surprise Attack

The Eisenhower and Eden proposals were advanced as inspection plans only
and were not tied to any proposal for specific force reduction. Both were, however, designed to demonstrate the technical feasibility of an inspection system
and to establish mutual confidence that would be the first stop on the road to general and complete disarmament. The Eden proposal, that the joint inspection
teams have complete freedom of movement and access at any time ". . . to units
or installations to check numerical strengths both of military personnel and equipment" was bound to be rejected by the secretive Russians as a form of legalized
espionage. Although Eden protested that the plan submitted was not to prejudice
a German settlement, it was clearly related to the confrontation along the line
separating the two Germanys and as such was opposed by the West Germans as
a step in the direction of recognizing the status quo. Both plans also called for
a stage-by-stage exchange of "blue prints" or tabulations of the forces in the area
to facilitate the inspection. Without such knowledge the aerial surveillance and
the inspection teams would not know what to look for. In the end, the Open Skies
proposal was rejected by the Soviet Union as an interest of intelligence services
that would contribute neither to disarmament nor to controls over reduction of
forces. The Eden proposal died quietly at the Geneva Summit Conference.

Nuclear Free Zones

The idea of a nuclear free zone as an arms control concept rests on one major assumption: that the removal of tactical or strategic weapons from an actual
or symbolic threatening position in Central Europe would reduce the apparent
danger of a general holocaust or would serve to inhibit escalation of local conflicts to a thermonuclear war. Unfortunately, the whole set of ideas related to
nuclear free zones is fundamentally asymmetrical in its potential impact on both
East and West. A removal of tactical nuclear weapons from Western Europe would

be giving up a major element of the NATO graduated deterrent and defense capability. NATO's conventional forces would then be expected to cope with the military threats of potentially preponderant Soviet conventional firepower. The point should be obvious that a removal of nuclear weapons from zones bordering on the Iron Curtain does not prevent the targeting of nuclear weapons from outside of the zone into this area. President Eisenhower pointed this out in a letter to the Soviet Premier:[1] ". . . there cannot be any great significance in denuclearizing a small area when, as you say, 'the range of modern types of weapons does not know any geographical limit' . . ." For example, the Soviets have some 700 IRBMs and MRBMs within their own territory clearly capable of unleashing a nuclear attack within any nuclear free zone. The West has a similar capability in the U. S. Minuteman and Polaris missiles, and in the NATO bomber and attack aircraft. In fact, a withdrawal of all nuclear weapons from a zone would appear to work counter to the objectives of arms control. The longer range weapons that might be called into play are more powerful, but lack the necessary accuracy to prevent severe collateral damage.

The Rapacki plan, to prohibit nuclear weapons in the two Germanys, in Poland, and in Czechoslovakia, was representative of the nuclear free zone idea. The Communists advanced some interesting arguments in its favor. To the West Germans, it was argued that nuclear rockets on German soil increased the likelihood of atomic war which would inevitably destroy German national life. Even if the war were limited to strategic nuclear exchanges, it would be necessary for the Soviet Union to strike the airbases and possible missile sites in West Germany that threatened Russia. The Soviets also objected to the stationing of foreign troops in West Germany and in other European countries as a scheme of the United States to involve the European NATO nations in American aggressive designs. To the Americans, the Soviets argued that stationing nuclear weapons in Europe would intensify the arms race and increase the chance of war. Besides inter-continental ballistic missiles made such new deployments unnecessary. Foreign bases could only promise to invite enemy strikes and enlarge the scope of the war. American foreign bases were springboards for attack against the socialist countries and were regarded as provocative threats by the Soviet Union that would have to be eliminated before permanent peace could be counted on. Furthermore, the Soviets doubted whether stationing nuclear weapons in Europe would strengthen American relations with its allies, for each would be ". . . compelled to sacrifice its independence for the sake of strategic plans that are alien to its national interests and to risk receiving a blow because of the fact that foreign military bases are situated on its territory."[2] In the French view, at least, the Soviet Union seemed correct on this last point.

Western objections to the Rapacki plan, and the later Gomulka plan (which in essence was merely a repeat of the first phase of Rapacki's plan), were based on military as well as political grounds. First, the superiority in conventional firepower of the Soviet Union, its easier logistic support, and its large mobilization base that called for NATO dependence on nuclear weapons in the first place would create an imbalance in the Soviet Union's favor. Second, a partial or regional solution that did not extend far enough to take care of the Soviet IRBM and MRBM threat was worthless. Third, there were no safeguards to prevent nuclear weapons from being introduced surreptitiously. Fourth, the numbers of nuclear weapons were so large and the size of many warheads so small that there was a question whether it would be feasible to verify that the area was indeed free of atomic weapons. Finally, there were the overriding political objections that the plan would freeze the status quo and would leave unsettled the question of German reunification.

One important argument against the nuclear free zone idea was not discussed, although it may have been recognized. A withdrawal of tactical nuclear weapons from Germany would foreclose on all the possibility of establishing a distinguishable firebreak or threshold of violence at a lower level in the escalation ladder by the use of battlefield nuclear weapons of low-yield and short-range, designed to confine the nuclear damage to a local situation only. Without this capability, the "firebreak" would be between conventional war and strategic nuclear strikes.

This is an important point. The whole thrust of the United States strategy is to make nuclear deterrence credible and defense feasible for Western Europe. The argument was advanced in Chapter 5 that this could be done best by a series of graduated threats and commitments. Doubts expressed by General de Gaulle and others about American nuclear commitment would become even more widespread if the United States were to withdraw its tactical nuclear weapons from Europe. In these circumstances, it is easy to develop an argument that a nuclear-free Europe would be an open invitation for a Soviet "quick grab" or fait accompli by decoupling the local tactical situation from nuclear deterrence. Whether we visualize the use of tactical nuclear weapons in conjunction with general war or as a separate kind of nuclear engagement, there is general recognition among all the allies that these weapons do play a part in deterrence. Whatever the validity of nuclear free zones as an arms control concept, it is just not acceptable to the Western allies in the present European context.

Disengagement

Three things are apparent in the European confrontation between NATO and the USSR. First, there are three major areas of military confrontation: the Arctic Frontier, the Macedonian-Thracian Frontier, and the Central Sector, which includes the Czech-German Frontier and the German "Zonal" Boundary. Second, there are great areas in between the northern tip of Norway and the Turkish straits where whole nations--neutral and neutralized--separate the two alliances: Yugoslavia, Austria, Switzerland, Sweden, and Finland. Third, the only confrontation where disengagements of a hundred or so kilometers can be considered is in the Central Sector. This is the only area in which trade-offs in terms of military "values" even approach symmetry. In the north, a pull-back of any significant distances would be overwhelmingly to the disadvantage of the Soviets because of their important defense installations around the Kola peninsula. In the South, the disadvantages of a reciprocal pull-back would be with NATO, due to the strategic importance of the Turkish straits.[3]

One of the disengagement schemes that would have the least effect on the military capabilities of either side is minor disengagement--i. e., demilitarized zones (DMZs) established with a width of twenty-five kilometers or less on each side of the border. The main difficulty with this measure would be at the political level, since any withdrawal or minor disengagement would involve a larger percentage of the population and the area of East Germany than of West Germany. Demilitarized zones of greater width (e. g., 100 kilometers) would force a major realignment of the NATO "Hawk Belt" and would affect the Warsaw Pact forces mainly through the loss of some forward airfields. Still larger demilitarized zones would have an even more serious effect on NATO by forcing a dangerous concentration of military forces--especially NATO nuclear forces that cannot be based in France. The Warsaw Pact powers might be less affected since a major portion of their logistic support installations are located outside East Germany.

If any major demilitarized zone were established in Central Europe, NATO forces would have to develop plans for defense against a sudden penetration of the disarmed zone by Warsaw Pact forces. Quick and strong reaction would be required of NATO forces to verify enemy intentions and to allow time for decisions at the highest political levels. Unless great care were exercised, a disarmed zone might provide the opportunity for Warsaw Pact forces to make an unopposed occupation similar to Hitler's occupation of the Rhineland before World War II (which was accompanied by a lot of noise but no serious combat) or to seize forward areas before NATO forces could be brought into action. Either move would present NATO with a fait accompli and place upon NATO forces the burden of deciding whether to sit down at the conference table, attempt to throw out the enemy forces by conventional means, or to take other military action at places and times of its own choosing--to escalate the conflict. In general, it is obvious that any large demilitarized zone along the Iron Curtain will offer opportunities for unopposed occupations or quick grabs even with an inspection system in force to give tactical warning that the DMZ has been violated. Reaction cannot be assumed to be automatic and there will always be delays while the information is being sifted to gauge enemy intentions and while decision-makers are making up their minds how to respond.

It would seem, on military grounds alone, that there are no significant sectors along the Iron Curtain where either East or West could afford to withdraw completely its military forces. Whereas this discussion has dealt with a possible Soviet attack, the conclusions would be the same for both sides if one conceived of a possible NATO attack. This particularly applies to zones which include large segments of population and industrial resources. By no means an insignificant consideration is the sacrifice of capital investment on both sides for bases and prepared defenses and the collateral requirement of obtaining additional military installations to replace them further back. As long as each side perceives a threat from the other, measures will be taken to guard against the threat.

There are, of course, related considerations to the strictly military problem. The Communist paranoia about espionage, and the West's only slightly less intense apprehensions about Communist subversion probably would make such a separation intolerable for both sides. To cap this, there are well-founded fears of the East Germans against permitting any of their population to exist outside of

their guarded frontier, or to come and go, as a matter of course, through them.
It must always be kept in mind that the Iron Curtain is primarily designed to keep
the people of the satellite states and the Russians "in" far more than to keep the
West "out." In addition, within the border, the Iron Curtain is designed to keep
the people under control of the Communist hierarchy. One alternative possibility
to a populated zone of disengagement is a cleared and evacuated strip on both
sides of the Iron Curtain. This would be out of the question on political grounds,
as it would imply a permanent division of the "two Germanys" and besides would
remove many acres of land from the agricultural economy.

Separate Commands for Nuclear Forces

One of the recurring suggestions for establishing constraints on the use of
nuclear weapons is to establish a separate command for these weapons. As the
late John Strachey argued, there is a strong feeling that "the tactical nuclear deterrent, however delivered, should be held well back, under a separate chain of
command."[4]

Some of the proposals for a separate nuclear command deal with strategic
deterrent forces for Europe leaving tactical nuclear weapons under the control
of SACEUR. Other proposals would put all nuclear weapons under a separate
command. Some of the difficulty one experiences in coming to grips with the idea
of a separate command is a matter of definition. In United States usage, a nuclear
weapons system which can strike the homeland of the enemy is regarded as strategic. A tactical nuclear weapon is designed for use against the enemy forces in
the field or against his military bases of support. Limited range and lower yield
are also considered as criteria for tactical nuclear weapons, although this is not
as important as the use for which the weapon is intended. In Europe, however, a
practical distinction between strategic and tactical nuclear forces cannot be made.
Nuclear weapons whose range limitation and yield makes them tactical as far as
the United States and the Soviet Union, might well be regarded as strategic by the
densely populated European NATO and Warsaw Pact nations whose cities might
suffer damage in the process of their use.

A distinction that is becoming increasingly more accepted and used in discussions of European defense is that between conventional weapons and "battlefield" nuclear weapons and the concommitant distinction between "battlefield"

and other "tactical" nuclear weapons. Battlefield nuclear weapons are usually considered to be weapons of low yield and of limited range to be used in the narrow area of contact with the enemy. Other tactical nuclear weapons are considered to be weapons of larger yield and greater range (although these attributes are not essential) to be used across the political boundary or beyond the battlefield, mainly in the role of interdiction.

The proposals that call for a separate NATO command of strategic nuclear forces, such as the American proposal for the Multilateral Force (MLF) and the British proposal for the "multinational" Atlantic Nuclear Force (ANF), are designed to give West Germany a participating share in Alliance nuclear strategy. Just about all of the conflicting national views on the question of political control of nuclear weapons are brought to focus in these two concepts. Neither of these separate strategic force proposals, which will be discussed later, address the problem of a doctrine of constraints in the use of tactical nuclear weapons. The nuclear weapons of these two proposed commands, if used at all, would be used only in conjunction with other strategic forces in the context of general war. A separate command for tactical nuclear forces in Europe at least addresses the problem of reconciling the contradictions between nuclear and conventional deployments for defense. Here we are faced with monumental practical difficulties. The proposal assumes that the present dual-capable forces would be supplanted by two separate forces having completely separate organizational structures and lines of command. The problems posed by such a separation include examining how separate forces can operate in the same space and over the same terrain, how communications and mutual support would be structured to ensure effective command and control of both forces and what doctrines of engagement would be followed by the two separate commands.

Schelling suggests having the nuclear armed forces physically distinct from the conventional forces, ". . . rather than to have a dual capability distributed throughout the troops." The purpose would be ". . . to be able to engage in large-scale conventional resistance with <u>conspicuous</u> withholding of nuclears."[5] (Emphasis added.) Technically or financially, doing away with dual capable weapons is an impossibility. Within certain limits, artillery that can shoot a conventional shell can certainly shoot a nuclear one. There is no way, technically, to make it <u>conspicuous</u> that the two capabilities have been separated. Conceivably, all

nuclear warheads for dual capable weapons now in the European arsenals could
be withdrawn and an entirely new set of nuclear-only weapons be created at tremendous cost. But this could not be done in a conspicuous and credible manner.

One thing that immediately becomes apparent is that more troops would be
required for two separate commands or a reduction of conventional forces in Europe would have to be accepted to create a separate nuclear command. We might
avoid the confusion of having the two kinds of forces operating in the same spa-
cial environment by stationing the nuclear command to the rear. But then there
would be the problem of conspicuously identifying the differences between the two
separate commands for the enemy. (Why else have two commands?) The logistics
for the conventional forces would have to operate through the zone occupied by
the nuclear force command. Then, when it was decided to introduce the nuclear
command into the action, the two forces would have to merge. There would be
also the siting problem of surface-to-air (SAM) defenses using nuclear warheads
versus the SAM defenses using conventional warheads; the problem of earmark-
ing certain airfields solely for aircraft to carry nuclear weapons; the problem of
liaison between separate commands. When broken down like this, the whole separate command concept smacks of "Alice in Wonderland."

This does not suggest that the idea of a separate tactical nuclear command
is entirely without merit. Certainly, we can conceive of separate nuclear battalions organized under corps command which could be made available to enter the
conflict in support of the U.S., British or German ground forces whenever the
U.S. Government decided that the Soviet Union was making a major effort to
break through. Such special weapons commands could rehearse with the NATO
divisions during field exercises in time of peace to insure tight and effective control. Such feasible organizational changes, however, are not usually the kind referred to when separate nuclear commands are discussed.

"No-First-Use," Sanctuaries and Nuclear Weapons for Defense Only

The whole set of arms control ideas embraced in these terms are subject to
the most serious political objections in Central Europe. To foreswear the option
of initiating the use of nuclear weapons would constitute a pledge to defend West
Europe with conventional forces only--a thing practically all military people regard as impossible in the light of the Soviet's superiority in conventional firepower,

their short and internal lines of communications, their ability to quickly reinforce their armies in contact, the density of population in West Germany and excellent east-west road network. To renege on the American pledge to defend Europe ". . . with every kind of weapon needed. . ."[6] could literally break up the Alliance and send Germany scurrying to acquire her own nuclear weapons.

"No-First-Use"

Except for this political objection, some analysts profess to see nothing wrong with an explicit "no-first-use" declaration. Some statements by the President and other administration leaders come very close to making such a "no-first-use" announcement.[7] Herman Kahn, for one, argues that it would be all right to make the "no-first-use" declaration because ". . . no one could wholly trust that the United States--or any nation--would stand by its declaration and refuse to resort to nuclear means if it were presented with a vital challenge."[8] In short, the United States could have its cake and eat it, too!

Quite obviously, the argument could be turned the other way. Even though NATO's declaratory policy is to use nuclear weapons under circumstances of NATO troops being overrun, no one could wholly trust that these nuclear weapons would in fact be used. In fact, de Gaulle and other Europeans already have expressed a lack of trust in American willingness to use these nuclear weapons in Europe unless the vital interests of the United States itself are threatened. Whereas the claim that they will be used does not introduce any more uncertainty in the equation than the claim that they would not be used first, the declaratory statement that they will be used slants the emphasis in favor of nuclear deterrence--a thing of great psychological importance to the Europeans. It may well be true, as argued by Herman Kahn, that the effects of actually using nuclear weapons on future "stability," the arms race, nuclear proliferation and other long-term objectives would justify a "no-first-use" policy.[9] But since a "no-first-use" declaratory statement would be disbelieved in any event, no useful purpose is served by making it. Unless NATO acquires the necessary conventional forces to make it safe to back off from reliance on tactical nuclear weapons, it would seem that Alliance cohesion would be better served by stressing a continued willingness to initiate the use of nuclear weapons in important circumstances. This willingness to initiate the use of nuclear weapons applies also to possible conflicts which might arise in East Germany--say, to relieve a besieged

Allied convoy along the autobahn or to prevent the Soviet occupation of Berlin.
Even if NATO acquires the necessary conventional forces to defend successfully
against a Soviet thrust into Western Germany, these same forces would not be
adequate to make an offensive penetration of East Germany to save Berlin. Furthermore, if NATO did in fact have superior conventional forces to do so, what
would prevent the Soviet Union from first using nuclear weapons and in defense
only?

Sanctuary

The idea that a part of Europe could be established as a sanctuary whereas
other parts would be used as battlegrounds suffers from the same objection of the
Europeans as the idea of fighting a war in Europe while leaving the United States
and Russian homelands intact. This does not suggest that sanctuaries are ruled
out entirely. Sanctuaries are elements of strategy. Sanctuaries were established
in the Korean War by both sides. The United Nations observed the Yalu River as
a line beyond which attacks would not be made. In return the airfields in South
Korea and the U.S. aircraft carriers were treated as sanctuaries by the North
Koreans and Chinese. The United States had observed the areas around Hanoi and
Haiphong in North Vietnam as sanctuaries until it appeared advantageous to bomb
the oil dumps near these populated centers. Even then extreme care was exercised
in avoiding the cities themselves. If sanctuaries were to be established in Central
Europe, they would be more likely to come about after conflict starts by tacit
agreement derived from the interpretation of each side of the statements and actions of the other. A sanctuary is not something on which one can reach agreement
with a potential enemy in advance. A sanctuary rests on the uneasy basis of threats
and counterthreats. A sanctuary will remain inviolate only so long as the opposing
sides perceive the relative advantages of refraining from extending the range of
combat to include the sanctuary as outweighing its disadvantages. This perception
is intrinsic.

Nuclear Weapons for Defense Only

The "Nuclear Weapons for Defense Only" concept embraces three different
ideas. First, the concept means to some the same as a no-first-use policy: nuclear weapons would be used only in defense against the enemy's nuclear weapons.
Second, the concept suggests to others that nuclear weapons would only be used
"for defense" on the defender's territory. It is conceivable that circumstances

might cause the fighting to be confined to the local battlefield only, with the rest of Europe, both East and West, treated as sanctuary. It is also conceivable that circumstances might establish the limits of a battlefield in West Germany only. To suggest, however, that a doctrine be adopted that nuclear weapons would be used only for defense on the west side of the political border, this would call for the most serious objections on the part of the West German government. Aside from the political aspects, the most serious objection to this idea is that it would foreclose on our option to use these weapons in East Germany during an armed conflict over Berlin that results in humiliation and defeat for the West. (Of course, one could claim that such use would constitute "defense only.") The third idea conveyed by the "defense only" doctrine is part of the United States strategy of flexible response. Implicit is the assumption that defensive wars are the only kinds of wars NATO or the United Sates would fight. In the name of defense we would use whatever weapon needed, even if it meant initiating the first use of nuclear weapons to stave off defeat. Conceived in this manner, the idea only serves to bolster a "moralistic" posture. As a practical concept of nuclear constraints, it is meaningless.

Constraints and Limitations on the Use of Nuclear Weapons

It is doubtful in the present climate that any scheme aimed at enhancing stability would be mutually acceptable to both East and West in an explicit manner. The only arms control arrangements that have been agreed to by both sides are peripheral ones, such as the military neutralization of Antarctica and the atmospheric test ban--neither of which really affects the current military confrontation in Europe. France, of course, has declined to subscribe to the partial test ban.

There is another course, however. Unilateral measures may be taken by the West to eliminate elements of instability in NATO's force posture with reference to, although without agreement with, the Soviet Union. These measures must be carefully calculated as to long-range purpose and effect. It does no good to carry out measures that give the West a so-called "military" advantage over the East, if in the process of interaction, the security of both sides is reduced by making the confrontation even more unstable. To achieve arms stability in Europe is a most complex strategic problem and the total environment must be taken into account. The intractable political problems which remain under the military

confrontation will undoubtedly continue. There will always be danger that attempts
to alter the political situation might result in upheaval and violence. A highly stable military posture might prevent possible ruptures in the political scene from
getting out of hand. This requires, as General Andre Beaufre said, "a strategy
more safe and perhaps less onerous than the one which we have." The military
mission, "deter, or if deterrence fails, prevail" is no longer adequate in Central
Europe. Under the concepts of arms control and stability, the mission becomes
"deter safely, or if deterrence fails, defend successfully without extending the
destruction to general war."

Since major readjustments in NATO forces to provide a viable conventional
defense/deterrence posture do not appear likely, there remains one other avenue
to follow: that of developing a workable plan of limitations or doctrine of constraints for the use of nuclear weapons that could possibly prevent the disastrous
consequences of general nuclear war. That the United States has no such workable
plan or doctrine became amply clear during the 1961 Berlin crisis. In working
out the United States strategy, a major premise was a willingness to face nuclear
war. But the option was undefined. Secretary of Defense McNamara and McGeorge
Bundy, the Special Assistant to the President for National Security Affairs, discovered that the existing military plans assumed an almost immediate resort to
nuclear war calling for a nuclear strike against the Soviet Union.[10] It is not necessary to be privy to secret war plans to assert confidently that a NATO doctrine
for local nuclear constraints still remains undefined.[11] For such constraints to
be made distinguishable to the enemy, they must be communicated openly by actions and pronouncements that are unambiguous or at least consistent with one
another. This has not been done.

In Chapter 5 a conceptual variation to the American concept of flexible response was proposed. The idea is to seek to establish additional firebreaks or
distinguishable thresholds of violence between the first use of nuclear weapons
and general war. If it were possible to do so, it was suggested, the danger of
escalation to general war might be diminished, the use of nuclear weapons might
be made less horrendous, and graduated deterrence would in any case be strengthened. The concept proposed is based on the conviction that armed conflict is not
a spectrum of one long continuum of violence. There are recognizable breaks in
the spectrum between cold war and border incidents; between border incidents and

civil disturbances; between civil disturbances and revolution; between revolution and intervention; between intervention and interstate warfare; and above all between conventional and nuclear conflict. Once nuclear weapons are used, however, a major threshold will have been crossed and there would be vast uncertainties as to the possibilities of creating further distinctions above that level. In theory, distinctions exist. Battlefield nuclear conflict is not the same as deep interdiction strikes; counterforce attacks are different from "civilian devastation" attacks. Making a distinction between thresholds is different from making a threshold distinguishable and thus convincing to the other side. There need be certain obvious and conspicuous characteristics that enable the enemy to perceive clearly the distinction one wants to make. Herman Kahn lists six major thresholds and forty-four "rungs" in the escalation ladder, with twenty-three rungs above the first nuclear use (Local Nuclear War--Exemplary).[12] But if the use of nuclear weapons were actually initiated at this level under present doctrine and circumstances, confining the fighting at this level or at any other level above would be a matter of the gravest doubt.

The problem in making such distinguishable thresholds in practice is exceedingly complex. The distinction of a threshold must be perceived and understood by both sides. This requires that the rules of the game or doctrine of constraints be consistent with both capabilities and announced intent. As pointed out earlier, NATO's avowed peaceful intent may be contradicted by certain elements in its force posture which are perceived by the enemy as offensive and provocative to the extreme.

Three things are required in an attempt to establish a distinguishable threshold between the first use of nuclear weapons in limited war and their use in general war. First, the technical possibilities of limiting a nuclear battle to the local battlefield in the light of the force postures adopted in Central Europe need to be understood. This requires an understanding of the possible consequences of using various kinds of nuclear weapons in conflict. Second, a plan of limitations and a doctrine of nuclear constraints need to be developed that are compatible with the concept of operations of the armed forces. Third, some readjustment in the NATO force posture is required to bring the doctrine of constraints developed and the capabilities of NATO forces in line with the Alliance's avowed peaceful intent. These matters are discussed in Chapters 8, 9, and 10, which follow.

THE TACTICAL USE OF NUCLEAR WEAPONS IN A LOCAL BATTLE

One of the most difficult problems facing the armed forces today is how to fight a nuclear battle. The armed forces have carried out many training exercises and field maneuvers simulating various kinds of nuclear battles that might be expected in war. Manuals on nuclear weapons employment have been published giving the effects in terms of blast, heat, and radiation; prescribing protective measures; giving target analysis factors for selecting the yield and characteristic of the nuclear weapon to be used on a specific target. In the final analysis, however, there is no operational experience to go on, and military analysts must resort to translating known characteristics of nuclear weapons, derived from controlled tests, into hypothetical operational settings whose only base of experience factors, data and insights are conventional combat situations. The results are often confusing and always inconclusive. Even the technical characteristics under field conditions could undoubtedly produce results dramatically different from the results of a controlled test. Whereas the weapon characteristics, the height of burst and horizontal aiming errors can be estimated and taken into account, the precise size, location and characteristics of the target are hardly ever known in battle. Even if they are known, at one moment in time, the fluidity of the battle may well cause such targets to dissolve before properly coordinated nuclear fire can be brought to bear on them. Or, on the other hand, the precise size of the target and its location might not be important as long as one knows from where the threat comes and nuclear weapons of sufficient size are used to compensate for target errors. But technical characteristics of yield and accuracy are not the governing considerations in calculating the probable number of casualties in a fluid combat situation.

115

Tactics, training, morale, manpower, weapons, terrain, transport and supply of nuclear weapons and conventional ammunition enter into the complex calculus.[1] Casualties would be high--even for "small" nuclear weapons. It would be pure speculation to here attempt to gauge the effect of these casualties on the outcome of a nuclear battle, since this might range from a standoff or even a local defeat for one side to a strategic nuclear exchange.

The psychological factor, for example, has always been important in ground warfare. Even in conventional defense, men must be motivated to move out of their foxholes and counterattack. We can only speculate about the psychological effect of a nuclear battle on the officers and men involved. Reconstituting a company or a battalion where a third or a half of the men might have become battle casualties of a single atomic burst is a major operational and logistics problem in itself; but it is equally a morale problem of great importance. The remaining troops might have none of it. Even the medical personnel sent to remove the casualties from the battlefield might have a difficult time overcoming the trauma of the experience. The morale factor might well be crucial in a nuclear battle, with one side using nuclear weapons not only for their destructive effects but as shock tactics to completely demoralize the opponent.

In examining the problem of fighting a local battle with nuclear weapons, the implicit assumption is made that certain restraints would be imposed that would make such a battle possible. At the very least, the assumption is made that somehow a local nuclear battle could be restricted by geography and could be divorced from events connected with strategic deterrence--the threat of a nuclear exchange on the homelands of the two super-powers. For if such a nuclear exchange should take place, the events on the local battlefield would be almost irrelevant--except, of course, to the military and civil populace in the area. The restraints assumed, however, go further. First, the assumption is made that the conflict would initially involve only conventional weapons and that at some point in the battle, a transition would be made to nuclear weapons. Second, it is assumed that nuclear weapons would only be used, initially as well as later, against lucrative or critical targets--concentrations of enemy troops, important logistic links, military bases, and supply depots. Third, the warhead yield and numbers of weapons used would be constrained according to the characteristics of specific target under attack. Fourth, attempts would be made to minimize or actually avoid civilian damage. These last three restraints imply careful deliberation and control right up the chain of command to the President initially and at least to the army corps or air force commander after blanket release had been made.

The assumption that these four restraints would be operable is necessary if the nuclear conflict is to be confined to the local battlefield. There may be others, but these are the key ones. They are logical restraints based on the fear of escalation to general war and, in part, on the assumption that the supply of tactical nuclear weapons would be limited.[2] The fact that we have 7,000 tactical nuclear weapons in Europe would indicate that the supply of weapons is not an important limitation. But these restraints are still assumptions. Whether the restraints would be observed in practice by one or both sides is a matter of speculation. Current U.S. Army doctrine on the use of tactical nuclear weapons is not as restrictive as it used to be.

Yet setting aside for the moment the speculative arguments that the use of one nuclear weapon would lead rapidly to general nuclear war, or the counterargument that the fearful effects of general war would cause both sides to do everything in their power to confine the nuclear conflict within definable limits, there are some tactical principles upon which most military analysts can agree.

Most warfare analysts would agree that concentrations of supplies and troops are extremely vulnerable to attack by atomic weapons. Accordingly, units of troops should disperse. Troops should also dig in for better protection. Mobility is also important. Troops can remain in one place once discovered by the enemy only by risking nuclear destruction. Massed artillery such as employed by the Russians in World War II could not be used over any length of time without providing a lucrative target for enemy atomic attack. Massing of fires according to current U.S. Army doctrine provides dispersion among batteries of a battalion at a sacrifice in concentration that can only be alleviated by increasing the range of guns. Troops may elect to engage the enemy closely and rapidly in a form of hugging tactic to prevent the enemy from using nuclear weapons against them without killing his own men. Supplies should be spread out and hidden. Aircraft should operate from a large number of airfields and the active bases should be shifted frequently. All these appear to be sound tactical principles until one attempts to visualize how they would work in practice.[3]

For instance, let us examine the matter of dispersal. This tactic is not based on thinning out troops over a wide area, but on separation of more or less self-sufficient units which can fight effectively. The theory is to separate these units so that only a small number of combat units (preferably only one) would be knocked out of the battle by one nominal tactical nuclear weapon. The units of dispersal could be company size or battalion size. The separation could be from one to five kilometers or more. The greater the yield of the enemy weapons, the more separation is required.[4] The more tactical nuclear weapons available to the enemy, the smaller the units of dispersal should be. Of course, there are practical limits imposed by the terrain, the need for mutual fire support and the operation of patrols between dispersed units (to prevent enemy infiltration) that impose practical constraints on distance of separation and size of combat units--if they are still to fight effectively.

Yet the numbers and yields of Soviet tactical nuclear weapons are unknown variables. If the enemy has only a small number of tactical nuclear weapons, he might elect to withhold them until he has reasonably reliable intelligence of lucrative targets that would justify their use. If he has large numbers, he might elect to use them on first contact with NATO patrols or on the basis of fragmentary intelligence. If the warhead yields are large (say of the megaton variety), the enemy might elect either to use them on blanket or saturation attacks over a wide area or to concentrate their use to clear the way of intended advance. In the case of blanket attacks, collateral damage to civilians undoubtedly would be high, while the NATO troops would suffer comparatively less destruction (being dug in and dispersed). In the case of concentrating their use for a breakthrough, collateral civilian damage might be low (if the advance is made over open terrain), while the NATO troops would suffer heavy casualties. In both cases, the impediment to ground advance caused by blowdown and radiation could change the nature of the battle.

Then there is the matter of digging in. According to the Army's training pamphlet[6] on nuclear weapons, troops in foxholes can weather in relative safety a low air burst of a twenty KT nuclear weapon (equivalent to 20,000 tons of TNT) if they are at least 1300 meters from ground zero. An entire battalion could be dug-in within this lethal radius. Foxholes and other prepared defenses are located on the basis of tactical considerations--usually to give the unit a commanding position for fire and mutual support. It might take twelve hours for a company or battalion to establish more elaborate defensive bunkers. Whereas such protective foxholes are useful in conventional as well as nuclear battle, the same foxholes may not in all cases be used for both. The transition from conventional to nuclear battle may require the abandonment of some foxholes dug for the first and rapid movement to the dispersed positions of the second. Therefore, during the critical transition period, the soldier may be either digging if he is not moving, or moving if he is not digging. This, in turn presents the discomforting thought that during the transition to a nuclear battle, the most exposed troops are the officers and the NCO leaders who are directing the movement, the emplacement of weapons, or the digging-in operations including the following checks of preparedness.

This brings up the problem of mobility on a nuclear battlefield. The requirement for rapid mobility is great. If a concentration of friendly troops is discovered by enemy patrols, the only salvation perhaps would be to move to another location before the arrival of a nuclear attack. Likewise if friendly forces detect a suitable concentration of enemy troops, they might have to withdraw quickly in order to be at a safe distance when our nuclear weapons arrive on target. Subkiloton weapons would of course allow friendly troops to remain quite close to the enemy and still be safe. If subkiloton weapons are used by the enemy, however, this would tend to negate the value of hugging tactics by our troops.

Nowhere is the requirement for mobility more important than during the transition from conventional battle to nuclear battle. This could happen quite suddenly if one side or the other determined that the concentration of the enemy and the factor of surprise made dramatic gains possible by using tactical nuclear weapons. On the defense, the most favorable circumstances for using battlefield nuclear weapons is when the enemy is deployed for conventional battle and is preparing to break through friendly defenses. On the offense, the best time for such weapons is when his advance is being checked by a formidable conventional defense. In either case, rapid redeployment is required by the side initiating nuclear battle if the full value of that initiative is to be maintained.

The transition to nuclear battle may not, however, come suddenly. There may be sufficient fear of escalation on either side to impose nuclear restraints while the troops are being deployed to more favorable positions in anticipation of using nuclear weapons in a more controlled and discriminate manner. Even here, however, the need for rapid mobility is great. True, conventional engagment cannot be broken off abruptly, nor can nuclear deployment be accomplished instantaneously. But the change in deployment cannot be carried out in a leisurely manner, either, since the other side might discover the activity and choose to preempt.

Whereas the two separate tactics of dispersal and digging-in on one hand and the hugging tactics of engaging the enemy closely for protection against nuclear attack on the other would not be adopted at the same time, there is an inherent contradiction in them. The first is based on the expectation that the enemy would use nuclear weapons; the second on the expectation that he would not, out of fear of hurting his own troops. Unrealized expectation in either case might be disastrous. In the first, the enemy might break through a dispersed deployment and seize its objective by conventional means; in the second, nuclear weapons might be used immediately to the rear of the engaged troops, cutting off supplies and reinforcements while the engaged friendly troops are being mopped up. In fact, the turn of the battle may well hinge on the destruction or containment of the reserves.

Then there is the question of logistics. Even if the troops can move about rapidly, disperse, dig in, and fight, they still have to be supplied. For example, fuel expenditure could jump by a factor of three when the ground forces shift from a conventional deployment to a nuclear deployment; maintenance problems would increase. Except for ammunition, which must be separated in small piles during any war for safety sake, it is more efficient to concentrate most supplies to the rear of large depots. In a nuclear environment, all supplies must be spread out in small hidden depots. Dispersed supplies in turn would require more vehicles for distribution than supplies concentrated in major depots. One can visualize large numbers of trucks and helicopters scurrying about trying to keep the mobile troops supplied with ammunition, food and fuel. If the combat forces are large or widespread, the number of supply vehicles multiply.

Under the flexible response concept of seeking initial combat with the enemy with conventional arms, such a dispersed supply system would be extremely disadvantageous. Such dispersal of supplies would be worth while only with the anticipated and actual authority to use tactical nuclear weapons. Alternately, small combat teams armed with nuclear weapons might move around the countryside and carry their own supplies.[6] These units might be resupplied at night from supply depots outside of the battle zone. It may be possible for these combat teams to acquit themselves well in nuclear battle and for enough of these combat teams to survive to maintain a viable front of FEBA (forward edge of battle area). But to do so would imply that the transition from conventional battle to nuclear deployment had been successfully carried out.

In short, the idea of fighting a ground engagement with nuclear weapons is full of contradictions. If the troops are dispersed, they cannot defend as well against an enemy that is concentrated for attack. The enemy can infiltrate a dispersed formation, thus building up pressures to use tactical nuclear weapons to prevent positions from being overrun. If the friendly troops are relatively concentrated, they offer tempting targets for enemy attacks with nuclear weapons. In the early stages, an area defense cannot remain static even in conventional battle. Some initial penetration will be made by attacking forces as the zone of combat evolves and as the intention of the enemy deduced. The conflicting requirements of dispersal and concentration, mobility and protection in battle ensures that the ground operations will take place in great depth. The greater the depth of penetration, the greater the pressures for using tactical nuclear weapons.

It may make good technical sense to have "dual-capable" weapons that can fire either a nuclear or a conventional warhead. It is quite impossible to have a "dual-capable" deployment scheme that would work for both nuclear and conventional battle. There are too many contradictions. As Otto Heilbrunn pointed out:

> Conventional deployment would invite nuclear disaster, nuclear deployment would deprive the defense of most of its traditional advantages and if nuclear deployment is superimposed on conventional deployment, the defense would suffer from the disadvantages of conventional deployment, require a very substantial number of troops and weapons, and may find itself impeded in the use of nuclear weapons. [7]

Then there is the role of aircraft in battle. Practically all of the aircraft of both sides, with the exception of helicopters and light liaison planes, are capable of delivering nuclear weapons. Even the helicopter could drop small atomic demolition mines along avenues of enemy advance. Aircraft present the most ambiguous force in local battle. In the first place, a defender cannot detect whether an aircraft in the air is armed with a nuclear weapon or not. Aircraft could be used for physical, target acquisition, or time-sensitive reasons to make nuclear strikes on battle field targets which are inaccessible to attack by ground forces. Aircraft could also be useful in conventional ground support. Here again, however, aircraft will suffer from the inability to have a "dual capable" deployment scheme that would work for both nuclear and conventional battle. Aircraft carrying conventional munitions do not normally at the same time carry nuclear weapons. The switch from one to the other requires going back to base. This not only takes time, but the aircraft are exceedingly vulnerable targets during the rearming. Alternatively, some aircraft might be held in alert status armed with nuclear weapons. Should these aircraft be kept on base where they are vulnerable to a Soviet preemptive nuclear strike, or should they be kept airborne in rotation?

It is important to recall that this discussion is based on the assumption that certain restraints would be observed to keep the battle localized. It may be argued that the term "local battlefield" defies definition and therefore does not provide a sufficiently clear distinction upon which restraints and limitations may be recognized and observed by both sides. Certainly, if aircraft are used to deliver nuclear bombs on air bases located outside of the immediate battle zone, the term "local battlefield" would lose many of the distinguishable features it might have possessed. The local battlefield would have been bridged, escalation would have been perceived to have taken place, and the whole idea of limitation would have received a serious setback.[8] On the other hand, if aircraft did not strike targets outside of the localized battle zone it would be evidence that the limitation was in fact distinguishable. If one side perceives the operation of such a restraint in the use of aircraft as a distinct limitation, the other side might also perceive the limitation--especially if it were advertised unambiguously as a restraint. If the other side did not perceive the limitation, it would be because it did not want to perceive it. If one side struck airfields outside of the battle zone, the action would be deliberate and not an unintentional violation of a limitation that the leaders have failed to perceive.

In any event, if this discussion of how to fight a local nuclear battle is to be kept in context, the assumption must be made that the geographical limitation would be observed. Regardless of how the troops deploy, move about, or dig in, it seems fairly certain that a local battle where both sides use nuclear weapons would result in a standoff. According to calculations based on the Department of Army Pamphlet "Nuclear Weapons Employment" an infantry battalion in a normal conventional defense deployment could suffer thirty per cent casualties and be effectively neutralized by a two- to five-kiloton nuclear burst. If the battalion were already deployed for nuclear battle, three or four small kiloton weapons or one or two larger weapons--about ten KT--would be required. Much would depend on whether the troops are in foxholes or in the open and whether the units of separation were one or two companies. In any event, sufficient casualties (from thirty to seventy percent) would occur to knock out the battalion combat team as an effective fighting unit.

One cannot specify how many nuclear weapons of what yield would be required to neutralize a division. The division could be concentrated for conventional attack, deployed for conventional defesne, or dispersed in battalion or company size units. Accuracy of target "acquisition" and terrain would change the calculation. With aimed nuclear fires smaller warheads may be used. Nevertheless, it seems quite clear that six to eight weapons with twenty-KT warheads in a salvo could knock out a whole division in conventional defense. It would take about thirteen weapons with twenty-KT warheads to render a division deployed for nuclear defense ineffective for combat.

The radioactive fallout from a nuclear weapon burst on or near the surface of the earth can extend the personnel casualty area of the weapon many times that circumscribed by the initial-effects circle surrounding ground zero. For example, the casualty-producing effects of a nominal ten-KT weapon, when detonated as an air burst against troops in open, will be contained roughly within a radius of one and a half kilometers from ground zero. If this same weapon were burst on or near the ground (i. e. , close enough for the fireball to intersect the earth), roughly the same initial-effects casualty circle would be produced. In addition, even with a moderate wind, a high-intensity, casualty-producing radioactive fallout would blanket the ground in a three-kilometer swathe reaching some twenty kilometers downwind from ground zero in less than an hour. Troops in the open caught in this pattern relatively close to ground zero would very quickly accumulate a lethal dose of radiation. At five kilometers downwind, for example, a lethal exposure could be expected in some ten minutes after fallout arrival, or about twenty minutes after burst. Personnel at the downwind end of the twenty-kilometer swathe would suffer a sickness dose, requiring hospitalization, if they were to remain in the fallout field about three hours. Of course, the tactically significant radioactive falluot field from this weapon would extend far beyond the rather ar-bitrarily chosen twenty kilometers, with lower and lower intensities being en-countered until it finally tails off some fifty or sixty kilometers downwind. At the same time, a normal shear wind would distort the idealized pattern discussed above, increasing its width by a factor of perhaps three or four, smearing the high-intensity field over a much larger area, and making accurate prediction of its eventual location extremely difficult if not practically impossible.

The immediate tactical effect of only a few ground or near-ground bursts is obvious. Not so obvious are the long-term disruptive effects on military opera-tions. The intensities of the fallout field decrease quite rapidly through decay over the first few hours. Days after burst the decay process becomes progres-sively slower so that, in terms of military operations, we are ultimately con-fronted with a large area that is permanently contaminated with low intensity radioactivity. Since radiation doses are cumulative over long periods of time, such an area must be either avoided or in some way decontaminated lest troop strength be seriously attenuated through repeated exposures.

Military professionals recognize and understand this problem as being the most dangerous and unmanageable aspect of the nuclear battlefield. Fallout pre-diction schemes, special protective clothing, radiation detection devices, decon-tamination systems, counter-radiation pills, automated foxhole diggers, height-of-burst indicators, and many other developments are being actively pursued as elements of an integrated defense against radioactive fallout. Yet the classic so-lution to the problem has been and remains today to keep the lid on this Pandora's box by detonating the weapons some distance above the fallout safe height-of-burst, thus restricting the effects to the rather neatly calculated casualty and damage circle around ground zero. Regardless of the accuracy of the height-of-burst calculation, however, there rides with every nuclear weapon employed a very low but quite finite probability of a surface burst. Sooner or later--and perhaps quite suddenly, the laws of probability being so capricious when applied to rela-tively short-term situations--the tactical nuclear battlefield is bound to become enmeshed in the toils of widespread radioactive fallout.

The possible dramatic results--unprecedented casualty rates, greatly ex-panded replacement requirement, vast destruction of equipment and supply--only emphasize the conflicting and competing tactical requirements for dispersal, shelter, concealment, and mobility. At the very least, the possible nuclear means are available on both sides to invalidate the ground tactics employed--even with the restraints assumed earlier. It may be perfectly feasible for either side to use nuclear weapons of sufficient yield to destroy enemy ground units in any sort of deployment either by aimed or blanket fire without causing large numbers of civilian casualties. This statement, however, is subject to several qualifications. Large yield weapons may not be used if their use would endanger friendly troops engaged in battle. Also, whereas it may be true, as Clark Abt points out, that ". . . less than one percent of Europe consists of built-up dwellings, homes, or factories,"[9] the countryside is also characterized by many small villages not more than two or three kilometers apart. It would be extremely difficult to avoid some civilian casualties. Unless deliberately deployed in or around cities and towns, where ground forces would be still vulnerable to nuclear fires and even more restricted in dispersal and mobility, it would appear feasible to select the proper numbers and yield of nuclear weapons to destroy "lucrative" targets without violating the geographical restraints or causing undue civilian destruction.

Most military analysts would agree that a localized battle fought with both sides employing nuclear weapons to achieve a localized victory would rapidly degenerate into a destructive stalemate. This poses the question whether a localized nuclear battle could be fought in any meaningful way with the large variety of nuclear weapons in the arsenals of both sides--especially since any relaxation of restraints by one side or the other would cause even more death and destruction. A possible answer is to tighten the restraints even further and allow only the use of sub-kiloton weapons--say of the explosive capacity of only five or ten times that of conventional weapons. But then we remember the intense destruction that took place at the St. Lo break-through in World War II with only conventional weapons. Such use of sub-kiloton weapons by both sides would hardly be less destructive. Provided such low-yield weapons are available in the arsenals, there may be strong incentives to limit the yield of nuclear weapons at least initially. The restraint that keeps the United States from using nuclear weapons in the first place would also tend to make it cross this nuclear threshold with care-- if for no other reason than to permit a controlled transition until redeployment is accomplished. The enemy might exercise the same restraints or employ larger nuclear weapons in retaliation. It would entirely depend on whether the enemy perceived an advantage in expanding the war or not. It is barely possible that the enemy would do neither if he felt that the gains made in the prior conventional action could be held while negotiations are carried out to terminate the conflict. But if large numbers of these sub-kiloton weapons were employed by the West to achieve a decisive local victory, the Soviet Union could hardly be expected to do other than respond with nuclear weapons also.

The battle might be fought on both sides with conventional weapons, with a great deal of restraint--a sort of limited sparring match--while the belligerents were seeking to gain some advantage by negotiations. Even here, however, there is always the possibility that the action would expand progressively as each side introduces more and more divisions into the fray until the battle reaches the scope of some of the actions in World War II. As one side or the other sees decisive defeat as the only alternative, the pressures to employ nuclear weapons on a wide scale would be tremendous. Likewise, if one side (presumably the enemy) employs nuclear weapons, the defense--deployed according to the flexible response doctrine for conventional action--would suffer such unprecedented casualties that unless defeat is accepted the impulse to retaliate with nuclear weapons could hardly be avoided. Such discussions of contradictions between conventional and nuclear combat do not really offer possible solutions to the dilemma, however, because each local conflict situation will vary according to the circumstances surrounding the initial crisis, the value of the objectives, and the conscious decisions of the two sides to join in battle to achieve a local victory.

This brings us to the point of questioning the use of tactical nuclear weapons to achieve a local victory. Perhaps there is something inherently contradictory between the means and aims of a localized nuclear battle. It would appear that if either side attempts to achieve a victory/defeat outcome with nuclear weapons the outcome would very likely be a tremendously destructive stalemate, or worse. This might very well be the reason why so many attempts to solve the local nuclear battle riddle ends up in failure. Perhaps the key to the riddle is in changing the purpose or aim of seeking local victory with nuclear weapons to something else. So far in this discussion we have tended to ignore the serious threat of escalation. It would seem that the fear of escalation to general war would provide the strongest incentive to keep the conflict limited--even from using nuclear weapons at all. Yet a credible willingness to use nuclear weapons, a known commitment, is an essential part of any realistic bargaining attempt to impose one's will--but necessarily for limited aims. The other side must be able to recognize the limits and to exercise an option that is less unfavorable than escalating the conflict to higher levels of violence. Whether this option can be provided by annihilating his ground forces with a wide range of tactical nuclear weapons in an attempt to achieve victory is at least debatable. A more discriminate and less-damaging use of tactical nuclear weapons, coupled with an unambiguous warning or threat to escalate to still higher levels of violence, would appear to offer more chance of success in terminating the conflict.

If a conflict expands to the point that battlefield nuclear weapons are brought into use it would be vital for both sides to seek means of limiting the nuclear conflict to the battlefield. Limited nuclear exchanges, restricted only to the battlefield, would likely result in a standoff with neither side obtaining a clearcut victory. Both sides would have the capability of neutralizing the other, i.e., causing fifty percent or greater casualties. This standoff would probably be only temporary in nature, however, if either side attempts to gain an advantage from the situation. On the other hand, fear of further escalation might result in an impasse with both sides attempting to negotiate a settlement along the lines of the status quo ante. This would seem to be the most advantageous termination of the conflict from the point of view of both sides. If the Soviets suffer a greater defeat, they might be tempted to exploit the significant advantage they hold in IRBMs and MRBMs. The only thing that might restrain them is a belief that the U.S. would raise the level to general war with Polaris and Minuteman.

At the battlefield level of nuclear war, NATO enjoys a qualitative and quantitative superiority in weapons. The value and significance of this, however, might be lost in widespread nuclear exchange since the Soviet weapons could make up for small yield and accuracy with higher yields. The true value would only be realized through the initial use of these most sophisticated weapons with such discrimination and control that aggression is stopped and nuclear retaliation by the Soviets is withheld.

The ultimate feasibility of using battlefield nuclear weapons in a local combat zone depends on preventing this level of conflict from escalating to a deep penetration nuclear exchange. In this sense, the objective of a nuclear constraint doctrine is not to determine the most efficient means to destroy enemy forces in a nuclear engagement on the battlefield, but rather how to communicate and bargain with nuclear weapons, and how to bring the hostilities to an end in this situation on terms least disadvantageous to NATO. This reinforces the need for a workable doctrine for using these battlefield nuclear weapons with discrimination and with control. However, there is no guarantee that the Soviets would not respond in kind with tactical nuclear weapons. If NATO battlefield nuclear weapons are used in a discriminate manner against an enemy, who by his very presence on NATO soil is the prima facie aggressor, there might be strong incentives for the Soviets to accept a standoff at this level and bring the hostilities to a close rather than risk the spread of nuclear destruction to Communist territory. Certainly, there is no assurance the Soviets would not use nuclear weapons in return, but there is a possibility they would exercise such restraint--a possibility that would appear to be many times greater if restraint in using nuclear weapons were used rather than if blanket release of nuclear weapons were given.

A DOCTRINE OF NUCLEAR CONSTRAINTS

In developing a doctrine for using tactical nuclear weapons in a localized battle, it is important to recognize that officers and men on the battlefield cannot be expected to assess the risks of escalation to general war. Combat is a straightforward undertaking for fairly clear objectives. A tactical nuclear doctrine needs to be as straightforward and clear. It must be based on a realistic appraisal of the possible consequences of a localized nuclear battle.

It is no doubt true, as Professor Schelling says, that the main consequence of limited war is to raise the risk of general war--particularly in an area such as Central Europe. Without question, the strategic nuclear forces in the background would be the main preoccupation of the national leaders. It might well be true that in a European conflict, the ". . . hour-by-hour tactical course of the war may not be even worth the attention of the top strategic leadership. . ."-- particularly in the initial stages of the conflict before tactical nuclear weapons are introduced.[1] But certainly, once tactical nuclear weapons are decided upon, the national leaders will be concerned because of a very real awareness of the danger of escalation. The specific use of nuclear weapons would in all likelihood be controlled from Washington, not to win a local war but as a bargaining tool to ". . . signal a heightened risk of general war, . . ." for the purpose of bringing the conflict to some sort of ending--either a truce, a slow-down, or an outright withdrawal by the enemy.[2]

If this be true, then there is all the more reason that some doctrine be established for the military forces so that they can be prepared to carry out the orders of the national and NATO command authorities in the discriminate manner desired. Equally important is a command, control, and communications arrangement that would enable selective-release and directed-use of tactical nuclear weapons to be effected in a timely fashion. Such a doctrine does not now exist, although there are elaborate procedures for requesting authority by and for authorizing release of nuclear weapons to the combat forces.

A doctrine for how and under what circumstances battlefield nuclear weapons might be used must be specific. To call for the use of nuclear weapons ". . .when NATO troops are in danger of being overrun, . . ." is not a doctrine. It is too vague. Views could diverge widely as to when this point is reached. Doctrine is codified common sense, or better, codified sense held in common. It is the philosophy to which strategy gives effect of substance; it is the common understanding governing the exercise of tactics. In short, doctrine tells a commander or soldier how to carry out orders. A doctrine of nuclear constraints must be compatible with the concept of operations. In particular, it must be workable during the most critical transition from conventional battle to nuclear battle. This transition cannot be carried out instantaneously; regrouping and redeployment are necessary.

Dr. Richard T. Loomis of Stanford Research Institute has developed a model illustrating a doctrine of nuclear constraints based on operations of the Seventh U.S. Army and the concept of operations of the U.S. ground forces. As taught in the Army's Command and General Staff School at Fort Leavenworth, there are four phases for joining battle:

1. Reconnaissance (or delaying) phase--the enemy is located and contact made to disrupt and divert initial assault.

2. Close Combat phase--the enemy is engaged and maximum casualties inflicted.

3. Destruction phase--the enemy's ability to fight is destroyed through a combination of fire and maneuver. In the forward strategy, this is the counterattack phase in which the U.S. forces take to the offense and destroy the continuity of the enemy attack.

4. Exploitation phase--the advantages gained during the preceding phases are fully exploited, the full destruction of the attack completed, and lost territory recovered.

During the reconnaissance phase the three forward, armored cavalry regiments (ACRs), which have been reinforced with artillery and engineers, keep the

front under constant surveillance. The U. S. forces in initial contact would be
fairly well dispersed--with a platoon or smaller unit guarding various road junc-
tures. Therefore, the deployment would be applicable to both conventional and
nuclear war. These reconnaissance units would fight a delaying action in order
to give the two armored divisions time to reach their forward position and make
contact with the enemy. Even here the armored divisions would be fairly well
dispersed and, furthermore, tanks give excellent protection against nuclear fires.
When the armored division reaches the front, the three ACRs fall back through
the forward edge of the battle area (FEBA) and become part of the mobile striking force assigned to the corps.

The two armored divisions then engage the enemy closely, while the three
mechanized divisions move into the combat position. At the proper moment the
two forces exchange positions, with the armored division passing through the
mechanized divisions to the rear where they join up with the ACRs as part of the
mobile reserve. At this juncture the major logistic elements have closed behind
the mechanized divisions and the battle has entered the close combat phase, with
the U. S. forces seeking to inflict maximum casualties on the enemy.

The destruction and exploitation phases are an extension of the close combat
phase in which the corps commanders, through the use of nondivisional artillery
battalions and the Pershing and Sergeant missiles, provide fire throughout the
entire sector. Conceptually, this firepower flexibility enables the corps and field
army commanders to influence the outcome of the engagement by adding weapons
of greater range and lethality to the field of battle in support of the close combat
units.

In summary, the doctrine of engagement for the ground forces envisions a
defensive posture structured around mobile, quick-reacting armored units with
heavy firepower. During the initial stages, these forces give some ground in order to gain time to marshall resources and define the size and direction of the
assault. Theoretically, by the time the mechanized divisions have engaged the
enemy, the battle zone will have stabilized, and the initiative will have passed
from the aggressor (Soviet-Warsaw Pact) to the defender (U. S. -NATO).

So much for the concept of operation in theory. It does not show, however,
the manner in which the transition would be made from conventional to nuclear
weapons. Loomis, using the Seventh U. S. Army as a model, suggests a three-
phase operation to bring about this transition.

Phase One remains essentially the reconnaissance phase. The three armored cavalry regiments fight a delaying action with conventional weapons and in the process cover the two armored divisions as they move up into position. In Phase Two, the three armored cavalry regiments retire to the rear and become part of the mobile reserve. They are reconstituted and equipped with nuclear weapons. In the meantime, the two armored divisions engage the enemy--still fighting with conventional weapons.

It is during Phase Three that the transition to nuclear battle can be made if so directed and authorized by the President, or by other national and NATO leaders. For now the battle has ceased to be a minor conflict. If two armored divisions cannot contain the enemy forces while all the other machinery of crisis management is at work trying to terminate the conflict, then the West must reckon on a major enemy invasion or a fight over something more than the restoration of the status quo ante bellum. As the two armored divisions retire, the three mechanized divisions move forward to the FEBA deployed and ready for nuclear battle. The three phases of this nuclear constraint doctrine are shown schematically in Fig. 5.

Of course, it should be emphasized that this is just a model to illustrate a doctrine of nuclear constraint. Nevertheless, the concept offers intriguing features.

At lower levels of violence this concept would tend to bring our nuclear forces into a deployment more in line with the strategic concept of testing enemy intentions with conventional weapons before resorting to nuclear weapons. The concept offers an alternative to the immediate use of nuclear firepower by removing our atomic weapons thirty to thirty-five kilometers behind the initial battle line. For the first twenty-four to thirty-six hours the ground forces would fight conventionally and, hopefully, would force a pause for negotiations. Establishing and advertising such a nuclear constraint doctrine could dampen the compulsion for either side to escalate quickly. Moreover, if a nuclear response became necessary, the space-time interval afforded should be ample to arrive at a decision and to send a nuclear release meesage to the combat forces.

From a military point of view, the increased time could substantially strengthen the field commander's tactical position by giving him time to determine the level of attack, assign weapons, and deploy his forces for nuclear engagement. This

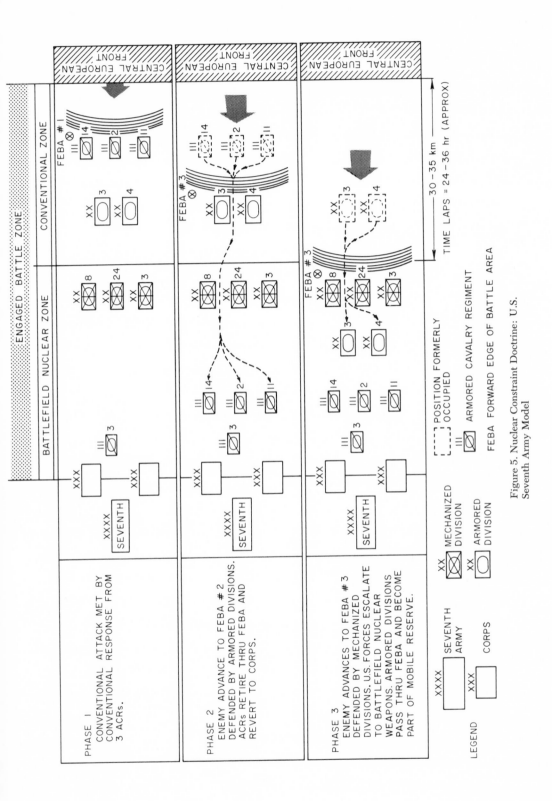

Figure 5. Nuclear Constraint Doctrine: U.S.
Seventh Army Model

time is needed. For, unlike strategic nuclear forces that have preassigned weapons for fixed targets, the tactical forces cannot assign weapons and targets until after the battle begins. The additional time that could be provided under this concept could give the field commander vital intelligence concerning (1) the type and location of targets, (2) target density, and (3) the type of weapon and rate of fire most appropriate to the occasion.

Of course, it could be argued that the first two phases of conventional defense might offer lucrative targets for the enemy's atomic attack. But then the conflict would immediately be transformed from one arising out of a crisis to a war for important objectives. No matter what doctrine of constraints is adopted, the possibility that the enemy would initiate the use of nuclear weapons cannot be prevented. On the other hand, the same disadvantage would hold true for the enemy. If the enemy dispersed as a prelude to the use of atomic weapons (a tactical maneuver that would undoubtedly be necessary), the NATO forces might possibly find out in time to take the necessary countermeasures by deploying themselves and initiating the use of tactical nuclear weapons.

Another weakness of this defense in depth is the possible loss of a large land area (up to thirty kilometers deep and of indeterminate length) to the Soviet forces. If this loss is forced upon NATO, however, then the intentions of the enemy would have become clear and NATO would probably call for the use of at least battlefield nuclear weapons. On the other hand, a well-advertised doctrine of nuclear constraints would eliminate the ambiguity in graduated deterrence. The closer the enemy approaches engagement with the three mechanized divisions in this model, the more he would have to reckon with the realization that NATO might use nuclear weapons. Some experts would then assert that such a doctrine would be an open invitation to the enemy, either to preempt with nuclear weapons or to seize territory to a distance somewhat less than thirty kilometers. In the first instance, should the enemy initiate the use of nuclear weapons in a preemptive manner, our ground forces in initial contact would be reasonably dispersed and protected by armor, and hopefully the mechanized divisions advancing to the front would be permitted to retaliate in turn. In the second instance, the important point to emphasize is that the line is not drawn at thirty kilometers but at the point of engagment with the three mechanized divisions that would be deploying to the front and digging in during the delaying action of the three ACRs and the two armored divisions. If the enemy should want to avoid nuclear battle with NATO, it would have every incentive to terminate the conflict before this point is reached.

The model treats only with the ground forces. What about the air forces? As the crisis develops, the air forces might be dispersed and placed on both atomic and conventional alert. If the issue is a local one--as it is most likely to be--it might be well to withhold the air forces (except for light reconnaissance planes) from the conflict in the initial stages while diplomatic channels are being used to resolve the crisis and snuff out the fight. Because of the ambiguity in the air force posture pointed out earlier, it becomes exceedingly difficult to devise a doctrine of nuclear constraint for the NATO air forces. The NATO fighter-bombers are generally (but mistakenly) regarded as a nuclear counterpart to the Soviet MRBMs and IRBMs--to be used in deep penetration nuclear strikes. If air forces are to have an unambiguous role in supporting the ground forces during conventional conflict, stringent constraints are needed to prevent aircraft from operating outside of the immediate battle area. Furthermore, these constraints must be well advertised so that the enemy would understand NATO's effort to limit the conflict while measures are being taken to terminate the battle. In the meantime, a substantial proportion of the fighter-bombers need to be placed on nuclear alert in the event the conventional conflict gets out of hand.

It seems almost heresy to suggest that NATO fighter-bombers should not be used to strike enemy airfields--except in retaliation. As pointed out earlier, the consensus among military analysts is that air superiority over the local battlefield in Central Europe is impossible without knocking out Soviet air bases in East Germany. Whereas it may be possible to destroy most of the enemy aircraft parked on air bases with modern conventional weapons in a massive saturation attack, the attrition to NATO aircraft would undoubtedly be high. Pressures by the military to use nuclear weapons to exact even greater destruction for the attrition cost would be strong. In any event, with or without nuclear weapons, the limitations that are necessary to keep a battle local could have been breached and escalation would most likely follow. There can be little question that if the conflict is extended beyond the immediate battle zone NATO military resources and bases would suffer more than those of the Warsaw Pact. With France out of reckoning, the ports, supply lines, and casernes of troops are concentrated close to the Iron Curtain in a wide area of very little depth. NATO would be at a serious disadvantage if the conflict enters into the phase of deep penetration strikes on both sides--either nuclear or conventional. If nuclear strikes are undertaken, the widespread devastation wrought would be such that it would be practically indistinguishable from general nuclear war.

If it becomes necessary for NATO to use battlefield nuclear weapons, every effort should be made to insure that the Soviets do not retaliate. One possible way of doing this is to establish by words and actions the ground rule for employment of battlefield nuclear weapons by NATO. First, they could be restricted initially to very discriminate and controlled use. The Soviets might recognize the nuclear constraints in these actions as well as NATO's resolve to defend its territory at whatever cost. Second, NATO could make it quite clear that Soviet use of nuclear weapons in NATO territory would result in extending the nuclear conflict to the Communist side. What should be left ambiguous to the Soviets, or even slanted to appear more menacing, would be the nature and size of the escalation step NATO would undertake. (As pointed out, Europe-wide nuclear warfare would likely be an extremely unstable level of violence that would be to the disadvantage of NATO to pursue.) One thing that should be made abundantly clear to the Soviets, however, is that Europe-wide nuclear attacks would draw retaliation to the Soviet homeland.

All things considered, there is no assurance that the first use of nuclear weapons will or will not escalate to general war. Even with discriminate use of small-yield battlefield nuclear weapons, however, a major threshold will have been crossed, and there is no guarantee that the Soviets would not respond in kind with larger-yield rockets. In fact, it is difficult to visualize, under present circumstances (since there is no workable and advertised doctrine of NATO nuclear constraints), that the Russians would not. In such an event, it would be reasonable to expect that the escalation that would rapidly follow would bring the war up to the deep penetration nuclear strikes where the USSR obviously has an advantage over NATO. At this level, however, the consequences in devastation of deep interdiction strikes would be practically indistinguishable from strategic nuclear strikes--at least as far as the Europeans are concerned. Nevertheless, a well-advertised doctrine of nuclear constraints, coupled with firm control over nuclear weapons, might bring about a more stable situation and make it possible to avoid the devastation of a general war if NATO found it necessary to use nuclear weapons.

The implied willingness to cross the nuclear threshold initially at the lowest nuclear level might well enhance the credibility and strengthen the effectiveness of deterrence. The U.S. advantage over the Soviets at the battlefield nuclear level could in this manner be exploited as an important element of graduated deterrence. The threat of escalation in any nuclear form exerts a powerful deterrent during conflict--a deterrent that affects all actions subsequent to the initial decision to resort to arms. A NATO threat to employ even a few small nuclear weapons in a discriminate manner at the scene of conflict has no other purpose than to deter Soviet actions with conventional arms. For, if the Soviets should have already employed nuclear weapons in the conflict, the NATO threat to use them as well would no longer deter. In other words, the threat of escalation deters actions below the level to which the threat applies. A NATO threat at the battlefield nuclear level deters a Soviet action at the conventional level. In like manner, the Soviets no doubt rely on their advantage in rockets and missiles at the deep penetration level to deter NATO at both the conventional and battlefield nuclear levels. But they must also realize that the indistinguishability of nuclear warfare once the battlefield limits have been bridged would almost certainly bring nuclear destruction on Russian homeland. Objectively, the Soviets must assess the overall hazards of such a widened nuclear response as less than a discriminate nuclear response at the battlefield level where there is a possibility--however tenuous--of making the distinction work.

On the other hand, let us suppose that the Soviets acquired large numbers of low-yield battlefield nuclear weapons and advertised a doctrine of nuclear constraint similar to the one proposed here which aims at making the battlefield level of nuclear warfare a distinguishable threshold. What would be the U.S. and NATO's reaction? The West could no longer emphasize a superior battlefield nuclear capability to offset an inferior conventional capability in the deterrence/defense equation. The Soviet superiority in conventional firepower and in interdiction nuclear firepower thus could be extended to superiority, or at least parity, in battlefield nuclear firepower as well. Under such circumstances the West might be expected to attempt to regain superiority or, to use Herman Kahn's terms, "escalation dominance," at one or more of these levels of conflict--in which case the outcome would be an arms race; or the West might be forced to change its strategic concept of graduated deterrence and bank all on the threat of massive retaliation with superior strategic forces as a deterrent--in which case deterrence might lose much of its credibility and effectiveness for possible Soviet aggression at lower levels of conflict.

This frankly speculative discussion only serves to indicate that the American concept of _graduated_ deterrence works best where it is backed up by recognized superiority at each distinguishable level of conflict. But this happy state is not attainable. The NATO nations have evidenced a pronounced aversion to provide the resources to achieve such superiority. Lacking superiority at a conventional level, the second best thing would be to establish superiority at the lowest nuclear level, provided this level can be made distinguishable. The matter of making the various levels of conflict distinguishable is an important feature. An unbroken series of indistinguishable steps from battlefield nuclear to strategic warfare makes most difficult the establishment of criteria to check escalation.

Much more is required than doctrine, however. The NATO defense posture would have to be altered so as to match the statements of our advertised doctrine of nuclear constraints.[3] This posture should look defensively strong to discourage Soviet aggression, but at the same time it should be reassuring and less provocative to the Soviets. A posture that appears provocative enhances uncertainty in the minds of the opponent and may lead to miscalculation. Provocation is an imponderable and incommensurable factor. Nevertheless, it is real and closely related to miscalculation. The Soviets provoked the U. S. in Cuba, which led to U. S. uncertainty as to Soviet intentions. U. S. actions in response proved that the Soviets had miscalculated our resolve. The whole immediate chain of events stemmed from the initial provocative action of the Communists.

The peacetime deployment of forces and means for controlling nuclear weapons should hopefully carry a message to the Soviets of our peaceful intent and firm resolve to use battlefield weapons with constraint if necessary to defend NATO territory. These actions would lend credibility to deterrence at low and intermediate levels, in an age of mutual strategic standoff. These actions may succeed in making it clear to the Soviets that a first use of battlefield nuclear weapons by NATO under the rules of engagement discussed above is not necessarily the signal for World War III. Hopefully, such a war could be terminated without extending the nuclear destruction further. It would at least place the burden of further escalation on the Soviets.

A NATO DEFENSE POSTURE

NATO is purely a nonaggressive alliance according to both its founding charter and its subsequent attitudes and policy. It has never contemplated any attack
on Eastern Europe or any other area outside its borders, except in retaliation.
Its policy statements have constantly emphasized its defensive nature. While policy statements are important, actions and their interpretations by others can be
even more important. Troops and weapon deployments and the commitment of
resources to the support of treaties are actions that potential antagonists will
see and interpret in the light of their own judgments. Lack of a coherent strategy
or consistent supporting actions could cause ambiguity despite any pronouncements
that might be made. This could be serious in politically unstable environments,
particularly where miscalculations of resolve and intent could lead to war.

A major military element in the NATO effort to deter or frustrate Soviet
attacks has been to date an air arm whose most obvious capability is to carry
nuclear destruction far into satellite territory. NATO ground forces and, in particular, the great Seventh U.S. Army, possess highly mobile, heavy armored
divisions armed with a great variety of nuclear weapons more appropriate for
attack than defense. On the face of it, Soviet analysis of NATO capabilities would
disclose offensive capabilities equal to or even greater than the ability to defend.
Despite the defensive philosophy and past actions of NATO, the Soviets appear to
be concerned about West German offensive capabilities, small as they are by comparison, on grounds of the bitter experience of World War II. If it were feasible
at comparable cost to constitute a force posture that had stronger defense capabilities at somewhat of a sacrifice in offensive capabilities, NATO would more
fully reflect its nonaggressive charter, philosophy and intent.

139

Such a posture then might reinforce the doctrine of nuclear constraints proposed. If it were feasible and if it could be made clear by our actions that NATO forces were not deployed or in some cases equipped for aggressive military operations, it would reduce the risks of war by miscalculation, reduce the chance of escalation, and reduce the amount of destruction to be anticipated from the initial use of nuclear weapons. Even more importantly, the adoption of such a clearly-defensive posture might help to create an atmosphere of increased mutual confidence in the stability of the military confrontation. These results might follow even if the posture were adopted unilaterally; they would probably be strengthened if both power blocs in Europe were to adopt postures characterized by relatively weak offenses and highly capable receptive defenses.

Dr. Russell Rhyne, of Stanford Research Institute, had developed a model of a NATO force posture that places emphasis on the aspects of "receptive defense." The force posture visualized would be able to repel enemy forces encroaching on NATO territory, to destroy them, and by limited counterattack to regain the territory initially penetrated by the invaders. It would emphasize the strengthening of defense and the deployment of weapons and forces clearly inappropriate for aggression, such as armored thrusts or deep interdiction air strikes.

There is little doubt that there would be important categories of attack, such as a rocket attack with nuclear weapons, where an economical defense that could await the attack and defeat it after launch is infeasible. In such cases, the threat must be deterred or met either by a blunting preemptive attack or by retaliatory destruction with surviving forces. However, there are other possible attacks at low and intermediate levels of violence where advances in technology appear to give advantages to the defense. The concept proposed by Rhyne for the defense of the Central Sector of Western Europe counts on repelling with a reorganized and re-equipped NATO conventional force the type of attack to be expected from the Soviet forces normally disposed in East Germany, but without necessarily being forced to use nuclear weapons. These are attacks that might arise out of a crisis or a miscalculated attempt by the Soviets to make a "quick grab." In the case of a major invasion by mobilized Soviet forces, nuclear weapons would be depended upon as a counter right from the start.

In Rhyne's model there would still remain a requirement for offensive capabilities to relieve the garrison of Berlin in case the Soviets attempt to take the city, or to rescue a convoy entrapped along the autobahn in East Germany. Thus, whereas the model stresses defense, it does not sacrifice offensive capabilities entirely. Offensive power would be reduced or constrained, however, to an extent that an effective offensive thrust into communist territory by NATO would be impossible without major reinforcement or redistribution of forces. The purpose of this would be to enable the Soviets to perceive that the offensive forces we have, conventional or nuclear, are not disposed for aggression and that the nuclear forces which do have the capability of striking deep into communist territories are sufficiently invulnerable to withstand a Soviet preemptive strike. As Bernard Brodie points out, ". . . the best way to reduce the danger of surprise attack is to reduce . . . the incentives to such an attack."[2] This end is served by promoting measures that enhance defense and deterrence rather than offense wherever the distinction can be made. To use a phrase of Thomas Schelling, it would greatly reduce ". . . the worry about his striking us to keep us from striking him to keep him from striking us . . ."[3]

Such a defense posture for NATO must at least be prepared to deal with a range of contingencies that could occur at a number of places along the Iron Curtain. The doctrine of nuclear constraints discussed previously would be invalid if the enemy were allowed to concentrate in secret and make a sizable penetration into West Germany before NATO forces could be deployed. Whereas a surprise attack may not be one of the more likely contingencies, it must nevertheless be considered in planning a force posture. The surprise, however, may take the form of a sudden uprising and a spilling over the border. The armored cavalry regiments and the German border guards are perhaps prepared to cope with such a crisis in the initial stages. However, any determined armed penetration at any point along the length of the Iron Curtain requires more.

Rhyne suggests a belt of conventional defenses about twenty-five kilometers deep, with variations in width and defense density as required by the proximity of high-value points that might be the limited objectives of an enemy incursion. The belt would contain field fortifications and barriers intermediate in quality between those that might be hastily constructed in the face of attack and the lavish installations of the Siegfried or Maginot Lines. The strength of this zone defense would be calculated to withstand the maximum conventional surprise assault that might plausibly be launched by Communist forces normally stationed in East

Germany and Czechoslovakia. This zone might contain some armor, for local counterattacks, but defense would depend primarily upon large numbers of widely-distributed weapons designed for the destruction of vehicles and personnel.

Field fortifications and associated barriers not only provide a degree of immediate protection against enemy fire, but also permit the forward defenders under some conditions of combat to call down supporting fire upon their own positions when they are overrun by attackers. Field fortifications also would permit harassing sallies to disorganize the attack. A force thus disposed could exert a given quality of defense over a wider front than would be possible with the same number of troops operating in unprotected positions. Political considerations would seem to eliminate only heavy permanent fortifications that would be construed as acceptance of a permanent separation of the two Germanies.

To provide a conventional defense such as described would, however, represent a major change in the NATO force posture, calling for changes in arms investment and making available about 500,000 troops along the Iron Curtain in times of crisis. The Allies have clearly indicated that they are not willing to provide additional regular army troops or to finance other major elements of infrastructure. In fact the trend is to cut back. Furthermore, even if provided, additional ground forces, organized in the kinds of armored and mechanized divisions now in West Germany, could only increase the provocative effect on the Soviet Union.

Nevertheless, we are dealing with the essence of the problem: how to provide the conventional defense that is necessary over the long pull for the success of the NATO forward strategy and for the doctrine of nuclear constraints proposed. If the problem were regarded not as providing more troops and equipment than already provided, the problem might not appear to be so intractable.

A primary requirement for a forward defense is speed of reaction. As Liddell Hart points out, a swift attack with a sustained speed of follow-through could actually split the defense ". . . so deeply and disintegratingly as to paralyze resistance, annulling the comparative advantage of numerical strength."[4] The speed of defense reaction however depends more on the quality of the defense than the numbers of troops. The Nazis overcame superior numbers of French forces in World War II by striking through the Ardennes and crossing the Meuse in one sustained drive. The French, with twenty-three divisions, failed to react in a timely fashion against the Blitzkrieg tactics of the seventeen German divisions and were defeated.[5]

The requirement for fast reaction is accentuated by the great length of front compared with the small depth that can be used for maneuvering. Defensive forces must either be in the right place to start with or be moved there at the time they are needed. Because of the wide choices usually open to an attacker and the initiative of the offense, the first alternative for defense would call for large numbers of infantry and antitank weapons more or less uniformly distributed over the entire front to be defended. The second alternative would require that a mobile force (say, NATO armor pitted against Soviet armor) maneuver to oppose the enemy at the point of attack. There are serious disadvantages to both. The first alternative requires that the unit price of infantry and antitank weapons be low enough and have a sufficiently high index of effectiveness to make the procurement and deployment of vast quantities over the entire front economically and militarily feasible. The second alternative requires something close to prescience, since there is always a time lag in detecting an enemy encroachment and gauging his intentions. If the defender does not guess right, his forces will not even be in position. If he does not back his guess with major commitment, the defenses that do come in contact with the enemy are likely to be overcome by superior numbers.

In either case quality and firepower are more important than numbers. Again, we can refer to the expert opinion of Liddell Hart. He estimates that a ratio of two to three should be safe insurance against a sudden attack. On this basis, seventeen fully-mobile, highly-trained and ready NATO divisions would be adequate to defend against a surprise attack by the twenty-six Soviet and East German divisions disposed in East Germany. But he emphasizes: "It is folly to imagine that it would be possible with forces of short-term service, even if their numbers were doubled or trebled."[6]

These requirements for quality, however, have not been met. Except for the Seventh U.S. Army, the bulk of the NATO forces in West Germany are provided by the Federal Republic whose twelve divisions, although improved somewhat over the last several years, still are deficient in several aspects. First, the Allies succeeded in demanding and fully achieving the complete breakup of the German Wehrmacht and general staff. The Bundeswehr had to be rebuilt practically from scratch. The experienced staff officers that formed the original nucleus in 1955 are being pensioned today and the new officers are not old and experienced enough to fill the gap created. There is a current lack of about 30 percent in officers and noncommissioned officers. Second, by placing the Bundeswehr directly under the Bundestag, many decisions that properly would be regarded the responsibility and duties of senior military officers in any armed service are made by "politicians" (as opposed to civil servants). This in turn affects discipline and esprit de corps. A third factor is psychological. Even today the military profession is disdained by much of the populace of Germany who regard officers and soldiers with distrust. There was a time in the mid-1950s when a German soldier in uniform walking down the street was reviled and spat upon. The young in particular see in the military a revival of nationalism that is contrary to their hopes for a wider Europe. As time goes on and the European dream begins to fade under the influence of de Gaulle's version of reality, there are incipient signs that the German people are beginning to develop a national consciousness that would make them more inclined to accept the military duties of a German citizen.

There is one possible solution to the forward defense dilemma. A German militia might well be used to man the forward barrier in much the same manner that the U. S. National Guard units are used in the United States continental air defense to man Nike missile sites. The cost of a fairly sizable militia force might be met by retiring or by not equipping two or three West German armored divisions.[7] This in turn would reduce the offensive capacity of the German ground forces-- presumably making them less provocative to the Soviets (and, it might be added, to some of the NATO allies).

The use of German militia to man the strong points along the border has some important advantages. In the first place, the overall quality of the troops could be improved greatly.[8] Citizen soldiers, living in the border areas, trained over a long period of time in the performance of one defense function, familiar with home terrain often reconnoitered, and led by officers who know the capabilities of the men in their units are troops who can be immediately available in the initial stages of conflict. A "cadre-conscript" army on the other hand must fill out its ranks at the very moment that a crisis evolves into open conflict. Frantic induction of re- serves, last minute training, and demands for replacements for combat casualties make it almost impossible for such a mobilization force to provide backup and sup- port for professional standing army divisions as the latter are brought up in contact with the enemy.

Second, from a technological standpoint, there are clear indications that conventional defensive weapons are gaining in the see-saw competition with offensive weapons. Light-weight antitank guided missiles such as the Vigilant and the French SS11 have a marked advantage over the weapons used against armor in the past. Other new machine guns and antitank weapons being developed promise even more lethality and relative invulnerability. These weapons are just the kinds of light-weight weapons a militia could employ to great advantage. They can be sited laterally some distance from the militiaman firing the weapon, who, because of his familiarity with the terrain, can select and prepare for himself a location of concealment relatively invulnerable to enemy counterfire.

A defense against armor founded on artillery and other armor must depend on mobility and extremely fast and accurate intelligence. Defense dependent on mobility and accurate intelligence requires a superior command-control-communications, a requirement all the more exacting because the defense does not enjoy the luxury of the preplanned operation accorded to the offense.

In contrast, diffused defenses with vast numbers of light-weight infantry weapons and homing antitank missiles are less sensitive to disruption, especially if the force is given a large measure of local autonomy. Less movement is called for, quicker local counteroperations can be mounted. A platoon task force would be able to handle many of its problems without reliance on system-wide decisions from above. A militia force living in the border areas could man the carefully planned barriers in an emergency. Utilizing prepared fields of fire, they should at least be able to slow down the advance of an attempted incursion through the border zone until the regular army units are brought into position.

In like manner, surface-to-air missiles have been improved to the extent that aircraft over an area with pervasive air defense would suffer casualties experienced in World War II, Korea, and Vietnam. A militia armed with light anti-air weapons such as Redeye or manning prepared and concealed antiair batteries near the border could cause great attrition to enemy ground support aircraft.

A third advantage of using German militia is more political. As time goes on, it appears inevitable that the United States and Great Britain will reduce their troops in West Germany--either for reasons of balance of payment difficulties or pressing commitments elsewhere.[9] A compensating buildup of regular German army units to replace the foreign forces withdrawn would cause anxiety not only

in Russia but also among Germany's European allies. Besides, there is a great
reluctance in Germany itself to see a revival of a strong military organization in
the Bundeswehr. A defensively-oriented militia, similar to that in Switzerland,
would still much of the fears. Further, it would be a shrewd move in the best
democratic traditions for Germany to create such a citizens' army organization
to defend its homeland. The fear of a revival of German militarism is not a fear
of a citizens' army whose ranks permeate the whole structure of a democratic
society, but rather a fear of the kind of separate military establishment such as
the old Prussian army, which regarded itself as a separate entity, free to influence if not determine the policies of the nation. That the German government is
alert to the danger of such a military revival is shown by the elaborate arrangements made to keep the Bundeswehr subservient to the German parliament. Without the backing of the Reichswehr, Hitler would not have been able to seize power.[10]

A fourth advantage may well be economic. The Germans have been unwilling
or unable to bring their twelve divisions up to combat readiness. There is a serious
deficiency in officers and noncommissioned officers. The only way to build up the
military ranks in the full-employment German economy is by offering more pay.
But military pay in Germany is matched to civil service pay and the cost would
go up all around. The militia would not be a drain on the economy: the members
could still hold down their jobs. Once trained, the troops could be organized in
units near their homes and become familiarized with the weapons and terrain over
a long period of time.

However, to provide a strong militia force that is well armed with modern
light-weight weapons would cost money, and something has to be given up. It might
be interesting to make a cost-effectiveness study to determine how many German
regular army divisions would have to be given up to provide the kind of militia force
envisaged. First, it would be necessary to calculate the numbers of militiamen
and the numbers and kinds of weapons required to cover the 1000 kilometers along
the Iron Curtain. This requires professional military judgment and knowledge of
the country. Second, the initial cost and annual operating costs on a five-year basis
of this force would be compared to the same costs of a regular standing army armored division. Unfortunately, such information is classified. Such an analysis
could be quite easily undertaken by any competent operations analysis organization
from classified and unclassified information available. If the number of divisions

to be given up are only a few, then the militia organization could be undertaken within the accumulated funds saved without sacrificing security. Three or four divisions, more or less, would not make much difference if in the exchange a competent militia barrier along the Iron Curtain is created.

One must be realistic, though, and recognize that a number of similar concepts and force postures have been proposed to improve the ability of NATO to defend the border areas of Central Europe without resorting to the immediate use of nuclear weapons.[11] None has been adopted. There may be another alternative. Serious thought should be given to whether the heavy-gunned and armored divisions of the NATO (especially U. S.) divisions are really the best organizations to cope either with the low level conflicts that might flash up along the border or with a limited nuclear conflict. There is something ambivalent about contemplating ground conflict in Europe. The composition of the Seventh U. S. Army, for example, is considered ideal for a fluid conventional battle in the traditional World War II manner. Yet in terms of either smaller conventional conflicts or in nuclear conflict, the ground force organization leaves much to be desired. Whereas the army has continued to gird itself with better and more powerful weapons and vehicles, there has invariably been a lag in developing imaginative tactics and doctrine for fighting the kind of warfare most likely to be encountered. Colonel George Reinhardt points out that France had both quantitative and qualitative tank superiority over Germany in 1940, but the Germans had more mobile forces and moreover had an operational doctrine for employment.[12] He points out that, historically, there has always been a lag in developing tactics and doctrines for effective combat use of new weapons.

We should at this point seriously ask the question whether light divisions such as the First Air Cavalry Division in Vietnam would not be as effective. For small uprisings or conflicts near the border, air cavalry units could move in armed troops to the crisis spot in a matter of a few hours. If the emphasis is on crisis management, it would appear that a flight of helicopters could do as well as a platoon of heavy tanks, particularly where quick action is essential to snuff out a conflict or to prevent a fait accompli. Even for nuclear operations, either in demonstration or "exemplary," in order to terminate a conflict that has somehow gotten out of hand, small mobile and dispersed units would appear to be of more use than a heavy concentration of armor and artillery.

The important point to emphasize, however, is that something must be done to provide a better border defense with at least sufficient conventional capability to cope with frontier incidents, crises, uprisings and even miscalculated attempts by the enemy to seize something of value on NATO territory. German militia may be part of the answer; mobile air cavalry units may be another.

Finally, we are faced with the crucial question of the NATO air force posture. The instability that the present air force deployment, capabilities and doctrine bring to the confrontation has been repeatedly emphasized. Concentrated as the NATO air forces are in West Germany, with flights of aircraft standing by on nuclear alert at all times, their survival in time of conflict depends on the forebearance of the enemy, on immediate use to avoid preemption, or on widespread dispersal. The first thing to do would be to reduce the impulse for preemption (by either side) by removing these aircraft from atomic alert--especially during peacetime. Having aircraft armed and standing by in peacetime for instant nuclear strikes deep into enemy territory is an anachronism in the current European climate. As it stands, the assigned missions of these atomic alert aircraft are, for reasons given in earlier discussion, incompatible with attempts to establish a distinguishable threshold of "firebreak" at the battlefield nuclear level. Even the most unlikely contingency of a deliberate Soviet invasion fails to justify this nuclear alert posture. Either the aircraft would be destroyed on base by the Russians, or they would be sent on a mission of deep nuclear strikes. In either case, NATO would have lost control over the dimensions of the conflict, and general war or at least Europe-wide devastation would result. If indeed the threat of deliberate invasion is not even in the cards and if indeed the most likely contingency would be a conflict that arises out of a crisis, then there would be ample time to disperse and alert these aircraft for whatever mission is required. Plans for dispersal do not, however, require all aircraft to be located in Europe. They could just as well be based in the United Kingdom or better, in the continental United States. The new fighter bombers (F-4s and F-111s) have the range to make the transoceanic deployment to the dispersed bases in West Germany. A squadron or smaller units of aircraft could be maintained on the present West German airfields, with periodic peacetime rotation with other air units based in the United States. Some physical presence of aircraft is obviously important--if for no more reason than to be a constant reminder of American and NATO capabilities.

Furthermore, the capability for nuclear arming and alerting these aircraft should be patently obvious--even though it is no longer necessary to keep these aircraft on nuclear alert during normal peacetime periods. We do not want to "clear the nuclear decks" entirely for conventional warfare. A potential aggressor must not be allowed to ignore our capability for tactical nuclear strikes as an element in graduated deterrence, nor should he be allowed to underestimate the severity of the West's reaction to surprise destruction of our airforces.

There are several advantages to such a dual-basing scheme. First, aircraft based in the United States are not as vulnerable to a preemptive attack. Second, deployment to the dispersed European bases during a crisis could be used as a diplomatic move to convey to the enemy U.S. commitment and resolve--similar to the dispatching of a U.S. battle group up the autobahn during the 1961 Berlin crisis. Third, the financial strain on the U.S. balance of payments would be relieved somewhat. Of course, this last is not a strategic justification, but merely a bonus. Yet it is the kind of political and economic consideration that determines much of strategy. The dual-basing idea could even be carried further to the basing of a large part of the German and British air forces in the United States. If dual-basing has validity for the United States, it would have validity for its allies. The basing of foreign air units on U.S. soil might be viewed as a symbol of Alliance unity and integration. It might undermine some of the political criticism of United States' presence in foreign countries.

The inertia to change, the continuing reluctance of NATO to meet its force goals, and the defection of France from NATO have left the present NATO fractured strategy and force posture in serious trouble. Without an improved capability to handle conflicts that might arise from crises along the border, NATO may be forced to base its plans on using nuclear weapons for even moderate sized conventional attacks. Such a dependence on nuclear weapons involves at least some chance of being regarded as incredible by the enemy. There will always be the chance that the enemy might believe that we or the Germans or the British or some other NATO partner might fear holocaust to such an extent that the political leaders would acquiesce to some minor incursion or peripheral grab rather than start nuclear war to prevent it. Furthermore, while escalation is no more inevitable than the reverse--a sort of quenching of conflict, it is nevertheless possible. The first use of nuclear weapons introduces the world to a chance of total calamity which does not exist so long as conventional weapons are the only destructive means employed. The doctrine of nuclear constraints proposed earlier was conceived in the framework of graduated deterrence. An improved conventional defense along the border is a necessary precondition to set it into operation in a measured, controlled, and discriminate manner.

PART THREE—THE CONTROL OF NUCLEAR WEAPONS

FRANCE, NUCLEAR CONTROL AND THE ATLANTIC ALLIANCE

Of all the problems that plague the Alliance, the problem of political control of nuclear weapons is the most vexatious. The conflicting strategic views among the major NATO nations on employment of nuclear weapons during war was discussed in the first part of this book. The practical problems relating to military constraints and doctrine in the use of nuclear weapons were examined in the second part. Political control of nuclear weapons within the Alliance, however, goes far beyond these strategic and military considerations. The problem of political control of nuclear weapons impinges on a national freedom of action during peacetime which is only indirectly related to the perception of military threats and feelings of national security. There are the important matters of political prestige and influence within the Alliance. No one can deny that de Gaulle's influence is enhanced in political circles by the possession of an embryonic nuclear striking force, no matter how credible and effective it may be as a deterrent. No one can deny that West Germany's freedom of action in the realm of foreign policy is severely limited by the institutional and other constraints imposed on her in the matter of nuclear weapons. The manifest opposition of the super-powers to further nuclear proliferation affects every nation in the Alliance that can afford and might want to pursue scientific knowledge, develop technical skills, and establish industrial capabilities in the nuclear field. One cannot overlook these aspects. But the essential issues are the national political choices available in times of crisis and the rights of sovereignty in time of war.

Every scheme that has been advanced to solve the problem of nuclear control --and there were many--has foundered on the basic issue of national sovereignty.

If there is any alternative, no nation gives up its freedom of choice in vital matters over the long term or entrusts its destiny to the dictates of another nation or even to an alliance of nations, except under the concept of unanimity. For a while after World War II, the European nations were forced by circumstances to entrust their security almost wholly to the United States. Even today, in the final analysis, their security depends on American strategic capabilities and the solemn commitment of the United States to come to their aid. No nation in the Atlantic Alliance wants to attempt to go it alone--not even France. In fact, de Gaulle's freedom of action in pursuing national policies regardless of the interests of the other allies is predicated upon the American nuclear commitment and the leverage France possesses in her independent nuclear force to influence American choices when survival may be at stake. For it is when survival may be at stake that the Allies want to assert their voice in the control of whether, when, and in what circumstances nuclear weapons would be used. It is a matter of choice and the one thing that the debate on nuclear control brings home clearly is that there is a lack of confidence in the United States' making the right choices in exercising its almost exclusive control over nuclear weapons within the Alliance. This lack of confidence is implied in Britain's demand for an opportunity to ". . . participate fully, intimately, and without limit in the formulation of ideas, policy, and strategy which together make up the doctrine upon which any particular decision of the President may depend."[1] The Germans, no less constrained in their aspirations, have, in addition, favored participating in some "hardware" solution that might give them a feeling of participating in a nuclear force, plus a stronger basis to be consulted on nuclear matters. With the recent change in government, the participating Social Democrats are demanding a Vetorecht--a right to veto the use of nuclear weapons from German soil or onto German soil. The lack of confidence is more explicit in France where President de Gaulle has expressed quite bluntly:

> For France to deprive herself of the means capable of dis-
> suading the adversary from a possible attack . . . would
> mean that she would confide her defense and therefore her
> existence, and in the end her policy to a foreign and, for
> that matter, an uncertain protector.[2]

Thus, the problem of nuclear control is essentially political. For if there were a community of interests among the allies such that the national interests

of the United States would be the same as the interests of the other allies, the
problem of control would not exist and the American insistence on centralized
control of strategic nuclear decisions would be acceptable to the members of the
Alliance. But such common interests unfortunately do not exist. Nothing brings
this home clearer than France's withdrawal from NATO, which has been dictated
by President de Gaulle's activist views of a different kind of Europe from that in
the past which has been largely under American hegemony. De Gaulle has a strong
desire to see France play a leading role in this new Europe as a counterforce
between the United States and the Soviet Union. Whether the French leader achieves
the continental rapprochement and the "European Europe" he seeks or not, he has
succeeded in disrupting the integrated NATO military organization and has placed
the problem of nuclear control into starkly clear focus.

The Military Implications of France's Withdrawal

As earlier stated, the withdrawal of France from NATO was not unexpected.
As early as March 1959, de Gaulle withdrew French naval units from the Allied
Mediterranean Command. The significance of this withdrawal was purely political.
In military terms, the withdrawal of the fleet units was almost meaningless. Nothing really changed except that de Gaulle would no longer permit these French
ships to participate in joint peacetime maneuvers. In wartime, these French naval units would be somewhat less significant during the initial stages of conflict
than the U.S. Sixth Fleet with its nuclear-armed, carrier-based aircraft. Furthermore, as a member of the Alliance, France could still and probably would
use these ships for the common defense--which was all that was asked of France
in the first place. France justified the withdrawal of her Mediterranean fleet
from NATO on three grounds. First, the ". . . zone of possible NATO action
does not extend south of the Mediterranean. The Middle East, North Africa,
Black Africa, the Red Sea, etc., are not part of it. Who can deny that France
may possibly find herself obliged to act in these different areas?" Second, both
the United States and Great Britain ". . . have taken steps to prevent the greater
part of their naval forces from being integrated in NATO." Third (and this was
de Gaulle's key consideration), the Alliance ". . . will be all the more vital and
strong as the great powers unite on the basis of cooperation in which each carries
his own load, rather than on the basis of an integration in which peoples and

governments find themselves more or less deprived of their roles and responsibilities in the domain of their own defense."[3]

The important thing to emphasize is that de Gaulle clearly affirmed at the
same press conference that France would remain in the Alliance, ". . . an Alliance which is unimaginable without the participation of France." Furthermore, he
pointed out that such a withdrawal would not prevent France from using her fleet
in a common battle in the Mediterranean. "Thus, there is nothing in this change
that might weaken the Alliance, . . ."[3] de Gaulle asserted.

The withdrawal of all the French armed forces from the NATO organization
is, however, a different matter. On the surface there are many similarities with
France's previous withdrawal of her Mediterranean fleet. After all, the forces
that have been withdrawn still exist. Ever since NATO adopted the Forward Strategy, French ground forces located to the rear of the U.S. Seventh Army generally
have been considered as reserves. They may still be so regarded, except that
France has now made it explicit that her armed forces would not in any case be
subordinated to an allied command. Nothing prevents France, however, from
using her armed forces "in a common battle." De Gaulle still affirms France's
adherence to the Atlantic Alliance. But here the similarities end.

The most serious military effect of France's withdrawal is the explicit refusal of de Gaulle not to be bound by any automatic commitment to assist France's
allies if one or more are attacked in Europe or North America, as required by
Article 5 of the North Atlantic Treaty.[4] De Gaulle still promises to fight along-
side France's allies in case of "unprovoked aggression," but France reserves
the right to determine whether the attack is provoked or not. The most damaging
effects to NATO's military posture, should France not join her allies in conflict,
would be to deny the NATO allies lines of logistics and dispersal airfields on
French territory and to split (in a geographical sense) the central sector from
the southern zone of operations.

In concrete terms, the withdrawal of France calls for the dissociation of
French military participation in joint planning and preparation. It calls for the
removal of the NATO military commands, SHAPE and AFCENT (Allied Forces
Central Europe), and the expulsion of foreign troops from French territory.
Some 70,000 American and other foreign troops and over 700,000 tons of stored
supplies are being shifted to other bases. French air units have been withdrawn

from Germany, but a new arrangement has been made for France to keep her

ground troops in Germany without being associated with NATO in any way.

The divorce is not complete. France permits the United States and NATO

to continue to use the communications network as a temporary expedient until

an alternate system is established. The 390-mile pipeline, under French man-

agement, can still be used in peacetime. France still permits allied military

planes the right of overflying French territory from month to month. Formerly

these overflight rights were granted on an annual basis. The most important ves-

tige of a tie with NATO is in France's participation in NADGE, the NATO air

defense network that provides radar warning, computes intercept data and com-

municates battle orders to the air defense forces. This participation obviously

serves France's own military security. Without it France would have little or

no warning of air attack until enemy planes cross its eastern frontier.

France's unilateral actions, damaging and costly as they are to the NATO

military posture, are not the only aspects to consider. There have been signif-

icant and little appreciated changes made by France in her own armed forces

over the last several years. These changes have been profound and have been

designed deliberately to support France's strategic concept--not NATO's nor

the United States'. First of all, to dissuade a potential aggressor, France de-

cided to build her own strategic nuclear force. Since the first operational test

of the atomic bomb in the Sahara on May 1, 1962, the progress has been rapid.

Sixty-two Mirage IV aircraft, capable of carrying a 60-kiloton bomb 3200 kilo-

meters without refueling and 5500 kilometers with air-to-air refueling, repre-

sents the first generation of the force de frappe. By 1969, twenty-five missiles

in underground silos will begin to take over the strategic role. These missile

sites are to be located in the eastern part of France in Haute Provence near the

low Alps. The nuclear warheads of these missiles will be at least four times as

powerful as those carried by the Mirage IV. The French hydrogen bomb is sched-

uled for test in 1968. These thermonuclear warheads are scheduled to be mated

with the submarine-launched missile in 1971. [5] The third generation of the stra-

tegic force will consist of three nuclear powered submarines, each carrying six-

teen missiles. The first is scheduled to be ready in 1970 and the two others in

1972 and 1974.

Parallel to the development of the strategic force, which enjoys top priority, is the rejuvenation and modernization of the maneuvering forces to be used for defense and intervention in situations where nuclear arms would be inapplicable. These forces, of course, would eventually be armed with tactical nuclear weapons as a supplement to strategic deterrence. The forces de manoeuvres would comprise five army divisions and the greater part of the air force and navy units. Due to the great cost involved in developing a strategic force, however, the maneuvering forces have been cut down in size. For example, the numbers of officers and men in France's armed forces have progressively been cut from a total of 1,023,000 in January 1962 to 581,000 in January 1967, a reduction of forty-three percent. [6] Although the French armed services are better equipped and the officers and men are better trained and have higher morale than any time since the Algerian rebellion, this reduction is a serious matter. The French action has completely dashed Mr. McNamara's hopes that the size of NATO's conventional forces could and would be increased. No matter how persuasive the United States is in persuading West Germany and the other European nations to increase their conventional forces, no additional European contribution will make up for the net reduction of over 440,000 personnel already made in France's forces de manoeuvre over the last five years. More importantly, de Gaulle has made it abundantly clear by his actions and by his refusal to be bound to any automatic commitment to France's allies in time of conflict that France could make it extremely difficult if not impossible for the United States and the other NATO allies to fight a sizeable conventional war in Europe in accordance with the American strategic concept of flexible response. France, theoretically, has the power to cut off logistics and reinforcements from the rear by declining to join the allies in combat, or alternatively by employing nuclear weapons before the United States is ready to use them--thus triggering a nuclear war. In any event, the American strategic concept of flexible response that calls for conventional defense with a high nuclear threshold would become impossible. The idea of fighting such a war, of course, is already unpopular with the British and the Germans. In fact, the British have indicated an extreme reluctance to increase their war stocks on the continent above ten days. It is quite obvious that there is a critical need to revise the American strategic concept to something more adaptable to the desires of the European nations--including France.

By severing all important military ties that might automatically commit France in the event of conflict, de Gaulle has attacked the very concept of integration of command and forces--regarded by most American military analysts as essential for defense in a nuclear age. It was generally appreciated that integration has never really applied to nuclear forces or weapons in the Atlantic Alliance. Neither the United States nor Great Britain (not to mention France) had ever agreed to assign control of nuclear forces or nuclear weapons to an allied command. Each has reserved the ultimate right of deciding on the use of these weapons as a matter vital to survival. Only in the use of conventional forces and weapons was there any semblance of integration.

But even here, the word "integration" must be qualified. In general, it signifies unity of purpose and direction. It implies that operational control rests in a central allied authority and that once forces are assigned to the allied command, the disposition and employment of these forces would be governed by the plans and direction of the allied command. But there are many limitations on this allied control. Each nation is responsible for the logistics of its national armed forces; each nation is responsible for training (although the allied command may attempt to establish standards of readiness). But most importantly, each nation in principle has the ultimate right of deciding to what extent to commit the national armed force contingent assigned to the Allied Command. Even before France's withdrawal from NATO, President de Gaulle had reserved for himself the right to decide whether, when, and in what manner French armed forces would be used. Quite obviously he considered this choice more theoretical than real. Because of the many institutional arrangements, such as infrastructure, basing rights, NATO Production and Logistics Organizations (NPLOs), French command and staff participation, there would always be the risk that France could get involved in conflict against her will. By pulling France out of NATO, de Gaulle has made each Alliance partner acutely ware that this risk of being involved in conflict against its will exists for each nation participating in the NATO integrated military organization. By breaking all ties with the Allied Military Command, and by insisting on a completely independent nuclear strategic force, de Gaulle has moreover emphasized the hazardous link between conventional conflict and nuclear war. In the final analysis, each NATO nation that takes part in conventional conflict, according to the integrated plans and direction of SACEUR or other allied commander, risks involvement in a nuclear war in which the decisions would be made independently by the nuclear nations in the light of their self-interests.

This is an important point. Until France withdrew from NATO, this risk was only vaguely understood. West Germany, for instance, was perfectly content to assign all her armed forces to NATO even in peacetime and rely on NATO to perform the military planning that other nations do themselves with their own national staffs. Now Germany is beginning to make explicit demands for a veto on the use of nuclear weapons from German soil and onto German soil. Even the smaller countries, which in the past were content to leave the problem of the control of nuclear weapons to the major NATO allies, are demanding a voice in nuclear plans and policy.

With France out of the picture as far as military planning is concerned, new initiatives are now possible for seeking an answer to the dilemma of nuclear control. But how much can be accomplished is debatable. France is still a member of the Atlantic Council and as such can exercise a veto on arrangements that affect her national interest. Whether a group of nations within the Alliance can make arrangements that deal with such an important matter as nuclear control against the express wishes of one of its members has really never been tested. On the one occasion, when some compromise over the American proposal for the Multilateral Force (MLF) and the British proposal for the Atlantic Nuclear Force (ANF) seemed close to being accepted, de Gaulle's explicit objection to giving Germany any share in the control of strategic nuclear weapons was enough to cause the United States to drop the idea. True, there have been other institutional arrangements within the Alliance in which only a few NATO nations have participated. For example, there are the bilateral arrangements between the United States and the nation concerned that govern the provision and release of tactical nuclear weapons. Even though location of American nuclear weapons on French soil has been forbidden since 1961, France nevertheless had participated in an arrangement--under the "two key" system--for her tactical aircraft formerly stationed in Germany. But when France left NATO, the United States abrogated the arrangement, and the French aircraft were withdrawn from Germany.

The Problem of Sharing in Control of Nuclear Weapons

The problem of control of nuclear weapons can be broken up into three elements. The first is ownership of weapons. The three nuclear powers within the Alliance guard carefully the special privileges which are accorded by virtue of ownership and possession of these weapons of mass destruction. None are ready to transfer control of nuclear weapons to another ally; in present circumstances at least, no nonnuclear power is likely to seek to have its own nuclear weapons under national control. This is not to say that at some long distant future date, Germany or even Italy might not seek ownership of nuclear weapons, but the circumstances would have to change markedly before further proliferation in the Alliance would come about. This is an alternative to consider; but especially in the case of Germany, it would require abrogating solemn treaty commitments. A country does not abrogate treaties with allies as long as the need for cooperation exists. Even France was careful not to withdraw from the Alliance, even though she departed from the integrated organization. The second element is planning--developing contingency circumstances in which nuclear weapons might possibly be used, determining how and where to deploy them, and what targets to select for nuclear fires. No contingency plan is automatic and there is always the need to decide what to do. The third element is the decision whether to use nuclear weapons, where to use them, when to use them.

One of the proposals advanced as a means to permit the West European nations to share in the ownership and the planning is an integrated NATO strategic nuclear force. The Multilateral Force (MLF) was to be such a force and, even though the MLF is now a dead issue, it is instructive to examine some of its aspects in order to gain a better understanding of the problem of nuclear sharing.

The Multilateral Force was conceived as a fleet of merchant ships armed with Polaris missiles and each manned by a crew of mixed nationalities. Physical safeguards--such as the permissive-action link (PAL) or, as some call it, positive arming link--were to be incorporated to prevent unauthorized firing of the missiles. Part of the force would always be at sea on ready nuclear alert. In fact, the most significant military advantage of the multilateral force concept was in basing the NATO strategic forces at sea. Despite the differences among our allies in nuclear strategic concepts, there is solid agreement on the advantages of sea-based deterrence. Without going into the many arguments for basing the deterrent force at sea, it is only necessary to point to the official position taken by the governments concerned.

The official British 1963 Statement on Defense as presented to Parliament states:

> . . . The Royal Navy is now to be entrusted with a most
> important additional task. It is responsible for creating and
> operating, in time to succeed the V-bombers, a force of
> Polaris-equipped nuclear submarines as Britain's independ-
> ent contribution to the long-range strategic forces of the
> Western Alliance.[7]

This decision was reconfirmed in the 1964 White Paper. This position has not been changed since the Labour government has come to power in Britain, even though, as an interim measure, the Labour government prefers to continue to maintain the V-bomber force and has contracted to buy some F-111s from the United States as eventual replacement.

Even France recognizes the advantages of a sea-based deterrent force. Defense Minister Pierre Messmer wrote an article in the Revue de Défense Nationale in which he spoke of the follow-on to the Mirage-IV strategic force:

> . . . The decision of a launch platform depends on technical
> factors, but also on strategic and, therefore, political ones.
> Technically, the launching from a mobile or stationary land
> platform, the latter often underground, is the most simple
> and most economical solution; militarily and politically, it
> is not without its drawbacks for a relatively small country
> such as France. That is why the nuclear-powered submarine
> has been selected as a launching platform.[8]

The position of Germany in favor of a sea-based strategic force can be inferred by its official preference for the sea-based MLF proposed by the United States over the land-based Medium Range Ballistic Missile (MRBM) concept proposed by General Lauris Norstad. However, there is little doubt that, unlike England and France, this preference is based mainly on political considerations.

The most important political advantage claimed was that it would provide a way, however limited, of providing Germany a means to share in the ownership and control of a strategic nuclear force without unduly provoking the fears of the Russians and Germany's NATO allies. Of course, these fears continue to be expressed by both Russia and by some of these NATO allies. But at the same time, there is a growing awareness that German aspirations to achieve a status in the Alliance commensurate with its importance and power must somehow be satisfied. The political and psychological advantages of "possessing the bomb" which have recently accrued to a backward industrial nation like China have not passed

unnoticed in the leading industrial country of Western Europe. Perhaps it was
once true that the German government went along with the MLF concept when it
was originally proposed more in response to American desires than from any
firmly held national aspiration to become a nuclear power. But there are now
clear indications that the German government attaches great importance to participating in some strategic nuclear force even today.

If one accepts the premise that Germany will not long remain willing to accept a subordinate position in the Alliance in regard to nuclear strategy and control, there exist only three alternatives. One, Germany may seek to become an
independent nuclear power--a move that would have serious consequences to Western unity and to the Soviet policy of "peaceful coexistence." Two, Germany may
turn to France and become associated with a purely European nuclear force--a
move that would clearly lessen American influence in European affairs. Three,
Germany may elect a closer attachment with the United States and its other NATO
allies in matters of nuclear policy, planning, and decision. The third course is
preferred by the German government today, and the MLF was seen as a partial
answer to implementing this alternative.

Unsettled, however, was the question of decision. Who could authorize the
use of nuclear weapons in this force? An integrated allied nuclear force was proposed in which each of the participants would almost certainly demand a veto over
its use in conflict. Of course, German Defense Minister von Hassel had suggested
an eventual system of weighted voting that would allow the use of the MLF even
with some dissenting votes among the collaborators in the project. But it is hard
to conceive that any nation--even a minority stockholder in the MLF--would agree
to permit a few Polaris missiles to be lobbed into Russia without its consent or
without being prepared to back up the action by the full use of its national military
resources. This applies to the United States as well as to the other nations that
might have joined in the project. Furthermore, the idea of having a veto loses
much of its significance as far as the European members are concerned should
the United States decide that strategic nuclear weapons will be used. There are
enough Minutemen and Polaris missiles available to the United States alone to
make the contribution of a separate NATO strategic command such as the MLF
almost irrelevant in terms of the actual physical destruction that could be inflicted
on the enemy. These arguments were used by many of the opponents of the separate

nuclear command who regarded the MLF as a mere super-addition to what the United States already has in nuclear strategic forces--except that the MLF would be paid for in part by the European nation members with funds that could be better spent on other military forces.

The real value of the MLF sea-based deterrent force, however, could really only be assessed in the light of the Soviet reactions to it. This depends not on the "facts" of its effectiveness and survivability, such as its damage-limiting features under attack, or the large Soviet effort required to counter it, or its mobility and versatility on a global basis, or its relative insensitivity to strategic warning prior to a first enemy strike--but rather it depends on Soviet perceptions of these "facts." It depends ultimately on whether the MLF strengthens the "disincentives" of the Soviet Union to embark on courses of aggression against NATO or whether it erects additional new "disincentives" in the event the major deterrence of the United States strategic forces loses some of its value. Viewed in this light, arguments that a NATO strategic force such as the MLF would add little or nothing to the size of Western strategic power become largely irrelevant.

Unfortunately, the question of how the Soviets would perceive our actions is largely speculative. Even the most dedicated Sovietologists in the West, immersing themselves in Russian history and culture, cannot make sure estimates of Soviet value judgments.[9] On the other hand, if Soviet official pronouncements and actions give any clue to their perceptions, an inference can be drawn that the Soviet deep-seated and emotional fear of the Germans is the basis of their vigorous opposition to the MLF or any other scheme that would give the Germans a share in nuclear control. This fear of Germany was probably also the reason the Soviet Union vigorously opposed the European Defense Community in 1954 and Germany's independent rearmament within NATO. There is also a more basic concern than emotional fear of Germany which accounts for Soviet opposition. The Soviet Union loses no opportunity to create disunity in the Atlantic Alliance. Whenever NATO undertakes a scheme for strengthening the military force, or for achieving closer unity, the Soviet Union is almost certain to object. These two considerations-- fear of the Germans and the demonstration of unity within the Alliance represented by any agreed upon scheme for a NATO strategic force--will continue to condition Soviet perception. Certainly, if low-level conflict were to break out in the Central European sector through a series of events or miscalculations in a crisis, the

Soviets could expect strong German pressure on the United States and on the other participating allies to commit the NATO strategic force to counter the Soviet strategic threat of 700 or so MRBMs and IRBMs capable of striking Western Europe.

In this sense, a NATO strategic force such as the MLF could act as an "intra-war deterrent force." It is arguable whether the Soviet Bloc would perceive a NATO strategic force in this light, or whether it would be more deterred by the knowledge that the United States has more than enough American ICBMs and Polaris missiles trained on Russia. A NATO nuclear force with Germany and other European nations participating may well strengthen the "disincentives" over any incentive the Soviets might have to exploit the threat of their home-based strategic rocket forces against Europe. These points, however, will remain uncertain.

It should be quite clear that the answer to the problem of the control of nuclear weapons--ownership, planning, and decision--could not be found in a NATO strategic force such as the MLF. The question of sharing in ownership would be only partially satisfied by the MLF; the question of sharing in planning could be satisfied by other means; the question of sharing in the decision remains unsolved. The lack of consensus in strategic concepts for the defense of Western Europe and the divergent national interests of the member nations outside of Europe will continue to make nuclear planning difficult. France's defection has only sharpened the focus on the issue of sharing in the nuclear decision. The problem is not one of giving the European nations a veto over American strategic nuclear power--a thing that is quite unthinkable in the context of the confrontation of the two super-powers, rather it is one of giving the European members a bargaining lever to convince the United States to come to their aid when their vital interests are threatened. The American view, of course, is that such a lever is not really necessary, since U.S. interests would demand our involvement if European vital interests are threatened. Since doubt is expressed about whether we will or will not, certainly a step in the direction of establishing even limited means to restore the confidence of our allies is needed. This is essential in making deterrence truly credible to the enemy.

Control of Tactical Nuclear Weapons

So much has been written about the political aspects of the control of strategic nuclear weapons that many observers tend to overlook the practical arrangements that have already been designed to control the 7000 tactical nuclear weapons stored in various Special Ammunition Storage (SAS) sites in Europe. The nuclear warheads are by U.S. law, in the custody of American military officers, with quite explicit and elaborate procedures for releasing them to U.S. and allied forces in time of grave crisis or conflict. Only the President of the United States has the authority to release these weapons and only the North Atlantic Council theoretically can authorize their use by an allied command. A "two-key" system, however, has been set up between the United States and the host country that at least gives to the host country a sense of confidence that, lacking unanimity in the Council, nuclear weapons would be released provided the United States and the host country determine that they are needed. This is an important aspect of the nuclear control problem. As pointed out earlier, in certain unlikely contingencies such as a massive invasion or a nuclear attack, tactical nuclear weapons might be used in conjunction with strategic weapons. Whether the decision to use nuclear weapons is made unilaterally by the President, or in conjunction with the exposed host country, the practical effect would be to by-pass any reluctant member in the Atlantic Council. Although France has withdrawn from NATO, she nevertheless might use her veto in the Council to contract out of the conflict--unless her own vital interest were threatened. Other member nations might follow suit. In any event, U.S. policy calls for an immediate nuclear response for such catastrophic contingencies. Here the problem of nuclear control centers on doubt that the United States would in fact carry out the policy in certain circumstances and on a fear that the United States would carry it out in other circumstances.

The real problem of nuclear control focuses on the more likely contingencies of conflict that arise out of crises or miscalculation where selected and discriminate use of nuclear weapons may be needed--i.e., whether to enforce a "pause" or to heighten the shared risk of escalation to general war. Here the most exact timing and control are required and this in turn makes it necessary to have the nuclear weapons in a state of readiness for instant use when ordered.

A complex system has been designed--but no system is fool-proof. Concern has been expressed that some of these weapons may be used by an allied commander without presidential authority despite the elaborate precautions designed. There is concern that the careful procedures, designed both for safety and to prevent unauthorized use of nuclear weapons, would slow down the authorization and release process so much that the warheads would not be available at the critical time and place to influence the course of events. The crucial issue is, as discussed earlier, an agreed-upon and practicable nuclear constraint doctrine that could cover a wide range of contingencies. Beyond that there are some practical problems of physical control and timing that might be overcome by technology.

Already installed is an electro-mechanical positive arming link (PAL) device that would make a warhead inoperative until a coded signal is sent by the President that would unlock the weapon mechanism.[10] The installation of a PAL on each weapon insures that the weapon cannot be used without authority. The PAL system in turn adds another procedure and potential delay to the authorized use of the weapon. There is no reason, however, why an improved version of the PAL might not be developed that could not only prevent the use of the weapon by unauthorized persons, but at the same time prevent the weapon from being used in a manner not prescribed. By such a device, the control as well as the physical custody of certain types of nuclear warheads (such as those required for air defense) could be given to the troops in anticipation of their use in a grave conflict. Already there are environmental sensing devices in warheads that allow explosion only at a prescribed height above the ground or in close proximity of a target. Sensing devices that would cause a weapon to "dud" or to disintegrate could be developed that would allow limits to be placed on the range of weapons, prevent surface-to-air weapons from being used in the surface-to-surface mode or even to prevent weapons from being used except in certain localities. If an unauthorized person tampered with the weapon in an attempt to make the nuclear warhead useful for any other purpose, a device could cause the warhead to neutralize itself and at the same time to notify Washington and Brussels.[11]

With such sensing devices, nuclear weapons could be distributed more widely. It would be possible for the President to permit certain categories of weapons to be readied for use by troops as soon as a serious crisis occurs. Whereas such a sensing device might permit the President to grant predelegated authority to SACEUR to use certain types of weapons under certain conditions, this would not be advisable before the initial use of nuclear weapons had occurred. The argument was advanced earlier that the selective use of tactical nuclear weapons in a limited war is part of a bargaining process of deliberately creating a risk of escalation and not a rational means of defense. If this argument has any validity, it would be absolutely essential that the first employment of nuclear weapons be centrally controlled by the President, who alone can control and coordinate all the military, intelligence, and diplomatic activities that might be able to shape the course of events. However, after the initial use of nuclear weapons, the President might --with the aid of these new sensing devices--grant an "anticipatory release" of certain types of nuclear weapons to be used by the Allied Commanders, under conditions precisely stipulated, with the assurance that they would not be misused. It would also be possible, as Sir John Slessor suggests, in peacetime to turn over custody of the storage sites to ". . . a specially recruited NATO corps of carefully selected international control officers drawn from all the allies, nuclear or other- wise. . ."[12] The custodial arrangements could be such that one of the control of- ficers in each unit would be from the nation where the special ammunition storage site is located. Such an allied custodial arrangement would have more than sym- bolic value since it could provide the European nations an effective veto over the American use of tactical nuclear weapons from a particular stockpile or weapon. Even though the President of the United States alone possesses the authority to release a nuclear weapon, the nation from whose soil and onto whose soil, the weapons would be fired would then have en effective veto over its use. This is something the Germans in particular desire. Such an innovation would require a change in Congressional law, of course. It might, however, give the NATO allies a practically meaningful share in the peacetime operations and control of nuclear weapons that they do not now possess, as long as custody of these weapons remain exclusively in the hands of American officers.

Permanent Nuclear Planning Group

The Western European nations are willing to accept or are resigned to the hard fact that the United States, France, and Britain are the owners of the nuclear arsenal in the Alliance. They are not willing to accept the fact that the control of planning and policy, and the decision to use or not to use nuclear weapons, should rest exclusively in the hands of the owners. Even the three owners are concerned: the United States is concerned lest France "trigger" the American strategic force; Britain is concerned on this point as well as to whether the United States would fully back Great Britain in circumstances considered vital to Britain; France is concerned lest the United States, in its role of "world policeman," might get France involved in a nuclear war against her will.

Before France's "defection," the coordination of nuclear strategy was theoretically the job of the Military Committee and the Standing Group in Washington. The Standing Group, consisting of the three nuclear powers--the United States, France, and Great Britain--was the executive agency of the Military Committee, with the task of coordinating defense plans and making recommendations to the Military Committee and ultimately to the Council. The Standing Group, however, was ineffective almost from the start. In the first place, the proximity of SACEUR (just outside of Paris) to the NATO Council resulted in the Council's seeking its military advice from the American officer who held the position of Supreme Allied Commander, Europe. In the second place, France consistently resisted the strategic concept of flexible response that the United States sought to impose on the Alliance and the American attempt to integrate strategic nuclear forces under the overall control of the United States. Finally, the Standing Group did not offer a truly viable means for the non-nuclear allies to share in the nuclear planning. With France's withdrawal, the Standing Group was dissolved.

In December 1966, a permanent nuclear planning group was established of four permanent and three rotating members of the Alliance to determine Western nuclear strategy. The United States, Great Britain, Germany and Italy are the permanent members. The first three rotating members, to be replaced after eighteen months are the Netherlands, Canada, and Turkey.

This permanent group started off under the auspices of the United States as the Select Committee of NATO Defense Ministers. The term "Select" was unfortunate, since it implied that the few members originally envisaged were somehow different from the other members of the Alliance. Italy immediately demanded the same permanent representation as Germany and the number of rotating members was increased from two to three because none of the smaller candidate members were willing to withdraw.

This permanent nuclear planning group of seven offers an opportunity for greater coordination and exchange of views regarding nuclear strategy. One cannot, however, help being pessimistic about its ability to do much about solving the problem of nuclear control and sharing. It has already become apparent that the views of the different members have not changed on certain fundamental issues. In the British view, the consultation group is the substitute for the formation of a NATO strategic nuclear force in which Germany would share in the ownership of nuclear weapons. The Americans do not see the permanent group as a substitute and they do not rule out eventual participation of Germany in the ownership of an Allied nuclear force. Germany, of course, still insists on a greater voice in how nuclear weapons would be used.

Nevertheless, the opportunity is there for the permanent group to go a long way toward solving the problem of nuclear planning. It depends on how much the United States is willing to allow European participation in the nuclear planning of the Strategic Air Command and the Polaris submarine fleet. In the long run, the nations that participate more closely with the United States, in planning and in the strategy for the use of nuclear weapons, may have more influence on American decisions than the nation that elects to go its own way.

The permanent nuclear planning group can come to grips with a number of critical questions. First, there is the question of formulating a NATO strategic concept, particularly in the matter of the possible first use of nuclear weapons. As the previous discussion has shown, neither a wholly conventional defense nor complete reliance on nuclear retaliation are capable of handling the possible range of armed clashes which might erupt during a crisis. Such conflicts could get out of hand. A strategy that provides the option of bringing battlefield nuclear weapons into the action earlier and in a more discriminate manner might find acceptance among the European allies, and especially Germany. Second, there is a dire need for a doctrine of nuclear constraints which is understood by friend and foe alike, lest the enemy detect in the first discriminate use of a battlefield nuclear weapon a signal that strategic nuclear warfare has begun. Third, there is a need to make ourselves, as well as our European partners, more aware of the difference between a nuclear strategy for deterrence and for defense. A more realistic understanding is needed of the technical and psychological possibilities of limiting a nuclear battle to the local battlefield, including the possible consequences of using various kinds of nuclear weapons in conflict. Fourth, there is a need to readjust the NATO force posture to eliminate potential instabilities, and to bring the doctrine of nuclear constraints developed and the capabilities of NATO forces in line with the avowed defensive intent of the Alliance.

Is a Solution Needed?

Perhaps, in the final analysis, the problem of nuclear control exists only in the minds of political leaders jockeying for influence in international matters. As

Marshall of the Royal Air Force Sir John Slessor commented in a letter to the

author:

> The United States need not insist on the de jure right of veto,
> because I am convinced, inevitably, such a veto will always
> exist de facto. . . . If the President of the U.S., having
> heard all the arguments, refuses to commit the U.S. to war
> then, again whether we like it or not, there will be no war
> and the question of using nuclear weapons will not arise. If
> war is forced upon us by open Soviet aggression, then the
> United States will be in it with us (whether they like it or not),
> and it is conceivable that such a war could be fought without
> using nuclear weapons.

The failure to recognize this truism accounts for many of the expressions of

doubt in the U.S. nuclear support. It is inconceivable that the United States can

sit back and observe the chain of events leading up to a crisis that may affect the

very survival of a NATO ally without stepping in and becoming involved also. Once

the United States becomes involved, the nature of the crisis changes and the play

would be taken away from the threatened nation. The United States' own national

interest would demand it.

There are some observers who refer to the "crisis" of the Atlantic Alliance,

which by definition is a juncture or decisive turning point. Certainly, France's

defection from NATO is a turning point. But the word "crisis" often has a conno-

tation of disaster. We can hardly expect a disaster to occur from de Gaulle's con-

trariness. The NATO patient therefore may well have passed the crisis and is in

the process of mending. Adjustements are badly needed in NATO's nuclear strategy

and military posture, as this book has endeavored to show. However, the neces-

sary changes won't be made by destroying institutions or by radically redirecting

the purpose for which the institutions were created. Institutions such as NATO

and the permanent nuclear planning committee are neither ends in themselves

nor means to predetermined ends. They are the means of reconciling differences

and accommodating interests. Even in the process of compromise and splitting

differences, the result is usually an upgrade of common interests. Even when

faced with the prospect of failure in arriving at a completely agreed-upon com-

mon strategy, some common stand may be adopted that protects other aspects of

Alliance cooperation. This is the spirit of the Atlantic Community; thus, when de

Gaulle acts without even consulting his allies, he may temporarily damage the

NATO institutions, but he cannot paralyze the will to agree of the remaining members.

As long as there is peace, the capacity to deter exists and the intentions of the two opposing sides favor a sort of stable military confrontation; then the problem of political control of nuclear weapons does not require a definitive solution. In many ways the problem of nuclear control is more apparent than actual. In our search for unity and agreement on a common strategy for NATO, we have used arguments that appeared logical, but turned out to be irrelevant or unfeasible in the real world of diverse national interests. If we focused on the practical results of our differences, however, we might find that they are not entirely bad. It is only realistic to recognize that some of the fundamental issues cannot be reconciled. The important requirement is to make sure that any decision made on the use of nuclear weapons can be executed in a timely and precise fashion. It is perfectly proper for the allies to participate in the arrangements to make this possible. But it is of course the nature of things that the most powerful nations will dominate alliances. No nation can confidently expect the United States to submerge completely her national interests within the Alliance, or to allow other nations to exercise a veto on her freedom of action outside of the Alliance; but in practice, constraints are there. The United States is not likely to act in ruthless disregard of the views of her allies, and an ally has every right to dissent and to take such action as it deems right for its own vital interests. There are limits of diversity, however, that can occur in an alliance without destroying it. As long as the dissenting actions do not contradict the joint purpose, the Alliance will remain vital.

A FINAL OVERVIEW

Traditional military planning has emphasized enemy capabilities over enemy intentions. This emphasis has led to establishing requirements based on the worst possible contingency, on the premise that if one is prepared for the worst war one can always handle the lesser conflict. This philosophy of preparation for the worst has caused the United States to devote extensive resources to large strategic nuclear forces and has enjoyed number-one priority for many years. In the nuclear age, however, it does not follow that the forces required for the worst contingency can satisfy the needs of lesser conflicts. It is just not true, as some officials have asserted, that if we have the strength required for global war, we could certainly meet any threat of lesser magnitude.

If armed conflict does occur, other choices of actions must be available. Some actions will undoubtedly create a risk of escalation, and some may even cause escalation to a greatly expanded conventional conflict. In these pages we have argued that, in Central Europe, the NATO allies should be prepared to use battlefield nuclear weapons in a highly selective manner before a conflict can expand into a major conventional war; and that this should not be done to prevent our conventional forces from being overrun, but to coerce the enemy by signaling to him in terms he best understands that a heightened risk of general war is shared by both sides. This "risk-sharing" process of bargaining cannot be postponed until the commitments of both sides become vital and irrevocable and the pressures for widespread use of nuclear weapons become irresistible. We suggest that the choice of using battlefield nuclear weapons in a selective and discriminate way should be carefully developed through a constraint doctrine, advertised intent,

and the practical command and control arrangements that will give NATO the
best chance to control events. As stated, there really is no assurance that things
would not get out of hand. In fact, the initial use of battlefield nuclear weapons i
in the manner previously described is calculated to increase the risk that things
would get out of hand. But this is an entirely different thing from insuring that
they will get out of hand by deliberate decision to go all out in nuclear battle or
general war before trying less catastrophic options.

Since the NATO allies cannot rely on worst-case military preparedness to
take care of lesser forms of conflict, it is only sensible to make estimates of
enemy intentions and the likelihood of possible conflicts as a basis for local force
postures. The Soviet threat is no longer an immediate military threat--if it ever
was one. But it remains, as before, an implacable struggle for political goals
that are diametrically opposed to those of the West. This political struggle is
backed by a strong and increasingly stronger Soviet military force in Central
Europe the presence of which cannot be ignored. As long as the Atlantic Alliance
presents a united political front backed by strong military capabilities, which the
Soviet Union cannot afford to ignore, a reasonably stable confrontation will continue to exist. The confrontation (there is no better word) remains because the
Soviet Union still contends with the West for political and economic domination
of Europe, still seeks to break up the Alliance, still maintains its hold on the
satellite nations, and still opposes reunification of Germany on terms compatible
with the ideals of freedom and democracy and the common interests of the members of the Atlantic Alliance.

In this context, there is no plausible way for a European war to occur except
out of a crisis or because of a serious miscalculation. That is to say, none of the
Soviet goals listed above require or merit a deliberate and rational decision to
resort to arms. A crisis can occur, but once the nature of a crisis is known, both
sides will be offered a choice of several courses of action. Some of the actions
available will undoubtedly increase the risk of conflict; some may even bring on
conflict. But neither side would initially consider as a serious alternative a direct course of action that would bring on nuclear war.

The kinds of choices available, especially with the departure of France from
NATO, do not include the ability to resist Soviet invasion with conventional arms.
Furthermore, if the assessment made in this study is correct there is no need

for this option. Any conflict in Central Europe involving United States and Soviet forces, however it might start, would be overshadowed by the danger of escalation to general nuclear war. Each incident would magnify this danger. Each battle maneuver or fire fight, each combat success or failure would bring general war nearer. The kind of NATO force posture needed is one that has the best chance of controlling these risks. It needs to be well forward to prevent a fait accompli; it needs to be structured to maximize nuclear deterrence at each stage in the conflict.

Yet deterrence in the final analysis requires a willingness as well as a capability to use nuclear weapons. A psychological posture is as essential as a military posture: we must create in the Soviets' mind a fear of or belief in our willingness to employ nuclear weapons in circumstances somewhat less than Armageddon. There is a world of difference between the calculated decision to use nuclear weapons in a selective manner to raise the risk of general war and the final desperate decision to hurl them at the enemy in the face of the threat of extinction. The attempt to make either the threat of massive retaliation with strategic nuclear forces, or the widespread use of tactical nuclear weapons cover every contingency is to confuse the reality of deterrent strength with the psychological state of mind in which will and fear determine the choices made. The will to defend resolutely should not engender fears that restraints will be thrown aside when nuclear weapons are needed. Potential instabilities and provocative elements in the NATO force posture need to be eliminated in peacetime if the confrontation in Central Europe is to remain stable during a crisis or low-level conflict.

Clearly, a workable doctrine of nuclear constraints is needed that is as convincing to a potential enemy as to allies. But no constraint doctrine will be convincing to the enemy so long as NATO has aircraft poised on German air bases in peacetime, ready to hurl nuclear destruction deep into enemy territory. No constraint doctrine will be convincing to allies so long as the United States continues to demand increasing buildups in conventional forces. No constraint doctrine will be convincing even to ourselves if it is imposed without consultation and agreement among our allies.

A nuclear constraint doctrine might be made believable by structuring the NATO defense posture in the manner suggested in Chapter 10. Such a posture, with emphasis on defense rather than offense, would provide a reasonable chance of success in defending against, and in gauging the intent and scope of, enemy incursion at any point along the Iron Curtain. Coupled with a willingness to employ selective battlefield nuclear weapons at a lower threshold, according to an advertised doctrine of constraint, the NATO posture would greatly improve graduated deterrence. In these circumstances, there no longer would be need for massive conventional forces. Some of the American ground and air forces could be withdrawn without degrading the deterrent and defense posture. This withdrawal will probably come about anyway, to solve the United States' and Great Britain's balance of payment difficulties. The withdrawal could be justified on strategic grounds if the NATO strategic concept is changed to fit the realities of the new situation. Furthermore, a NATO force posture that is less provocative and more clearly designed for defense may in time create a climate of confidence between adversaries that would enhance the chances of arms control arrangements and permit further reduction of military forces of both sides in Central Europe.

However one views the future of Europe, however one desires a solution to the division of Germany, however one strives for a détente or rapprochement between West and East, it is clearly to the interest of both NATO and the Warsaw Pact that the confrontation remain stable while the complex political, economic, and social processes of change are at work. It is only too obvious that the prevailing stability has been largely achieved in peacetime. Whether it can be maintained in time of crisis depends on whether the potential instabilities are corrected and whether the NATO nations can find some measure of agreement on a NATO strategic concept for employing nuclear weapons. Even then there is no assurance that general nuclear war can be forestalled. But the chances of survival would be improved.

NOTES

NOTES

Chapter 1

1. Dwight D. Eisenhower, State of Union Message, 7 January 1954; New York Times, 8 January 1954, p. 10.

Chapter 2

1. Secretary of Defense Robert S. McNamara, statement before the House Armed Services Committee on the Fiscal Year 1966-70 Defense Program and 1966 Defense Budget, 18 February 1965.

2. Secretary of Defense McNamara, speech at Ann Arbor, Michigan, 16 June 1962.

3. Secretary of Defense McNamara, speech at Ann Arbor, Michigan, 17 February 1962.

4. Secretary of Defense McNamara, testimony before Subcommittee on Defense, House Appropriations Committee, 6 February 1963, p. 130.

5. Secretary of Defense McNamara, statement before the House Armed Services Committee on the FY 1966-70 Defense Program and 1966 Defense Budget, 18 February 1965.

6. Secretary of Defense McNamara, testimony before Subcommittee on Defense, House Appropriations Committee, 6 February 1963.

7. Dialogue between Senator Margaret Chase Smith and Secretary of Defense McNamara, 20 February 1963, "Military Procurement Authorization, Fiscal Year 1964," hearings before the Committee on Armed Services, U. S. Senate, 88th Congress, 1st Session (Washington, D. C. : United States Government Printing Office, 1963), pp. 84-90.

8. Secretary of Defense McNamara, testimony before the Subcommittee on Defense, Senate Appropriations Committee, 23 February 1966.

9. Secretary of Defense McNamara, testimony before the Subcommittee on Defense, Senate Appropriations Committee, 23 February 1966.

10. The choices available among <u>controlled</u> tactical nuclear responses and the various alternative conventional options that are considered commensurate with the provocation are often referred to as the <u>flexible response.</u> The connotation, however, implies that conventional conflict would probably take place first.

11. These three situations are briefly postulated only to pinpoint the European objections to the American strategic concept of flexible response. All are implausible and extremely improbable. A fourth hypothetical case of a Soviet invasion--where the Soviets themselves initiate the use of nuclear weapons--is perhaps more plausible, given the Soviet announced strategic doctrine. However, this situation would not be relevant to this hypothetical scenario illustrating flexible response, but would call for immediate nuclear retaliation. A more detailed analysis of strategic concepts is made in Chapter 5 and Part Two.

12. In the "Carte Blanche" exercise of June 1955 it was conservatively estimated that 1.7 million Germans would have been killed and 3.5 million more wounded had the exercise been an actual wartime action. Bogislav von Bonin, <u>Atomkrieg--unser Ende</u> (Düsseldorf, 1956), pp. 22 ff., cited by Hans Speier, <u>German Rearmament and Atomic War</u> (Evanston, Illinois: RAND, Row, Peterson and Co., 1957), p. 144.

13. Some nuclear scientists will disagree that nuclear weapons cannot be judged by their yield. Certainly, there is a difference between a fraction of a kiloton weapon and a megaton weapon. But in situations where only tactical nuclear weapons are used, it is difficult to imagine an accurate distinction being made by troops in the confusion of battle between, say, a 30-kiloton tactical weapon that may be aimed either badly or accurately and a 10- or 50-kiloton weapon.

14. Stewart Alsop, "Our New Strategy: The Alternative to Total War," <u>The Saturday Evening Post</u>, 1 December 1962.

15. Robert E. Osgood, <u>NATO, the Entangling Alliance</u> (Chicago: University of Chicago Press, 1962), p. 156.

16. T. C. Schelling and M. H. Halperin, <u>Strategy and Arms Control</u> (New York: Twentieth Century Fund, 1961), pp. 141-42:
"Surely arms control has no monopoly of interest in the avoidance of accidental war; anyone concerned with military policy must be concerned with the danger of accident, false alarm, unauthorized action, or misunderstanding, that might lead to war. Arms control has no monopoly of interest in reducing the destructiveness of war if war occurs; military policy, too, should be concerned with the survival and welfare of the nation."

17. The Hot Line is a direct communication link between Washington and Moscow, to be used only in emergencies.

Chapter 3

1. Committee on Foreign Relations, United States Senate, <u>Documents on Germany 1944-61</u> (Washington: U.S. Government Printing Office, 1961).

2. For an excellent discussion of the German nuclear defense problem, see Uwe Nerlich, "The Nuclear Dilemmas of the Federal Republic of Germany," <u>Europa-Archiv</u>, 10 September 1965; <u>Strategie</u>, September 1965.

3. Fritz Erler speech in the Bundestag, 6-7 July 1956, Verhandlungen, pp. 8777-78, quoted by Nerlich, op. cit.

4. New York Times, 13 July 1956.

5. Vice-Admiral F. Ruge, Deputy Inspector-General of the Bundeswehr, "Prerequisites for Effective Defense," Survival, Vol. II, No. 6 (November-December 1960), quoted in Alastair Buchan, "NATO Divided," The New Republic, Vol. XLVII (29 December 1962), 15.

6. Vice-Admiral F. Ruge, "German Views on Nuclear Weapons," paper prepared for Stanford Research Institute, 1965.

7. Excerpt of a speech in 1961 quoted in L. Beaton and J. Maddox, The Spread of Nuclear Weapons (New York: Praeger, 1962), p. 117.

8. Frankfurter Allgemeine, 16 December 1961, pp. 1, 4.

9. "Die weltweite Dokumentation für Politik und Wirtschaft," Archiv der Gegenwart, 22-28 July 1962, p. 1006, cited by Vice-Admiral F. Ruge.

10. Defense Minister Kai-Uwe von Hassel warns that the U. S. concept of flexible response ". . . must not be interpreted to mean that the so-called atomic threshold can be raised unduly high, without reference to political considerations. Apart from the fact that this would lead the potential aggressor to think that he could calculate his risk, it would create a situation in which he could seize pawns for future negotiations." Kai-Uwe von Hassel, "Organizing Western Defense," Foreign Affairs, Vol. XLIII, No. 2 (January 1965), p. 211.

11. Many commentators who criticize the FGR on this point apparently do not realize that one does not give up bargaining points in advance of negotiations.

12. Von Hassel, op. cit., p. 214.

13. Terrence Robertson, Crisis: The Inside Story of the Suez Conspiracy (New York: Atheneum, 1965), pp. 252-54.

14. No longer secret, the contents have been reported in the press and other places. (See New York Times, 5 December 1958; Times (London), 5 December 1958; Time Magazine, 29 December 1958; Dirk Stikker, "The Weakest Link in NATO," Life International, 20 December 1965.) The text of Eisenhower's letter to de Gaulle, and the Department of State memorandum recording the events surrounding the French proposal were released on 11 August 1966 (see Atlantic Community Quarterly, IV, 3 (Fall 1966), pp. 455-58.

15. Department of State memorandum released 11 August 1966.

16. Major Addresses, Statements and Press Conferences of General de Gaulle (19 May 1958 - 31 Janaury 1964), (New York: French Embassy, Press and Information Division). Press Conference of General de Gaulle at Elysée Palace, 25 March 1959.

17. Loc. cit., address by President Charles de Gaulle outlining the principles of French foreign policy, 31 May 1960.

18. Loc. cit., fourth press conference by General de Gaulle at the Elysée Palace, 11 April 1961.

19. Loc. cit., sixth press conference by General de Gaulle at the Elysée Palace, 15 May 1963.

20. Loc. cit., seventh press conference by General de Gaulle at the Elysée Palace, 14 January 1963.

21. New York Times, 22 February 1966, Sec. C, p. 6.

22. An apocryphal story is told that a ranking member of the U.S. State Department had asked in 1965 what de Gaulle proposed for changing NATO. The French president drew himself up haughtily and said, "De Gaulle does not make proposals." No doubt the unceremonious disposal of his 1958 proposal to Eisenhower and MacMillan still rankles.

23. New York Times, 22 February 1966, Sec. C, p. 6.

24. New York Times, 1 April 1966, p. 11.

25. General C. L. M. Ailleret, "An Opinion on the Strategic Theory of the Flexible Response," Revue de Défense Nationale, August 1964.

26. Pierre Messmer, "Notre Politique Militaire, " Revue de Défense Nationale, May 1963.

27. Le Monde, 19 January 1965.

28. New York Times, 22 February 1966.

29. General Ailleret, op. cit.

30. Editorial, Le Monde, 31 July 1964.

31. President de Gaulle's letter of 7 March 1966 to President Johnson, New York Times, 25 March 1966.

32. Pierre Gallois, "The Case for France," Diplomat, April 1966. Hans J. Morgenthau, "The Four Paradoxes of Nuclear Strategy," American Political Science Review, March 1964.

33. Raymond Aron, The Great Debate (New York: Doubleday, 1965), p. 135.

34. General André Beaufré, "French Divergences on Nuclear Strategy," paper prepared for Stanford Research Institute, 1965.

35. "Defense: Outline of Future Policy," presented by the Minister of Defense to Parliament April 1957 (London: Her Majesty's Stationery Office, Cmnd. 124).

36. Statement on Nuclear Defense Systems, agreed to by the President of the United States and the Prime Minister of Great Britain at their meeting held in the Bahamas December 18-21, 1962 (London: Her Majesty's Stationery Office, Cmnd. 1915, December 1962).

37. Prime Minister's Statement to the House of Commons, 30 January 1962. (Reported in the Times, London, 31 January 1962).

38. Ibid.

39. Statement of the Defense Estimates, 1965, February 1965 (London: Her Majesty's Stationery Office, Cmnd. 2592).

40. Prime Minister Harold Wilson, Statement Before the House of Commons, 16 December 1964 (Hansard), 5th Series, Vol. 704, House of Commons Official Report, Session 1964-65 (London: Her Majesty's Stationery Office, Cols. 432-435).

41. Statement on Nuclear Defense Systems (Nassau, Bahamas, December 1962)

42. Resolution of the British Labour Party at the Brighton Conference, 1960. (Cited by Leonard Beaton, "Would Labour Give up the Bomb?", Sunday Telegraph, August 1964.)

43. Statement on the Defense Estimates, 1966, Part I: The Defense Review, February 1966 (London: Her Majesty's Stationery Office, Cmnd. 2901).

44. Ibid.

45. Jack M. Schick, "The Berlin Crisis of 1961 and U.S. Military Strategy," Orbis, VIII, 4 (Winter 1965), pp. 822-23. Also see Arthur M. Schlesinger, Jr., A Thousand Days (Boston: Houghton Mifflin, 1965), pp. 380-81.

46. New York Times, 1 June 1965.

Chapter 4

1. It is noted that the Soviet Union did not occupy Finland or attempt to impose a Communist regime on Finland at the end of World War II. But the Soviets did succeed in stabilizing the northern flank by annexing some territory from Finland. Sweden does not present a serious threat to the USSR. Had Finland been communized, Sweden might have elected to join NATO and Norway might have allowed the introduction of U.S. nuclear weapons and forces on her soil during peacetime.

The author put a direct question to a member of the Soviet Embassy in Washington as to the reasons the USSR did not impose a Communist regime on Finland. The reply was that the USSR did not "impose" Communist regimes on anyone. Wherever Communist regimes appeared, it was because the situation was ripe for a "socialist" revolution. Naturally, the presence of the Red Army helped. The government of Finland, unlike the Satellite states, had not lost the support of the people. Hence no "socialist and democratic" changeover.

2. Marshall V. D. Sokolovsky, Military Strategy (New York: Praeger, 1963), p. 42.

3. Arthur M. Schlesinger, Jr., A Thousand Days, pp. 358-78.

4. Sokolovsky, Military Strategy, p. 171. The text of Khrushchev's statement is to be found in Soviet News, No. 4131, 14 October 1959 (London: Press Department of the Soviet Embassy in London), p. 38.

5. Major General N. Talenskii, "On the Question of the Laws of Military Science," Military Thought, September 1953, cited by H. S. Dinerstein, War and the Soviet Union (New York: Praeger, 1959), pp. 37-63.

6. For a more complete discussion of preemption in Soviet strategy see Thomas W. Wolfe, Soviet Strategy at the Crossroads (RAND RM-4085-PR, April 1964), pp. 64-69.

7. Hearings on Military Posture, U. S. Congress 88:1, House Committee on Armed Services, 30 January 1963, p. 308; Bulletin of the Atomic Scientists, April 1963, p. 38.

8. Dinerstein, op. cit., pp. 37-63.

9. Wolfe, op. cit., chapter on the "Doctrine of Military Superiority"; see also Arnold L. Hordick and Myron Rush, Strategic Power and Soviet Foreign Policy (Chicago: University of Chicago Press, 1966), pp. 196-203.

10. Sokolovsky, op. cit., p. 189.

11. Ibid., p. 195. The word "our" was inserted before "achieving" in the second edition.

12. Stefan T. Possony, "U. S. Intelligence at the Crossroads," Orbis, IX, 3 (Fall 1965); and "Analysis of Khrushchev Speech of 6 January 1961," Hearings before Subcommittee to Investigate the Internal Security Act and Other Internal Security Laws (16 June 1961).

13. V. I. Lenin, Selected Works, Vol. VIII, "The Period of War Communism (1918-1920)," A. Fineberg, ed. (New York: International Publishers, n.d.; first published in USSR). Selection entitled "Report of the Central Committee of the RDP (Bolsheviks) at the Eighth Party Congress, 18 March 1919.

14. Khrushchev's Report to the 20th Party Congress, Current Digest of the Soviet Press, VIII, 4 (7 March 1956), 11.

15. Marshall R. Ia. Malinovskii, Bditel'no Stoyat Na Strazhe Mira (Vigilantly Stand Guard Over the Peace), (Moscow: Voenizdat Ministerstva Oborony SSSR, 1962), p. 23. Published by the Military Publishing House, November 1962, and cited by Thomas W. Wolfe in "A Postscript on the Significance of the Book 'Soviet Military Strategy' " (Evanston, Illinois: RAND RM-3730-PR, July 1963), p. 33.

16. Robert D. Crane, "The Structure of Soviet Military Thought," Studies in Soviet Thought, scheduled for publication in March 1967, to which he has kindly permitted the author to make reference.

17. Sokolovsky, Voyennaya Strategiya (second edition), p. 96; cited in Joint Publications Research Service, Military Strategy (a comparison of the 1962 and 1963 editions), JPRS 22,451; 24 December 1963, p. 20.

18. Wolfe, Soviet Strategy at the Crossroads, pp. 143-54.

19. Kommunist Vooruzhennykh Sil No. 10, May 1963, pp. 11-12, cited by Wolfe in Soviet Strategy at the Crossroads, p. 146.

20. Sokolovsky, Voyennaya Strategiya, p. 374, cited in JPRS 22,451, p. 91.

21. Crane, op. cit.

22. Victor Zorza, "Soviet Strategy Revised," Manchester Guardian Weekly, XCIII, 18, 4 November 1965.

23. Premier Alexei Kosygin, speech to the Supreme Soviet 3 August 1966 (see Survival, October 1966, p. 323).

24. Warsaw Pact Statement on European Conference, 9 July 1966 (see Atlantic Community Quarterly, IV, 3 (Fall 1966), 445-46).

Chapter 5

1. Henry A. Kissinger, "NATO's Nuclear Dilemma," The Reporter, XXVIII, 7 (28 March 1963), 27-28.

2. Bernard Brodie, "Anatomy of Deterrence," World Politics, II (January 1959), 177.

3. Robert E. Osgood, The Case for the MLF (Washington Center of Foreign Policy Research, 1964).

4. Prime Minister Harold Wilson, Parliamentary Debates (Hansard). Fifth series, Vol. 687, House of Commons Official Report: Session 1963-64 (London: Her Majesty's Stationery Office, Col. 445).

5. Glenn H. Snyder, Deterrence and Defense (Princeton: Princeton University Press, 1961), pp. 8-9. Snyder makes the distinction between deterrence by denial and deterrence by punishment. The "capacity to deny territory to the enemy, or otherwise to block his aims, may be a very efficient deterrent."

6. New York Times, 2 June 1965.

7. T. W. Stanley, NATO in Transition (New York: Praeger, 1965), p. 246.

8. Lewis Carroll, "The White Knight" in Through the Looking Glass, Chapter VIII.
"I was wondering what the mouse-trap was for," said Alice. "It isn't very likely there would be any mice on the horse's back."
"Not very likely, perhaps," said the Knight; "but, if they do come, I don't choose to have them running all about."
"You see," he went on after a pause, "it's as well to be provided for everything. That's the reason the horse has all those anklets round his feet."
"But what are they for?" Alice asked in a tone of great curiosity.
"To guard against the bites of sharks," the Knight replied. "It's an invention of my own."

9. Secretary of Defense McNamara before the House Armed Services Committee on the FY 1966-70 Defense Program and 1966 Defense Budget (18 February 1965), p. 47. There is something inherently inconsistent with these figures. They represent an inability to be accurate except within a range of twenty-seven million yet they suggest that one can be precise within one or two million on the upper and lower figures. Perhaps "over 100 million" would be a more general and representative figure. Mr. McNamara goes on to suggest that these figures could be reduced by about one-half with adequate fallout shelters.

10. Arthur M. Schlesinger, Jr., A Thousand Days, pp. 379-80.

11. Ibid., p. 391.

12. It is suggested that the geographical position of France permits her to entertain the concept of nuclear retaliation even for a "probe," since a probe must first strike Western Germany, and by the time it threatens France it is no longer a probe. General Pierre Gallois, a French strategic theorist, in discussion with the author, suggested that if the enemy threatened France from "outside the gates of Strasbourg," the appropriate reply would be to strike Russia with nuclear weapons. This viewpoint indicates the kind of situation in which the French

might regard nuclear retaliation as an appropriate response. Unanswered is the question of how the Soviets achieved this position "outside the gates of Strasbourg" without "bloodying" quite a few American and German allies in the process.

13. For a more detailed discussion of this point see the author's "Psychological Effects of Nuclear Weapons," U. S. Naval Institute Proceedings, April 1960, p. 34.

14. Quoted in Schlesinger, op. cit., p. 853.

Chapter 6

1. Secretary of Defense McNamara, statement before Subcommittee of the Appropriations Committee, House of Representatives, 14 February 1966 (figures are for mid-1966).

2. Institute for Strategic Studies, The Military Balance 1966-1967, London, September 1966.

3. U. S. News and World Report, 4 January 1965, pp. 32-33.

4. Source: Institute for Strategic Studies, London; Seventh U. S. Army Briefing; "Vater, Bruder oder sonst wer," (Father, Brother, or Anyone Else) Der Spiegel, No. 23/1965 (2 June 1965), 34-44.

5. S. L. A. Marshall, Men Against Fire (New York: Apollo Publishing Company, 1961).

6. Quincy Wright, Problems of Stability and Progress in International Relations (Berkeley: University of California Press, 1954), p. 245.

7. Neither general war nor limited war, nor even low-level conflicts are probable contingencies in Central Europe. They are "not probable" in large part due to the military balance, so there is certainly something to be said for assessing imbalances. A serious imbalance could change the probabilities markedly. However, if there is any degree of difference in probabilities that are extremely low, the "low-intensity conflict" idea is the more likely.

8. This apt phrase was coined by James E. King in his paper delivered at the Arms Control and Disarmament Seminar in Ann Arbor, Michigan, January 1964.

9. "Vater, Bruder, oder sonst wer," loc. cit., pp. 34-44.

10. This brief discussion of invasion routes is based on Dr. Robert B. Johnson's assessment in "The Context of the European Arms Control and Disarmament Problems Through 1970," Stanford Research Institute Research Memorandum, DAC-RM-11 (November 1963), and its companion atlas also by Dr. Johnson, "An Atlas of the Arms Control Context and the Disengagement Concept for the Europe of the 1960s," Stanford Research Institute Research Memorandum, DAC-RM-13 (March 1964).

11. A "division slice" comprises all the combat forces and logistic elements supporting the division.

12. "Bedingt Abwehrbereit" (Conditionally Fit for Defense), Der Spiegel, No. 41 (10 October 1962), 32-53.

13. "Vater, Bruder oder sonst wer," loc. cit., pp. 34-44.

14. General André Beaufré, Nato and Europe (New York: Alfred A. Knopf, 1966), p. 50.

15. Institute for Strategic Studies, Disarmament and European Security, Vol. II: Tables, August 1963.

16. V. D. Sokolovskii, Soviet Military Strategy (New Jersey: Prentice-Hall/RAND Corporation, 1963), p. 352.

17. Source: Institute for Strategic Studies, USAF Jet Navigation, Planning and Pilotage Charts JN-9m GNC 4N, PC E-2B, PC 231A, PC 231B.

18. Jane's All the World's Aircraft, 1964-1965, John W. R. Taylor, ed. (New York: McGraw-Hill, 1964).

19. Secretary of Defense McNamara, speech to Economic Club of New York, 18 November 1962 (DOD Office of Public Affairs No. 1486-63), p. 12.

20. Secretary of Defense McNamara, statement before the House Armed Services Committee on the FY 1966-70 Defense Program and 1966 Defense Budget, 18 February 1965.

21. Derek Wood, Interavia, No. 1/1966 (January 1966), 78.

22. New York Times, 30 June 1966.

23. Calculated on the experience in locating tanks and delivering weapons with pinpoint accuracy. Napalm and modern rockets would permit improvements.

24. J. S. Butz, Jr., "Those Bombings in the North," Air Force and Space Digest, April 1966, pp. 42-54.

25. U.S. News and World Report, 14 June 1965, p. 10. Also, Secretary of Defense Robert S. McNamara before the Senate Subcommittee on Department of Defense Appropriations, 23 February 1966. On 13 August 1963, Mr. McNamara informed the Senate Committee on Foreign Relations that "we maintain a total number of nuclear warheads, tactical as well as strategic, in the tens of thousands." See Secretary of Defense Robert S. McNamara before the Committee on Foreign Relations, United States Senate on "The Nuclear Test Ban Treaty," 12-27 August 1963.

26. New York Times, 24 September 1966, p. 1.

27. "Vater, Bruder, oder sonst wer," loc. cit., pp. 34-44.

28. G. C. Reinhardt, Nuclear Weapons and Limited Warfare, RAND P-3011 (November 1964), p. 2.

29. The Military Balance 1966-1967, p. 14.

30. Military Review, November 1964, p. 103.

31. The Military Balance . . ., p. 44.

32. The same rationale of course applies to NATO aircraft capable of reaching the Soviet Union. However, the Soviets do have extensive air defenses-- surface-to-air missiles, antiaircraft artillery, and modern interceptors--whereas they do not have a reliable ballistic missile defense.

Chapter 7

1. President Dwight D. Eisenhower, White House Press Releases, January- April 1958, for release on 13 January 1958, p. 4 of release text.

2. Documents on Disarmament, 1945-1959, Vol. II, 1957-1959, Department of State Publication 7008, released August 1960 (Historical Office, Bureau of Public Affairs): Doc. No. 237, "Letter from the Soviet Premier (Bulganin) to President Eisenhower, 10 December 1957," p. 921.

3. "Disengagements as Arms Control Measures in the Europe of the 1960's," Documents on Disarmament, 1945-1959, Vol. II, 1957-1959. Also see Robert B. Johnson, "An Atlas of the Arms Control Context and the Disengagement Concept for the Europe of the 1960's," Stanford Research Institute Research Memorandum, DAC-RM-13 (March 1964).

4. John Strachey, On the Prevention of War (London: Macmillan and Co., Ltd., 1962), p. 112. Actually, in a sense, a separate tactical nuclear command already exists if one conceives of using American strategic nuclear forces (Polaris and the Strategic Air Command) in a tactical supporting role--say against targets in East Germany.

5. T. C. Schelling, "Nuclear Strategy in Europe," World Affairs, April 1962, p. 426.

6. Secretary of Defense McNamara, testimony before House Commitee on Department of Defense Appropriation, 6 February 1963.

7. In his message to Congress 28 March 1961, President Kennedy said, "Our arms will never be used to strike the first blow in any attack . . . in the area of general war. This doctrine means that such capability must rest with that portion of our forces which would survive the initial attack. We are not creating forces for a first strike against any other nation." Congressional Record, Vol. 107, Part 4, 87th Congress, 1st Session, p. 4954. On another occasion, however, President Kennedy said, "Of course in some circumstances we must be prepared to use the nuclear weapon at the start, come what may--a clear attack on Western Europe, for example." Stewart Alsop, "Kennedy's Grand Strategy," Saturday Evening Post, 31 March 1962, p. 11. Christian A. Herter has also stated, ". . . I can't conceive of the President of the United States involving us in an all-out nuclear war unless the facts showed clearly that we are in danger of devastation ourselves, or that actual moves have been made toward devastating ourselves." U.S. Senate Committee on Foreign Relations, Hearing on the Nomination of Christian A. Herter to Be Secretary of State, 12 April 1959. Dr. Alain C. Enthoven, Deputy Assistant Secretary of Defense, stated, "Now that the Communist Bloc is armed with nuclear weapons, we cannot successfully fight conventional wars except under the umbrella of nuclear strength. This nuclear strength is required to deter the Communists from escalating a non-nuclear conflict which is not going well for them into nuclear war, and to convince them that an act of nuclear aggression would lead to their defeat

and possibly to the destruction of their society." U.S. Senate Committee on Armed Services, Military Procurement Authorization: Fiscal Year 1964, Hearings on H. R. 2440, 88th Congress, 1st Session, 1963, p. 170.

8. Herman Kahn, On Escalation (New York: Praeger, 1965), pp. 102-103.

9. Ibid., pp. 105-33.

10. Schlesinger, A Thousand Days, p. 388.

11. Secretary of Defense McNamara has defined at least three different strategic options in his University of Michigan address: counterforce, countercity, or both. These, however, could hardly be classed as local constraints. (Ann Arbor, 16 June 1962.)

12. Kahn, op. cit., p. 39.

Chapter 8

1. Conventional weapons create casualties, too! As Thornton Reed suggests, "To try to understand tactical nuclear war in terms of nuclear weapons and delivery systems would be like trying to understand conventional war solely in terms of artillery."

2. In a so far unpublished book, James E. King points out that many military analysts have treated this restraint as "military" in the sense that all battlefield supply problems are military. The assumption was "that the supply of nuclear weapons, despite their increasing availability, would continue to be limited. That is to say, in a sense that was never true of nonnuclear weapons, the designers of model tactical nuclear battlefields invariably assumed fewer nuclear weapons than targets for nuclear attack." He goes on to point out several consequences. In the first place, if relative availability is a critical consideration, then the assumption that the United States and its allies were more generously supplied with a more varied stock of weapons would be an advantage. Second, because of the scarcity, "there must be deliberate target selection to prevent the available weapons from being wasted, with the consequence of delays both in attacking targets of opportunity and in providing nuclear support for friendly troops under attack." Third, nuclear scarcity would slow down the rate of weapon expenditure. And fourth, nuclear scarcity would dictate that the combat would still be conducted in large part with conventional weapons.

3. An excellent summary discussion is contained in Seymour J. Deitchman, Limited War and American Defense Policy (Cambridge: M. I. T. Press, 1964), Chapter 7.

4. Of course, safety considerations for the enemy's troops would establish upper limits to the yields of weapons that may be employed once combat is joined.

5. Nuclear Weapons Employment, Department of the Army Pamphlet No. 39-1.

6. Major General Hamilton H. Howze, "The Land Battle in an Atomic War," Army, July 1961, pp. 29-48.

7. Otto Heilbrunn, <u>Conventional Warfare in the Nuclear Age</u> (New York: Praeger, 1965), p. 83.

8. Many military analysts find it most difficult to visualize a localized nuclear battle in which the air forces do not perform a dominant role. This perhaps stems from the time when the U. S. Air Force practically monopolized the atomic bomb and questioned the utility of the first 280-mm nuclear gun and the Matador missile. The doctrinal emphasis on interdicting enemy airfields as a means to gain air superiority continues to foster the belief that a nuclear battle would not be confined to the localized battlefield.

9. Clark C. Abt, "Tactical Nuclear Operations in Limited Local Wars," <u>Army</u>, October 1964, p. 42.

Chapter 9

1. T. C. Schelling, "Nuclear Strategy in Europe," <u>World Politics</u>, April 1962, p. 424.

2. <u>Ibid.</u>, p. 427.

3. This does not mean that actions and words can have only one interpretation. Interactions among nations and alliances take place through real actions and pronouncements where the actions are clarified and slanted by the words. The point made is that actions should not be inconsistent with the statements. As pointed out by Professor Eldridge, "Actions speak louder than words, although words make the meaning of actions precise as well as loud, soft, or tangential." ("Projecting Western Realities," <u>NATO Letter</u>, June-August 1963.)

Chapter 10

1. Some offensive capacity is needed for counterattack--an essential element of defense.

2. Bernard Brodie, <u>Strategy in the Missile Age</u>, p. 301.

3. <u>Ibid.</u>

4. B. H. Liddell Hart, <u>Deterrent or Defense</u> (New York: Praeger, 1960), p. 165.

5. <u>Ibid.</u>, pp. 103-104.

6. <u>Ibid.</u>, p. 166.

7. Malcolm W. Hoag, "Rationalizing NATO Strategy," <u>World Politics</u>, XVII, 1 (October 1964), 131 ff.

8. A most persuasive case is made for a militia in Frederick Martin Stern's <u>The Citizen Army</u> (New York: St. Martin's Press, 1957).

9. The United States has 81,000 fewer troops in Europe than in December 1961 after the buildup during the Berlin Crisis. Britain has also pared its troop strength to 51,000 from the 1954 Western European Union commitment of 78,000.

10. Stern, op. cit., pp. 70-101.

11. Such as the proposals of Colonel Bogislav von Bonin, Chief of Planning in the German "Blank" Office (Predecessor to Ministry of Defense); Vice-Admiral Freidrich Ruge, former Deputy Inspector-General, German Armed Forces; Adelbert Weinstein, German military commentator; Malcolm Hoag, RAND Corp. ; James E. King, Jr., Institute for Defense Analyses; and Rear Admiral Sir Anthony Buzzard, Institute for Strategic Studies.

12. Colonel George C. Reinhardt, U.S. Army (Ret.), "The Doctrinal Gap," Proceedings, U.S. Naval Institute, XCII, 8 (August 1966), 62.

Chapter 11

1. P. C. Gordon Walter, "The Labor Party's Defense and Foreign Policy," Foreign Affairs, XLII, 3 (April 1964), 393.

2. Le Monde, 18 April 1964.

3. First Press Conference held by General de Gaulle as President of the French Republic in Paris at the Elysée Palace, 25 March 1959. Major Addresses, Statements and Press Conferences of General Charles de Gaulle, May 1958-January 1964 (New York: French Embassy, Press and Information Division).

4. Article 5 leaves to the choice of each member "such action as it deems necessary." This is highly subjective and the promise to "assist" could be interpreted as meaning little more than an agreement not to join forces with the enemy. However, the supplemental arrangements made in the North Atlantic Treaty Organization have established institutions and procedures that in actual effect insure that the armed forces of the members of the Atlantic Alliance would be committed "automatically" in the event of attack. By withdrawing from NATO, France has eliminated these automatic arrangements.

5. "Une certitude: La technique seule vaincra," France Demain, No. 2, 19-25 (December 1966), 20-21.

6. Ibid., p. 36.

7. Statement on Defense 1963 Including Memoranda to Accompany the Navy, Army, and Air Force Estimates 1963-64 (London: Her Majesty's Stationery Office, Cmnd. 1936).

8. Pierre Messmer, "Notre politique militaire," Revue de Défense Nationale, May 1963.

9. A Soviet military officer who had defected to the West recently told the author that Mr. McNamara's "no cities doctrine" confirmed Soviet leaders' fears of "war-mongering Americans" attempting to find ways to fight a nuclear war. This reaction, if true, might or might not be the reaction Mr. McNamara would seek.

10. U.S. News and World Report, 19 October 1964, p. 48.

11. Edward Teller, "Planning for Peace," Orbis, X, 2 (Summer 1966), 357.

12. Marshall of the Royal Air Force Sir John Slessor, "Atlantic Nuclear Policy," contribution to a Stanford Research Institute study.

INDEX